Shakespeare: A Complete Introduction

To the family

Shakespeare: A Complete Introduction

Michael Scott

First published in Great Britain in 2016 by John Murray Learning
An Hachette UK company.

This edition published in 2016 by John Murray Learning

British Library Cataloguing in Publication Data: a catalogue record for this title
is available from the British Library.

Library of Congress Catalog Card Number: on file.

ISBN: 9781473612785

eISBN: 9781473612792

1

Typeset by Cenveo® Publisher Services.

Printed and bound in Great Britain by CPI Group (UK) Ltd, Croydon, CR0 4YY.

John Murray Learning policy is to use papers that are natural, renewable
and recyclable products and made from wood grown in sustainable forests.
The logging and manufacturing processes are expected to conform to the
environmental regulations of the country of origin.

John Murray Learning
Carmelite House
50 Victoria Embankment
London EC4Y 0DZ
www.hodder.co.uk

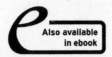

**Also available
in ebook**

Acknowledgements

This book could not have been written, produced or published without the help and support of my wife, Eirlys, who worked tirelessly on it with me from its inception, but who sadly died before its publication. My thanks are incalculable, my love immeasurable. She wanted the book to be dedicated 'to the family'. I wish it also to serve as a tribute to her memory and to her love for us all.

My thanks to Professor John Drakakis, friend and colleague, who has diligently read through the typescript, making suggestions and comments which I have invariably included. Thanks also to Terry Hands, former Artistic Director of the Royal Shakespeare Company and subsequently of Clwyd Theatre Cymru, a good friend with whom I've discussed elements of this book and who has inspired generations of theatregoers.

I am grateful to my publisher and editor, Victoria Roddam, for her professionalism, guidance and timely notes of encouragement through the writing period, and to my project manager, Sarah Chapman, and my literary agent, Charlotte Howard at Fox and Howard Ltd, for their advice and support.

I owe a debt of gratitude to all my teachers and colleagues at the various universities at which I've studied or taught and to those teachers and members of my family who in my schooldays gave me my first insight into the joy of Shakespearean performance and study. Too many are, sadly, now long gone but will never be forgotten. Thanks also to Medwin Hughes, Vice Chancellor of University of Wales Trinity St David for his support and encouragement. I am grateful as always to my daughters, sons-in-law and grandchildren for the joy they give us as a family, which encourages the writing.

Finally, I acknowledge with gratitude all those writers and scholars referenced and/or quoted in this book and, of course, the students I have been privileged to teach, both in the UK and abroad.

WITHDRAWN Contents

Preface

Shakespeare wrote for everyone, whoever they were, from Queen or King to the most menial, and all came to see the plays. He is as comprehensive in his entertainment as he is in his audiences. For years, certain factions in society have tried to claim him for themselves and in so doing have deterred others, perhaps even you, from appreciating and enjoying his work. This book wishes to set him free for everyone to enjoy. It aims to introduce and explain the plays by looking at how they work, taking you on a journey through the genres of comedy, history and tragedy. It is the process of this journey, with its various landmarks, which is the book's purpose.

We will also consider various critical perspectives that will help you clarify various movements or issues concerning Shakespeare's work that we will meet along the way. Broad definitions of various critical movements, for example, can be found in Chapter 24. Obviously, as with any guide, I have to be selective. Each of Shakespeare's plays is mentioned but we will spend more time discussing the best known and popular of the plays. Nevertheless, even plays in which Shakespeare may have had only the briefest creative and collaborative interest as a writer, get at least a mention, as do the poems, although I do not dwell on them in any detail.

There are plenty of good biographies of Shakespeare, and I spend a little time identifying some of the more recent ones but, throughout our journey, aspects of his life are referenced in the discussion. The book follows a logical framework, on which I comment in the conclusion, but I've taken care, I hope, to enable you to dip in and out of various chapters as you wish and to provide you with a wide range of references.

Hodder & Stoughton invited me to write this book following the publication of *Shakespeare's Comedies* (2014) and *Shakespeare's Tragedies* (2015), which I wrote for its All That Matters series.

I draw on material from those books in some of the chapters. That being said, let's 'stiffen the sinews' and begin.

Michael Scott

A NOTE ON THE REFERENCES
Unless otherwise stated, the text used for all quotations and references to acts, scenes and lines is *The Arden Shakespeare Complete Works* edited by Richard Proudfoot, Ann Thompson and David Scott Kastan, reissued edition 2011, paperback (London: Bloomsbury Methuen Drama).

1

Releasing Shakespeare

William Shakespeare has been hailed as one of the greatest thinkers of all time, one of the world's finest artists, poets and dramatists. His plays are discussed in the context of their language, philosophy and 'meaning'. Nowadays people study them and are assessed on his work in examinations. So intense has the Shakespeare 'industry' become that, in any single year, there are probably more words written about him or spoken of him than he wrote himself. He is a complex phenomenon that can cause us problems as we approach his work, whether on the page or the stage.

When we put this prodigious reputation together with the distance of four hundred years since Shakespeare died, we need to remember that there have been major changes in language, social values and perceptions. The medium of poetry in which much of the drama is written reflects the verbally dominant styles of communication and entertainment of his time that have become primarily visual today. In view of the vast amount of scholarship about the man and his work and an apparent elitist culture that has grown up around him, it is no wonder that some people approach his plays with trepidation.

Shakespeare the entertainer

Shakespeare was in the entertainment business. He made his living mainly from writing and acting in plays. He was so successful that he became a 'sharer' in his company, the Lord Chamberlain's Men, and in their theatre, the Globe. The company name indicated that the Lord Chamberlain was the patron of the company. Without having a patron it was against the law to act in plays professionally, but this did not mean that the Lord Chamberlain actually subsidized the company. Through his name the actors were protected; without it they could have been prosecuted as vagabonds and vagrants.

'... all Fencers Bearewardes Comon Players in Enterludes & Minstrels, not belonging to any Baron of this Realme or towardes any other honourable Personage of greater Degeree; all Juglers Pedlars Tynkers and Petye Chapmen; ... [who] shall wander abroade and have not Lycense of two Justices of the Peace at the least, ... shal bee taken adjudged and deemed Roges Vacaboundes and Sturdy Beggers.'

Act for the Punishment of Vagabonds 1572 (quoted in Gurr, A. [1970: 19], *The Shakespearean Stage, 1574–1642*. Cambridge: Cambridge University Press

The Globe Theatre was not the first theatre where the Lord Chamberlain's Men acted or for which Shakespeare first wrote plays; that playhouse was 'The Theatre', situated north of the city of London. The lease for that playhouse ran out in 1597, so for the following year the company played at the neighbouring theatre, the Curtain, before moving to the Globe, which opened in 1599. The actors had to run their theatre and company as a commercial concern. Later, Shakespeare took a business interest in a further smaller indoor theatre, the Blackfriars, where the company could perform in winter. After the accession in 1603 of James VI of Scotland to the English throne as James I, the King became the patron of the company, which then became known as the King's Men.

The Red Lion (1567) in Whitechapel was probably the first public theatre in London. In 1576 it was replaced by 'The Theatre', built by James Burbage in Shoreditch just outside the city walls. Burbage had been a carpenter and in 1575 had worked at Kenilworth Castle on the creation of the stage for the entertainment planned for the visit of Queen Elizabeth I to the Earl of Leicester, who owned the castle. Kenilworth was not far from Stratford-upon-Avon where Shakespeare lived. The Queen's visit was a great occasion for the locality and occurred when Shakespeare was just 11 years old. We can only speculate about whether the boy went to the castle in the hope of seeing the Queen or whether he heard talk of it. Leicester entertained Elizabeth for 19 days, from 9 to 27 July. We know also that travelling players regularly performed in Stratford during Shakespeare's childhood. There are, of course, no records of Shakespeare's engagement with them but entertainment appears to have got into his blood from somewhere.

Key idea

Shakespeare's works are easier to enjoy and to put into context if he is freed from the carbuncles of history and cultural elitism that have grown up around him. We may then get back to the purpose of the plays – to attract people from all strata of society to what is popular entertainment.

There is much speculation about Shakespeare's life before he arrived in London in the early 1590s, when he is first mentioned as an actor and a writer. We will come to that speculation later but it is held that in 1594 a playwright, Robert Greene, reportedly on his deathbed, complained that Shakespeare was taking and using the work of other dramatists to make his way in the theatre. Greene, apparently out of resentment, calls him an 'upstart Crow'. Whether it was Greene or another writer – for example Thomas Nashe or Henry Chettle who wrote the *Groatsworth of Wit* but published it under Greene's name – is a matter for debate. (See, for example, Katherine Duncan-Jones [2010: 48–56].) It is said that Greene died from 'a surfeit of Rhenish wine and pickled herring'!

Whoever made the 'upstart Crow' accusation, it's apparent just
from looking at Shakespeare's plays and consulting his sources
that he adapted and rewrote some known plays and to great
effect, since it appears that he was making them more popular
and enduring with his audiences.

Spotlight

For the majority of his plays throughout his career, Shakespeare used
known stories, plays and other sources to create his dramas, and to bring
people into the theatre to entertain them and to make money for his
company and for himself.

Shakespeare the businessman

As a 'sharer' in the company, Shakespeare had part-ownership
of the company and the properties, the scripts and the costumes.
It was what we might regard as a communal business with
the risks shared, at first, between eight and, later, 12 fellow
members of the company. Their business manager was John
Heminges, one of the two men who later published the First
Folio of Shakespeare's works in 1623. When Shakespeare
retired, in 1613 or thereabouts, he was quite a wealthy man,
owning handsome properties in Stratford and London and some
land. He was also involved in a controversy over a proposal to
enclose some of this land, which would have allowed him to
make more money but at the expense of poorer people. As it
happened, the particular proposal was not successful. We know
that he also loaned money and that he purchased a large house
in London, which he rented out.

Shakespeare wrote his plays primarily for the company in which he had a business interest, and they were usually performed in one or other of the theatres in which he had a financial interest. Thus he was not only a poet and dramatist but also what we would today term a businessman.

Key idea

There appears with Shakespeare to have been no separation between the ownership of the means of production and the participation in the means of production – the plays in performance. Shakespeare was working at a time when capitalism was in its infancy and when modern industrial relations had yet to be developed. His theatre was in the business of generating income and was therefore at the centre of commercial activity, although there was a general cultural suspicion of the process of commodification that resulted from the growth of a market economy.

Shakespeare through time

Shakespeare was born in 1564, probably on 23 April, which is St George's Day (the patron saint of England), and he died in 1616, possibly on his birthday. The actual dates of birth and death are speculative; they are mainly based on the dates of his christening (26 April 1564) and burial (25 April 1616), although the bust of him that was erected some time later in Holy Trinity Church does give 23 April as the date of his death, at the age of 53.

We might consider whether Shakespeare believed that as a dramatist he would be so highly regarded four hundred years after his death. He certainly had the desire, and he thought he would gain immortality through his non-dramatic poetry, as shown, for example, in Sonnet 60 where he writes that although 'Time' brings youth and beauty to an end when '… nothing stands but for his scythe to mow', he yet hopes that his writing will last: 'And yet to times in hope my verse shall stand,/Praising thy worth, despite his cruel hand.' But like a number of his contemporaries, with the exception of Ben Jonson, he may have regarded his plays as ephemeral and, as far as we know, he did not himself seek to have them published. He may have distinguished between his non-dramatic poetry and a play such as *Love's Labour's Lost*, which is critical of 'fame', although Kiernan Ryan believes that he was aware that future audiences would see his plays.

'To grasp a Shakespearean play as fully as possible at any point in time is to recognize that its gaze is bent upon a vanishing point at which no reader or spectator can hope to arrive. Like the hat that the circus clown kicks out of reach every time he steps forward to pick it up, final comprehension of the play is perpetually postponed by each act of interpretation. Built into Shakespeare's plays, as into his poems, is the expectation that whatever eyes are viewing them at a given moment, other "eyes not yet created" (Sonnet 81) will one day view them in another light.'

Ryan, K. (2001: 198), 'Shakespeare and the Future', in Cartmell, D. and Scott, M., *Talking Shakespeare*. Basingstoke: Palgrave

His trust in the endurance across time of poetry to praise the lover is a powerful theme exemplified also in Sonnet 55, where he exalts both the art of the poet and the lasting memory of the one to whom it is addressed.

Not marble, nor the gilded monuments
Of princes, shall outlive this powerful rhyme;
But you shall shine more bright in these contents
Than unswept stone, besmeared with sluttish time.
When wasteful war shall statues overturn
Nor Mars his sword, nor war's quick fire, shall burn
The living record of your memory:
'Gainst death, and all oblivious enmity,
Shall you pace forth; your praise shall still find room
Even in the eyes of all posterity
That wear this world out to the ending doom.
So till the judgement that yourself arise,
You live in this, and dwell in lovers' eyes.

Of his 37-plus plays (as we will see in Chapter 27, scholars claim that he had a hand in more plays, usually as a collaborator, and it is now generally accepted, for example, that a 38th, *The Two Noble Kinsmen*, was written by him and John Fletcher), only 18 were published during his lifetime. All of these, except *Pericles*, were republished with the other 19 in the first collected edition of his works, prepared seven years after his death by two of his friends and fellow actors in 1623: John Heminges, referred to earlier, and Henry Condell. This collected edition, known as the First Folio, did not include *Pericles*, which was subsequently ascribed to him. (*The Two Noble Kinsmen* was published in a single edition in 1634, naming John Fletcher and William Shakespeare as the joint authors; that text was reprinted in 1679 in the Second Folio of Beaumont and Fletcher's *Comedies and Tragedies*).

Single editions of the plays were known as quartos, and in Shakespeare's case those published had usually been authorized by his company. Some 'pirated' editions, however, as we will see in Chapter 21, were also published without his or his company's approval.

Spotlight

The words 'folio' and 'quarto' refer to the size of a book's leaves. For a folio edition, the standard sheet of paper of about 340 × 430 mm (13.5 × 17 inches) was folded once, making two leaves or four pages. For the smaller quarto the standard sheet was folded twice, making four leaves or eight pages.

This dramatist, who never went to university, came from a relatively modest background; his father, John Shakespeare, was a glover and, although a prominent citizen and one-time alderman of Stratford-upon-Avon, found himself in serious financial trouble. Yet by the early nineteenth century, as we will see, his son William became almost deified in the way in which intellectuals regarded him.

Shakespeare's reputation in schools – and beyond – is often framed by difficulty. You might yourself have made or heard such statements as 'I was put off Shakespeare at school', 'Shakespeare's not for the likes of me', 'I don't understand the words', 'It's boring' or 'I don't know what it means'. For Shakespeare, I would imagine, these statements would be anomalous, even heartbreaking, so try not to let negative statements put you off.

For example, after working on a Shakespearean play for a short time, a student said, 'I don't understand this play.' 'What don't you understand?' I asked. 'The words,' he replied. 'Which words?' 'All of them,' he answered! Of course, he did understand most of the words but was fearful of the poetry at first. He persevered by allowing the words to flow over him and, as he became more engrossed in the story, so he started to enjoy and appreciate the play.

Key idea

Shakespeare wrote plays not for an elite but for people from all strata of society to enjoy. His theatre, the Globe, was in an area of London where there were bear-baiting pits, brothels and taverns. The plays were written as popular entertainment and they worked as such. They brought in the crowds. They made money for him and his fellow actors in the theatre.

What I want to do in this book is to allay the fear of Shakespeare, and take you, the reader, back to how Shakespeare developed and constructed his plays for popular entertainment. I am, of course, part of the Shakespearean 'industry' but I want to release Shakespeare from the confines of the layers of commentary that have grown over his dramas. I want to concentrate not on what the plays mean, but how they work, and I want you to come with me on a journey through the plays, as I introduce you to their structures, their plots and language, so that you too might be entertained by them. Certainly, I will attempt to demystify the jargon and delineate the various critical schools and approaches, but we will concentrate on how the plays work and how we, four hundred years after their creation, can respond to them.

2

The framing of Shakespearean comedy: *The Comedy of Errors* (1594)

Many writers strive for a structural formula for their work, which will ensure sustainable success. Modern crime writers, for example, may decide to start their work with a murder and then create a detective to work through various clues in order to discover the perpetrator. Alternatively, they might start by revealing the murderer to the reader or the audience and work through the book or play by showing how he or she avoids or tries to avoid being caught. These are simple structural decisions to be made. In a complex play it is not always easy to perceive the structure underpinning the plot at first, but the writer usually needs one in order to hold the play together.

When Robert Greene, or whoever, accused Shakespeare of borrowing other people's ideas he was, in a sense, right. Shakespeare learned from ancient and contemporary plays but framed what he learned into something new, or he discarded old formulae in order to give a freer rein to his imagination by innovating, adapting or even adopting new structures for his plays.

Some modern critics accuse Shakespeare of being too formulaic. James Shapiro, a respected, historically oriented scholar, for example, considers *Twelfth Night* (1601), one of Shakespeare's most celebrated and performed comedies, to be formulaic. If this is so, it is probably because Shakespeare, in one of his earliest comedies, *The Comedy of Errors*, not only employed a dramatic formula derived from the Greek philosopher Aristotle (384–322 BCE) and the Latin classical dramatist Plautus (c.254–184 BCE), but began to frame a formula of his own which was to influence the later *Twelfth Night*. His sources for *The Comedy of Errors* were two plays by the Roman dramatist Plautus – *The Brothers Menaechmi* and *Amphitryon* – that he may have encountered while at school, as well as an old classical story, *Apollonius of Tyre*. He was probably also influenced by the Latin comedies of Terence (c.190–159 BCE), which were themselves based on plays from classical Greece.

The three Unities

Neoclassical writers and critics in the sixteenth, seventeenth and eighteenth centuries referred to Aristotle's work *Poetics* and used the work of Greek and Roman writers and dramatists as a measure for evaluating the success of a play. They judged that a play should follow Aristotle's rules for drama, which were called the 'three unities' – that is, of time (a single day), place (a single location) and action (a single plot) – if it were to be judged as being of quality.

At the beginning of his career in *The Comedy of Errors*, and in *The Tempest* towards the end of his career, Shakespeare adhered to the three Unities but for the majority of his plays he ignored them. With *The Comedy of Errors* the discipline of keeping to Aristotle's three Unities worked but, although he had devised the details of his plot mainly from Plautus, he nevertheless introduced further complications to it.

The plot of the play

In the play's main source – Plautus' *The Brothers Menaechmi* – there is only a single pair of twins but in *The Comedy of Errors* Shakespeare introduced a second set of twins to complicate the action, creating the potential for more identity errors and thereby more humour. Antipholus of Ephesus has a servant called Dromio. Antipholus of Syracuse, who has arrived in Ephesus searching to find his lost identical twin brother, also has a servant called Dromio. Egeon, a rich Syracusian merchant and the father of the twins Antipholus, bought the twins Dromio to act as his sons' servants. It is a farcical situation, which is explained by Egeon in the opening scene of the play:

> ... she (my wife) became
> A joyful mother of two goodly sons,
> And, which was strange, the one so like the other,
> As could not be distinguish'd but by names.
> That very hour, and in the self-same inn,
> A mean woman was delivered
> Of such a burden male, twins both alike;
> Those, for their parents were exceeding poor,
> I bought, and brought up to attend my sons.

(1.1.49–57)

Key idea

Try to watch as well as read *The Comedy of Errors*, which is a very funny play about the confusions that arise from mistaken identities. Highly entertaining, it is also a 'foundation play', which can help you to understand how many of Shakespeare's later plays work. Widely available, Trevor Nunn's 1978 RSC musical production with Judi Dench and Michael Williams stands the test of time, but there are plenty of other recordings of this play on DVD and the Internet.

The play opens with Egeon being arrested and sentenced to death by the Duke of Ephesus. Ephesus and Syracuse are at war and unwittingly Egeon has landed in the Ephesian port, looking for one of his lost twin sons. Now a captive, he narrates the story of his life to the Duke in order to explain why he has arrived at Syracuse: 'A heavier task could not have been impos'd,/Than I to speak my griefs unspeakable' (1.1.31–2). In the process he tells the incredible story of the birth of his twin sons and the twin servants years ago in 'the self-same inn'. He continues by describing how, on their sea voyage home, a storm blew up and the sailors abandoned the ship they were on, leaving them alone. In order to save themselves, Egeon and his wife fastened one of their baby twins and his servant to one end of a 'small spare mast' (1.1.79) and the other twin and his servant twin to the other end. The wife and Egeon then fastened themselves to either end of the mast.

So they floated, carried by the 'stream' or current (1.1.86) until the storm subsided and the waters calmed, allowing them to see two ships coming towards them, one 'of Corinth', the other 'of Epidaurus'. A further mishap then occurred as they hit a rock that split 'our helpful ship' down the middle, separating them from each other. The wife, with the one twin and the one servant twin, were lighter than the husband and his 'burden' and were rescued by the ship from Corinth, while the other ship rescued Egeon and the other twin son and his servant twin. That ship travelled more slowly than the Corinthian ship and so the family was separated.

He explains that, at the age of 18, his twin son, together with his servant, both of whom had retained the names of their lost brothers, ventured abroad in search of them. He now having lost all his family followed in a search to find the twins whom he had brought up. After five years of searching, he had landed in the hostile town of Ephesus (now in present-day Turkey) where he says he will be content to die and end his misery.

It is a story of a man apparently beset by tragedy but his predicament is so ridiculous as to make it farcical. This is, as the title of the play has announced, a comedy. The Duke's reaction to the tale is to take pity and give Egeon a single day to find the money to pay a ransom for his life. Of course, the money and its passage through the play will be an important stage prop along with others in the development of the comedy.

Key idea

The Unities define the play's structure: a single day, a single place and a single action, the search to find the means of reprieve, which will actually be accomplished through Egeon's discovery of all the twins and his long-lost wife.

The Duke says:

> ... I'll limit thee this day
> To seek thy health by beneficial help;
> Try all the friends thou hast in Ephesus,
> Beg thou, or borrow, to make up the sum,
> And live; if no, then thou art doom'd to die.

(1.1.150–54)

In Trevor Nunn's 1976–8 Royal Shakespeare Company (RSC) musical production of the play, these lines are turned into a song-and-dance routine, thereby contributing to the comical nature of what might otherwise become an outwardly sombre, potentially tragic denouement.

Spotlight

Throughout the farcical story, but one that retains a degree of credibility, the audience is given signals that Egeon's escape from death will be as a result of acquiring the sum needed for his release, and that he will recover his lost sons. In the process, and with the arrival – unknown to him – of Antipholus and Dromio of Syracuse in Ephesus on a similar quest, a series of mistaken identities ensues as the two sets of twins get thoroughly confused with one another. As an audience, we sit back to enjoy the comic 'errors' that begin in the next scene when Antipholus of Syracuse, with his Dromio, arrives in Ephesus but is warned that a Syracusian merchant has been sentenced to death, and therefore not to divulge his Syracusian identity.

Dromio of Syracuse is sent off to the Inn with Antipholus' money and the farce ensues as Dromio of Ephesus arrives on the scene and is mistaken for Dromio of Syracuse. The play moves along as a comic romp of mistaken identities, involving sexual innuendo, a frustrated marriage, a courtesan, a merchant, an officer of the law, a fake exorcist magician and, finally, the Duke himself. The situation becomes so chaotic that no one, not even the Duke, can sort out what is happening. But at this point the dramatist engineers a discovery. It is prompted by the local Abbess, into whose 'house' Antipholus and Dromio of Syracuse escape to seek sanctuary. She turns out to be the long-lost wife of Egeon, and her recognition of her husband is the first step towards a resolution of all the errors that have arisen.

Spotlight

In its denouement the play is following a classical discipline that allows resolution through what Aristotle termed *anagnorisis*, or discovery, although he uses this term primarily in relation to tragedy. Anagnorisis is when the characters on stage recognize the errors of the action of the play and so bring it to a conclusion through a discovery. Anagnorisis often involves a process of 'self-discovery' and comes usually towards the end of the play, although we will see that later, in *King Lear*, Shakespeare will frustrate its placement to great, if controversial, effect.

In *The Comedy of Errors*, anagnorisis occurs in Act 5, scene 1 when the Abbess, on seeing her long-lost husband, says:

> Whoever bound him, I will loose his bonds,
> And gain a husband by his liberty.
> Speak old Egeon, if thou be'st the man
> That hadst a wife once call'd Emilia,
> That bore thee at a burden two fair sons?
> O, if thou be'st the same Egeon, speak –
> And speak unto the same Emilia.
>
> (5.1.340–46)

Egeon replies:

> If I dream not, thou art Emilia;
> If thou art she, tell me, where is that son
> That floated with thee on the fatal raft? (353–5)

So it is that the Antipholus twins are then recognized, as are the two Dromios. This also completes the quest of Antipholus of Syracuse to establish his own identity in a world where identities can be duplicated. Finally, Egeon is pardoned and the assembled company (as well as the audience) is able to laugh at the potentially disastrous errors that have taken place, leaving the two Dromios on stage to exit harmoniously 'hand in hand, not one before another'.

The play concludes with a family united after adversity, but may possibly leave members of the audience ruminating on what might happen once the twins are again separated from each other. This, however, is a play, not real life. Nothing will happen because the characters are part of a fictional story. From the very beginning of his career Shakespeare innovates, drawing his audience into the narrative of the play.

The structure of the play

This early comic play is nearly perfect in structure – in presenting a problem, an action and a resolution. Some critics (for example Bertrand Evans) have noted that the Abbess is introduced only at the end of the play to resolve the action and does not feature in the errors throughout, which suggests that there might be some slight artistic imperfection in the play's overall structure. That, however, is at most an academic nicety, and not entirely consistent with the story that Egeon unfolds at the beginning of the play. Given the series of comic coincidences that occur throughout *The Comedy of Errors*, the appearance of the Abbess at the end is in keeping with the play's comic ethos, and in production doesn't detract from the hilarity of the farce or our enjoyment of it. The *Comedy of Errors* is a neoclassically well-structured and hugely entertaining play.

Some critics may demean the play precisely because it does what it sets out to do. It is written as a farce and does not have the 'weight' of the later comedies. Others, such as L. G. Salinger for example, see far too much emotion in it to characterize it simply as a farce. When this play was first performed, the mature romantic comedies were still to come but there is, nevertheless, a foretaste of them here. If we wish to see how Shakespeare's plays work, *The Comedy of Errors* actually starts to map out a template on which much of Shakespearean comedy was later to be developed.

'The fact is that the serious elements are in some danger of going unobserved, while no one is likely to miss the fun, especially in the distorted and jazzed-up versions of the play which are commonly staged.'

Foakes, R. A. (1962: xlix), 'Introduction' *The Comedy of Errors, The Arden Shakespeare*. London: Methuen

In farce, characterization is not developed in detail since the figures are primarily types. The main interest in this play is the characters' immediate reactions to the chaos being created around them and to which they contribute, often inadvertently. The misunderstandings that produce the hilarity are, at this stage, superficial, and we do not get too close to the predicaments in which the characters find themselves.

But in the play there are already pointers towards what will be developed in more sophisticated comic form, and also in tragedy, in the later plays.

As early as Act 1, Scene 2, when the merchant who has helped Antipholus of Syracuse commends him to his 'own content', Antipholus replies:

> He that commends me to mine own content
> Commends me to the thing I cannot get.
> I to the world am like a drop of water
> That in the ocean seeks another drop,
> Who, falling there to find his fellow forth,
> (Unseen, inquisitive) confounds himself.
> So I, to find a mother and a brother,
> In quest of them, unhappy, lose myself.

(1.2.33–40)

This is an early example of **soliloquy**, whereby a character left alone on the stage is revealing something of himself to the audience, reflecting on his situation. It also points up the issue of 'identity' that is crucial here, and is a theme taken up in plays that follow.

We find later in the play that Adriana, the wife of Antipholus of Ephesus, is distraught at her husband's neglect of her and jealous that he may be looking elsewhere for female company. She laments; but Shakespeare places her dissatisfaction within a comic framework by having her sister Luciana point out the flaws in her argument:

> ADRIANA   Are my discourses dull? barren my wit?
>
> ...
>
> My decayed fair
> A sunny look of his would soon repair;
> But, too unruly deer, he breaks the pale
> And feeds from home; poor I am but his stale.
> LUCIANA   Self-harming jealousy! fie, beat it hence.

(2.1.92, 99–103)

In later plays, most notably *Othello* and *The Winter's Tale*, Shakespeare explores jealousy at a much deeper level while still exposing errors of perception. The answers the characters give to the errors that occur in *The Comedy of Errors* result often in what we might call 'slapstick' or 'pantomime violence', or in claims and rumours that Ephesus is haunted by magic, as Antipholus of Syracuse notes:

> They say this town is full of cozenage,
>
> As nimble jugglers that deceive the eye,
>
> Dark-working sorcerers that change the mind,
>
> Soul-killing witches that deform the body,
>
> Disguised cheaters, prating mountebanks,
>
> And many such-like liberties of sin.

(1.2.97–102)

Later, Dr Pinch the conjurer is called upon to exorcize Antipholus of Ephesus in an attempt by Adriana to 'Establish him in his true sense again' (4.4.50). Magic, violence, misunderstandings, discontent, loss of identity – all are encompassed but within the recognizable farce of the play. The combination of these elements rarely fails in performance.

Innovation in *The Comedy of Errors*

The unities of time (a single day), place (a single location) and action (a single plot) in *The Comedy of Errors* give the play its structure but the comedy is so successful that it allows Shakespeare, even at this early stage in his career, to innovate. In other comedies he moves away from the stranglehold of the unities, giving himself greater freedom and the opportunity to ask of his characters and his narrative the question 'But what if?' This allows him to free up the formula for his romantic comedies and in doing so to experiment even further in the tragedies, and with the other plays over whose classification critics continue to argue.

From this early farce, we can discern the formula that Shakespeare is to develop. The action will begin with certain characters embarking on a search in order to find themselves and to achieve peace of mind. That search begins with danger and even the possibility of death. The search for contentment may involve pretending to be from somewhere where you are not and/or being someone you are not. You may, thereby, be displaced from your normal surroundings and alienated in some way or deliberately adopting a persona, or as in the later *Twelfth Night* it could be all of these. But these journeys relate to the characters themselves being lost, that is, in their very identity, and subsequently found.

The formula or structure involves the sorting out of errors in relationships, certainly with the opposite sex and possibly with the same sex, finding reconciliation in love, as occurs (it would seem) with Antipholus of Ephesus and Adriana or with the reunion of Egeon and his wife the Abbess. These searches lead to a recognition scene, to Aristotelian anagnorisis. Shakespeare keeps this classical focal point in the construction of many of the comedies and tragedies later in his career. But what happens if that scene is cruelly contrived by one character, as in *Measure for Measure*, or deliberately frustrated by the dramatist, as in *King Lear* or in *Cymbeline*? In *The Comedy of Errors* Shakespeare lays the foundations for the development of the mature but more flexible structures of the plays to come. *The Comedy of Errors* is one of the most valuable means by which we can gain an introduction to Shakespeare's craftsmanship. It is also one of the best plays to watch as an indication of his entertainment value.

3

Critical perspectives 1: Neoclassical and Romantic approaches

Approaches to Shakespeare have varied from age to age since the plays were first performed and published. One of the difficulties for sixteenth- and seventeenth-century critics was the problem that, if Shakespeare flouted neoclassical rules, how is it that he is so good? The Romantics' concept of 'the organic nature of art' provided an answer to the question but as a result they began to venerate him, which led to the rise of 'bardolatry'.

The fact that Shakespeare did not generally follow the neoclassical rules for dramatic writing is one of two major criticisms that have bedevilled him. The second is the claim that this man from the parochial town of Stratford-upon-Avon, who had received no university education, could not possibly have written the plays. In one sense the two issues – the divergence from neoclassical rules and the authorship question – are grounded in social perceptions, prejudices and intellectual elitism, all of which have been exposed by contemporary criticism.

Spotlight

The allegation that he could not have written the plays is still levelled by some against Shakespeare, despite historical evidence to the contrary and the weight of mainstream literary scholarship that has supported his authorship. It is the subject, for example, of the film *Anonymous*, which peddles the theory of the Earl of Oxford as the writer of the plays, with little understanding of how the myth began or of how impossible the claim is.

If you read, for example, James Shapiro's *Contested Will* or Michael Wood's *In Search of Shakespeare* or Jonathan Bate's *The Genius of Shakespeare*, you will see that the authorship question has surfaced many times since Shakespeare's death but that it was based often on misleading or fraudulent evidence. Michael Wood discusses the quality of Shakespeare's grammar school education in Stratford and provides a useful account of the influence of his family, especially Mary Arden his mother, and his general upbringing, on the development of his imagination.

The seventeenth century

From Robert Greene's 1592 'upstart Crow' complaint onwards, Shakespeare has often been viewed with some suspicion – even, at times, hostility. How could this non-university-educated newcomer to the literary and theatrical scene be so good? Plays in English were not considered 'literary works' until Ben Jonson in 1616 published a folio edition of his own plays, calling them *Works*. In Shakespeare's own day, some of his poetry – surprisingly not the *Sonnets* – was highly successful and well regarded, but the fact remains that he was neither aristocratic nor highly educated. Even Ben Jonson, while admiring his unique, timeless talent, quipped, perhaps ironically, that Shakespeare had 'small Latin and less Greek'. But, as modern historians have noted, such was the educational system and the standard of the Elizabethan grammar schools that a boy on completing his school education may have been as proficient in Latin as Classics graduates are today. Ben Jonson was not university educated either but he was an exceedingly good classical scholar, so the description 'small' has to be put into perspective.

Throughout the seventeenth century, Shakespeare was considered, not only by Ben Jonson but also by later poets such as John Milton (1608–74) and John Dryden (1631–1700), to have been a 'natural genius'. But do natural geniuses actually exist? Perhaps it is no small wonder, given the breadth of material in the plays, that claims – sometimes based on fraudulent evidence – were made that Shakespeare could not have written them but was merely a front man for an intellectual or aristocratic writer such as Francis Bacon or the Earl of Oxford who wished to remain anonymous. None of this squares, however, with the facts as we have them or the contemporary evidence concerning Shakespeare's authorship, although later in his career he did collaborate with younger dramatists. The way in which he has been regarded, nonetheless, and the reputation he has acquired over the last four centuries, help shape the way we now approach him.

Spotlight

Milton saw Shakespeare as the supreme English poet but both he and Dryden still had difficulty with his apparent failure to obey the neoclassical rules; they blamed the 'fury of fancy' for transporting Shakespeare beyond the bounds of judgement. *Antony and Cleopatra*, for example, darted from city to city and country to country over several years and contained multiple plots and subplots. This kind of structure went against what was regarded as the disciplines of the art form. Dryden's own play *All for Love* (1678), a version of the Antony and Cleopatra story, is in the neoclassical disciplined style, and is occasionally produced on the modern stage in repertory with *Antony and Cleopatra*. It is a good play but it lacks the breadth of imagination and the theatrical presence of Shakespeare's masterpiece.

As early as 1681, Nahum Tate regarded Shakespeare's *King Lear* as 'a house of unorganized treasures', and he rewrote the ending in order to allow Cordelia to fall in love with Edgar and let Lear survive. Tate's version commanded the stage for the next 150 years. In a more seriously critical vein, in 1697 Thomas Rymer had declared *Othello* to be a 'bloody farce, without salt or savour'. Shakespeare's tragedy did not harmonize with the taste of the age or its literary sensibilities.

The eighteenth century

The late seventeenth-century criticism of Shakespeare continued into the eighteenth century. In France, Voltaire declared Shakespeare to be an 'English buffoon', describing *Hamlet* in 1748 as 'a vulgar and barbarous drama, which would not be tolerated by the vilest populace of France or Italy'. His choice of the phrase 'vilest populace' is of interest to us, especially when we recall the location of the Globe theatre in the suburbs, in what we might now call a red-light district just beyond the boundaries of the city of London.

Shakespeare developed his theatre for all, but in the late seventeenth century and into the eighteenth literary intellectuals regarded Ben Jonson as the purer craftsman. Nonetheless, it was Shakespeare whose reputation grew in spite of his apparent failure to follow neoclassical rules.

The influential scholar Samuel Johnson (1709–84), in his *Preface to Shakespeare*, rejected the concept of the Unities as an appropriate measure of quality for drama. He saw Shakespeare as depicting 'life' and advised that we should consider most of the plays as 'tragic comedies'. Johnson was, however, critical of some of Shakespeare's dramatic poetry: he wished to expunge the famous lines in Macbeth 'Here lies Duncan, his silver skin laced with his golden blood' with 'an universal blot'. He also expressed great difficulty with the harrowing final scene of *King Lear*.

'*Shakespeare's plays are not in the rigorous or critical sense either tragedies or comedies, but compositions of a distinct kind; exhibiting the real state of sublunary nature, which partakes of good and evil, joy and sorrow, mingled with endless variety of proportion and innumerable modes of combination; and expressing the course of the world, in which the loss of one is the gain of another; in which at the same time, the reveller is hasting to his wine, and the mourner burying his friend.*'

Johnson, Dr S. (1765). See Powell, R. [1980: 141], *Shakespeare and the Critics Debate*. Basingstoke: Macmillan

Key idea

Dr Johnson's perspective is that Shakespeare does not adhere to the Unities because he has imagination to portray a common humanity, which is not modified by the constraints of time and place.

In the latter half of the eighteenth century Shakespeare was regarded as being able to deal with generalized passions. If you want to know about jealousy, refer to *Othello*; if you want to know about young love, refer to *Romeo and Juliet*; for mature love, see *Antony and Cleopatra*; for debilitating ambition, see *Macbeth*; for procrastination, see *Hamlet*, and so forth. Shakespeare's genius is thereby considered to lie in the portrayal of a human nature to be found in young lovers and ageing monarchs. His characters are types, displaying human passions.

> '… he was the man who of all Modern, and perhaps Ancient poets, had the largest and most comprehensive soul. All the Images of Nature were still present to him.'
>
> John Dryden in Powell (1980: 140–41)

Nevertheless, as we have suggested, Samuel Johnson is still critical of the dramatist. There is little moral purpose behind the plays; the plots are loosely constructed and even though the Unities are rejected there is no sense of time or place – no clear geographical location whether the setting be Rome, Egypt or Venice. But even more problematic for Samuel Johnson and eighteenth-century Augustan cultural attitudes is the fact that Shakespeare is seen to be deficient in language and decorum, having a laboured narration. In language, Shakespeare's use of the pun, for example, irritated Johnson as being tedious. It was, he claimed, Shakespeare's 'fatal Cleopatra'. This is indicative, perhaps, of what Johnson regarded as a general deficiency in gentility and the protracted narrative scope of some of the plays.

Today we recognize that Samuel Johnson is judging the plays by the social attitudes and ideologies of his own age. Despite his rejection of the Aristotelian Unities, he remains bound within the neoclassical tradition, with eighteenth-century notions of decorum and the mindset that accompanies them. Such an eighteenth-century taste for decorum and elegance did not sit easily with what then might have been considered the crudity of Shakespeare's frequent use of the pun. Today, however, modern criticism appreciates the pun's social and political subversive nature – as noted, for example, by Peter Davison:

'The pun – and again, the bad pun especially – as used by Shakespeare, plays not only upon the word but upon the individual's relationship with the community, within the play-world and the real-world. It epitomizes both our individuality and, through the response, that we have a place in the community. Of all literary devices it is the one that, in a hierarchical community, can most readily transcend class ... The bad pun may be said to be the epitome of "popular appeal", demanding of an audience to a play conscious awareness of, and response to, extra-dramatic, social, relationships.'

Davison, P. [1982: 78], *Popular Appeal in English Drama to 1850*.
Basingstoke: Macmillan

If the pun caused Dr Johnson unease, so too the ending of *King Lear* undermined his sense of decorum and violated his eighteenth-century commitment to a kind of poetic justice:

'... if my sensations could add anything to the general suffrage, I might relate that I was many years ago so shocked by Cordelia's death, that I know not whether I ever endured to read again the last scenes of the play till I undertook to revise them as editor.'

Johnson, Dr S., in Woudhuysen, H.R. (ed.) (1989: 222–3), *Samuel Johnson on Shakespeare*. Harmondsworth: New Penguin Shakespeare Library

Nahum Tate's 1681 adaptation accorded with natural justice until a revival of something like the original version of *King Lear* in the early nineteenth century, when in 1823 the actor Edmund Kean and later in 1838 Charles Macready moved performances away from Tate's happy ending and gradually reinstated the ending of Shakespeare's tragedy with which we are familiar today, and of which Charles Dickens approved.

The late 1780s proved a great turning point in the history of the Western world with the American War of Independence in 1787 and the French Revolution in 1789. It was perhaps as seismic a shift in cultural and social perceptions as was the European Reformation and Henry VIII's revolt against Rome in the sixteenth century, both of which had such a profound effect in Shakespeare's lifetime. The French Revolution was not only a political but an intellectual movement, which had an effect on the emergence of the European Enlightenment and Romanticism at the end of the eighteenth and the beginning of the nineteenth centuries, and which paved the way in turn to the growth of realism as the nineteenth century progressed.

Romanticism

The Romantic Movement fundamentally changed attitudes towards Shakespeare. English Romantic critics and poets and writers and poets in Germany regarded poetic expression as the pinnacle of philosophy. If Shakespeare were the supreme poet, then he was to be venerated as the greatest of all thinkers, paving the way for 'bardolatry' to take hold.

Hector Berlioz (1803–69), an intensely romantic composer who composed the wildly macabre *Symphonie fantastique* and works based on Shakespeare's plays, regarded him as 'the living and loving God':

'Shakespeare! You were a man. You, if you still exist, must be a refuge for the wretched. It is you that are our father, our father in heaven, if there is a heaven... Thou alone for the souls of artists are the living and loving God. Receive us, father, into thy bosom, guard us, save us! De profundis ad te clamo. What are death and nothingness? Genius is immortal!'

Berlioz, H.; see Bate, J. (1989: 247), *Shakespeare and the English Romantic Imagination.* Oxford: Clarendon Press

In England, the influential Romantic poet Samuel Taylor Coleridge (1772–1834) concentrated attention on language and the characters that spoke it. The question of genius was resolved through an understanding of language and character as the fundamental components of the plays.

Coleridge developed the notion from German philosophy of the organic form of the play as opposed to the mechanical and rustic forms identified by earlier criticism. A. W. Von Schlegel (1769–1845) between 1808 and 1811 had challenged the rules that neoclassicism had imposed upon plays. In his view, it was this imposition that had produced a lifeless garden of artificial flowers, but for him true art had to be organic. Art changes from principles within itself; it is innate and unfolds like a flower according to its own organic nature. The consequence is that you don't criticize one flower because it is not like another one. You appreciate it for itself, for its own innate nature.

'Form is mechanical when, through external force, it is imparted to any material merely as an accidental addition without reference to its quality ... Organical form ... unfolds itself from within, and acquires its determination contemporaneously with the perfect development of the germ. We everywhere discover such forms in nature ... In the fine arts, as well as in the domain of nature – the supreme artist – all genuine forms are organical, that is, determined by the quality of the work.'

Schlegel, A. W. von; see Bate, J. (1989: 12–13), *Shakespeare and the English Romantic Imagination.* Oxford: Clarendon Press

Applied to Shakespeare or other great poets, this approach insisted that the artist might not be aware of the organic laws governing the unfolding of the work of art, since it is a combination of the unconscious and the conscious mind in cooperation that creates the poem or the play.

'... the poet, in his dreams, institutes, as it were, experiments which are received with as much authority as if they had been made on waking objects.'

Schlegel, A. W. von; see Bate, J. (1992: 97), *The Romantics on Shakespeare.* Harmondsworth: Penguin Books

The primacy of language

The Romantics held that the uniqueness that informs everything emerges from the creative process. Language is thus regarded as the living principle of the play rather than the coat with which its thought is clothed. The play grows out of the words and thus, to understand the play, you need primarily to appreciate the language. Language, metre, poetry are a tripartite living principle. To understand the organic nature of the plays, you must first savour their language. As the twentieth-century critic L. C. Knights was to argue, the better the language the better the play. It is the language, the poetry that is paramount and continues to this day to be seen by many distinguished Shakespearean scholars and directors as the primary element of Shakespearean drama.

'[Shakespeare] creates people, talking really, within a poem. There is poetry in structure, in juxtaposition, in rhythm. A poem is communication through image – and it is an ambiguous communication at that. Each individual image defies analysis, and together they add up, not to a thesis but to an experience. The ambiguity is intentional. The less it is explained by decor and costume, the greater is its richness. Whatever else we attempted or achieved in the production ... everything – rehearsals, staging, performance – was aimed at communicating its poetry. Not just the spoken word, but the real poetry of the whole. The golden armour of the French ... the follow spots ... canopies ... music, the empty stage, the actors' changing styles and utterances, all were images within the overall poem.'

Terry Hands, former artistic director of the Royal Shakespeare Company, quoted in Beauman, S. (ed.) (1976: 26–7), *The Royal Shakespeare Company's Production of* Henry V *for the Centenary Season at the Royal Shakespeare Theatre.* Oxford: Pergamon

Further, as the plays are composed of elements, the critic must search for the organizing principle of the play from within. For nineteenth-century commentators, influenced by developments in the novel as a literary form, this was located not in the plot but in 'character'.

Organic growth, language and character, the determining features of the emerging novel form, become, through Romanticism, the dominant criteria of literary criticism for the nineteenth and early twentieth centuries. Characterization starts to be seen as the determining force of the drama. Beginning with Maurice Morgann's 1777 *Essay on the Dramatic Character of Sir John Falstaff* and developed in William Hazlitt's *Characters of Shakespeare's Plays* (1817), attention was focused on close textual analysis of what characters say of themselves as individuals whose lives extend beyond the actions in which they are involved. It is almost as if the characters are real people, and judgements are made about them as organic individuals. It was a critical trend which developed into the twentieth century with the appearance in 1904 of A. C. Bradley's *Shakespearean Tragedy*, but which still retains a certain respectability. It is an approach, as we will see later, that began to be challenged in the 1930s, but which has also been challenged vigorously by more recent twentieth- and twenty-first-century criticism.

4

A Midsummer Night's Dream (1595–6) and *Romeo and Juliet* (1595–6)

The dream is a complex theatrical metaphor. It is the double vision that allows us to watch, listen, consider and reflect – but rarely, if ever in comedy, to apportion blame. In this chapter we will consider two plays: *A Midsummer Night's Dream* and *Romeo and Juliet*, written at almost the same time (1595–6). These can be seen as mirror images of each other, working from a similar structural foundation to produce in the one, comedy, using the dream metaphor, and in the other, tragedy, with reference to a particular dream. But the concept of dream itself is multi-layered, since plays in the theatre are also often described as dreams or fantasies. In these two plays metaphors accumulate, thereby opening to question and constantly challenging the audience's perception.

A Midsummer Night's Dream

You might ask what kind of dream it is that Shakespeare creates in *A Midsummer Night's Dream*. Whose dream is it? How does he create it?

Let us take the second question first. As we have seen, Shakespeare elaborates on a basic formula that he develops for his drama. In this romantic comedy it begins with a problem, a serious threat, even of death. A geographical relocation or the taking on of a disguise then occurs until an awakening happens – a discovery – which brings about reconciliation and, in comedy, the resolution of the initial problem and the neutralization of the threat of death.

This is the structure underlying *A Midsummer Night's Dream* which holds the play together. In *The Comedy of Errors* Shakespeare had two pairs of identical twins, whose escapades generate the hilarity of mistaken identities. In *A Midsummer Night's Dream* he takes two couples, Lysander and Hermia and Demetrius and Helena, who enter a forest. It is a 'wood', which is a word that also meant 'mad' in Elizabethan colloquial speech. Here they become embroiled in a fairy world in which a third couple, Oberon, King of the Fairies, and Titania, Queen of the Fairies, are quarrelling over the ownership of a 'changeling boy'. In fairy stories 'a changeling' is a child that has been exchanged for another at birth – a child that is of wronged or mistaken identity.

In this play Lysander and Hermia have fled to the forest from the Athenian court because Hermia wishes to marry Lysander, but her father Egeus (representing old age), wants her to marry Demetrius. The Duke (representing authority) rules in favour of the father and threatens the choice of death or the cloistered life of nun for Hermia if she does not obey. So the flight of the lovers is to escape the threats of age and parental authority. They wish to be free in their choice of partner and to establish an identity for themselves. Helena tells Demetrius, whom she loves but who does not love her, about the flight of Hermia and Lysander, thinking that the knowledge will make him love her. It does not, and he pursues Hermia and Lysander into the forest and Helena, in turn, pursues him. In going to the forest, unwittingly they are entering a 'mad' fairy world at odds with itself because of the quarrel between Oberon and Titania.

The King and Queen of the Fairies correspond to Theseus, the Duke of Athens, and his bride-to-be, Hippolyta, the Amazonian Queen. Indeed, both have past connections with Oberon and Titania in the fairy world. The audience sees in one set of characters a reflection of another set; in this case Oberon and Titania are reflections of Theseus and Hippolyta and vice versa, through what is known as **correspondence**. One set of characters corresponds to another set.

'... the power of suggestion is the strength of the double plot, once you take two parts to correspond, any character may take on mana *(an expression of an unseen force), because he seems to cause what he corresponds to or be* Logos *(the resulting word), of what he symbolizes.'*

Empson, W. (1935: 34), *Some Versions of Pastoral.* New York: New Directions

(For more about mana and logos, see the key terms at the end of this chapter.)

THE SEARCH FOR THE SELF AND THE SELF'S LOVE FOR ANOTHER SELF

In some old medieval stories – such as the one recounted by Chaucer in *The Wife of Bath's Tale* – the question arises of what a woman wants to be. The answer is to be herself, like any man. So the lovers flee to the forest to be or to find themselves. But what is that self, what is self-identity? What is the difference between being in love and being infatuated or self-deluded or merely self-gratifying? How do you find your own identity and reality? In this play, despite the opening threat of death, the search is for identity, for the self and the self's love for another self, and they are portrayed through comic mistakes of identity and excursions into 'madness' brought about by Oberon and his mischievous attendant fairy, Puck.

We know from the start, of course, that this is a comedy and that all will, ultimately, be resolved happily. Compare this with *Romeo and Juliet,* written probably in the same period. Here Shakespeare changes the genre from the comic to the tragic within the play. Romeo, at first, is in love with Rosaline but his love changes from his own fancy almost as swiftly as Lysander's changes in *A Midsummer Night's Dream* under the influence of Oberon's magic potion that is wrongly applied by Puck. Romeo gives up Rosaline for Juliet, even though we know that both the houses of Montague and Capulet are involved in a long-standing feud. His friend Mercutio tells him that being in love is being enslaved by the Fairy Queen, Mab, and soon after this the potentially romantic story turns sour. At the midpoint of the play, Mercutio, the cousin of the Prince, is killed in a fight with Juliet's cousin, Tybalt, leading Romeo in the heat of the moment to avenge his friend's death by killing Tybalt. Although the Prologue to the play has informed us from the start that the play will show that the lovers will take their own lives, it is at the point of Mercutio's death (3.1.75f.) that the play moves into the tragic mode. The Queen Mab dream turns into a nightmare, with Mercutio's death leading eventually to the tragic deaths of Romeo and Juliet.

In *A Midsummer Night's Dream* there is a blurring between dreaming and waking, between the 'dream' and 'reality', but in *Romeo and Juliet* the opposition is ultimately between life and death. In both cases, but in different registers, the stage imitates issues of uncertainty that pervade existence. While I was writing this chapter, my three-year-old granddaughter, playing with her toys and lost in a fantasy world, suddenly stopped and asked, 'I am real, aren't I? I'm not pretend?' She was told that she was not pretend and went happily back into the imaginative fantasy world in which she was playing.

Key idea

In *A Midsummer Night's Dream* the question 'I am real, aren't I?' is being asked by some of the characters as they eventually awake from their dream. What is it to be awake or asleep, to be real or pretend? How does a child, a lover, know what is real, know what love actually is? What is it to be oneself? This is not a problem for aristocrats alone or one for the learned. It is a question for everyone, whatever their station in society as they start to define their individuality through that society.

Identity and the individual

As we will see later in our discussion on tragedy, the concept of the individual as defined by the society in which he or she lives was beginning to be understood at the time of the Renaissance and Reformation. As England, Wales, Scotland and Ireland as geographical locations were becoming important in the formation of a sense of national identity, traditional religious explanations concerning truth and authority, society and the individual were being questioned. With the growth of Protestantism and the challenge to the authority of the Catholic Church, the concept of a secular individualism was developing in an increasingly commercial society that was on the cusp of developing into what we now recognize as capitalist.

THE DREAM METAPHOR

The dream metaphor in *A Midsummer Night's Dream* is used to generate the humour of the mistakes that are made. The love potion placed on the wrong lover's eyes by the fairy, Puck; the punishment meted out to the Fairy Queen, Titania, for not doing as the Fairy King wants; the translation of Bottom, the weaver, into an ass with whom Titania falls in love: all these events border on cruelty and the grotesque but are rescued for comedy by a certain distancing of the action. The characters affected by the potions administered to them by Puck are in a dream, but we as an audience are both self-conscious and at the same time open to the prospect of being bewitched as we enter into the play's bewitched narrative. We are watching a dream by being in the theatre, but we are also drawn into it.

'The whole night's action is presented as a release of shaping fantasy which brings clarification about the tricks of strong imagination. We watch a dream; but we are awake, thanks to pervasive humour about the tendency to take fantasy literally, whether in love, in superstition, or in Bottom's mechanical dramatics.'

Barber, C. L. (1959: 124), *Shakespeare's Festive Comedy.* Princeton, NJ: Princeton University Press

While more recent criticism has shifted emphasis to the social and historical context of the play by pointing to the political realities it exposes, Barber's comments still hold some force, although they need to be tempered. Towards the end of the twentieth century, the cultural materialist critic James H. Kavanagh argued from a more politically oriented position:

> '[The play exposes] a set of pre-conscious image-concepts in which men and women see and experience, before they think about their place within a given social formation, with its specific structure of class and gender relations.'
>
> Drakakis, J. (ed.) (1985: 145), *Alternative Shakespeares*. London and New York: Methuen

There is no doubt that, politically, Shakespeare had to be very careful within the play; as it was probably watched by Queen Elizabeth I, he didn't go too far in drawing contemporary parallels. The Queen herself was known as the 'Fairy Queen' or the 'Virgin Queen', so to have a Fairy Queen 'enamoured of an ass' – a creature renowned for its large genitalia – could have had serious consequences for the dramatist if not handled carefully within the framework of comedy. The Queen at the end of the play is assured that, as with other members of the audience, she has been witnessing the comedy, and like the audience generally she, too, has been dreaming:

> If we shadows have offended,
> Think but this, and all is mended,
> That you have but slumber'd here
> While these visions did appear.

(5.1.417–20)

Key idea

The concept of the play as a dream isn't uniquely Shakespearean.
The Elizabethan dramatist John Lyly perhaps set a precedent in the Prologue to his play *Sappho and Phao* (1584), when he entreats the Queen to imagine herself at the conclusion to have been in 'a deep dream'. Dream poetry is also notably plentiful in medieval English literature.

Shakespeare asks that the play itself be regarded as a dream, in which the characters themselves enter into a dreamlike world in which they are subject to a wide range of fantasies. For example, Hermia, having fallen asleep, wakes from a nightmare:

> Help me, Lysander, help me! Do thy best
> To pluck this crawling serpent from my breast!
> Ay me, for pity! What a dream was here!

(2.2.144–6)

But she finds that Lysander has left her alone because he is now under the influence of the love potion and has gone in pursuit of Helena. The dream motif in the play is multilayered. Hermia has had a dream of danger and, in the story of the play, has awoken to the 'dream' of the forest, and yet all this occurs for the theatre audience within a performance that the dramatist is encouraging it to regard as dreamlike.

On awakening, the lovers talk of their experiences. Demetrius says, 'These things seem small and undistinguishable, / Like far-off mountains turned into clouds' and Hermia remarks, 'Methinks I see these things with parted eye, / When everything seems double' (4.1.186–9).

Bottom, on awaking from his ridiculous fantasy, thinks he is still rehearsing the Mechanicals' play for the wedding of Theseus and Hippolyta, 'When my cue comes, call me and I will answer. My next is "Most fair Pyramus"' (4.1.199–200). But, finding himself alone, he reflects on the events of his own dream: 'I have had a dream, past the wit of man to say what dream it was' (203–5); he concludes that his fantasy should be made into a ballad written by Peter Quince, to be sung at the end of their performance before Theseus and Hippolyta. This is an example of **metatheatre**, in which the character refers self-consciously to the nature of the play, the story of which he says should be made into a 'ballad', into an entertainment, which, of course, is what the play actually is.

ELIZABETH, THE 'IMPERIAL VOT'RESS'

In all of this, Shakespeare flatters Queen Elizabeth by simultaneously associating her with Titania and yet almost simultaneously deliberately distancing her from that association. Queen Elizabeth's virginity was part of the myth of the authority that surrounded her person, as demonstrated in her 'chastity', 'constancy' and her 'marriage' to the realm. So, in Act 2, Scene 1, lines 158 and 161–4, Shakespeare has Oberon tell Puck that he once saw Cupid shooting an arrow at 'a fair vestal, throned by the west', that is, the English Queen, but that the 'fiery shaft"/[was] Quench'd in the chaste beams of the watery moon;/And the imperial vot'ress passed on,/In maiden meditation, fancy free.'

There is a reference here also, perhaps, to Elizabeth's visit in 1575 to the Earl of Leicester at Kenilworth Castle. The visit might have suggested a possible romance between the Queen and her vassal, ending in marriage, but on this occasion it did not. The 'imperial vot'ress' departed 'in maiden' determination to remain wedded only to her realm. As we will see in discussing *Richard II* and *Macbeth*, for example, Shakespeare had to take great care not to be seen to insult his monarch Elizabeth and, later, King James. Who actually knows what happened between Leicester and his monarch in 1575?

CRAFTSMANSHIP AND RESOLUTION
A further element of the dramatist's craftsmanship in the work is that, within the construction of this dream play, Shakespeare uses some sublime poetry to transport the audience into the realms of fairyland. Oberon uses the full resources of poetry to instruct Puck to administer the love potion to her eyes:

> I know a bank where the wild thyme blows,
>
> Where oxlips and the nodding violet grows,
>
> Quite over-canopied with luscious woodbine,
>
> With sweet musk-roses, and with eglantine.

(2.1.249–52)

It is as if the language within the dream of the play actually takes the audience to the place where:

> … sleeps Titania sometime of the night,
> Lull'd in these flowers with dances and delight;

(2.1.253–4)

Oberon, the King of the Fairies, has the power within the play to correct Puck's errors and his own vindictiveness towards Titania, but he can also ensure that the love potion is correctly administered to the two pairs of earthly lovers. In the end, he releases Titania from the spell, lifts the ass's head from Bottom's shoulders and allows the lovers to find the correct partner, which leads to the marriages they wish for and to the assent of the reluctant Egeus. Through **correspondence** – Oberon with the Duke Theseus and Titania with Hippolyta – Shakespeare implies moreover that the resolution in the fairy kingdom guarantees the resolution in the earthly one.

In modern performances the same actor occasionally plays Theseus and Oberon and the same female actor – in the Elizabethan theatre a boy actor – Hippolyta and Titania. The plot, developing from the foundations of the structure, allows for reconciliation and a 'happy ending'. In *A Midsummer Night's Dream* the disasters are averted first of all by the corrective authorized by Oberon and secondly by the way in which the potentially tragic performance of Pyramus and Thisbe by the Mechanicals is subjected to a hilariously comic treatment, the result of their own thespian incompetence. With *Romeo and Juliet* we find some of the same ingredients but they are treated very differently.

Romeo and Juliet

In *Romeo and Juliet* we see that the reverse occurs in the end, since the attempts by a controlling agent to bring about reconciliation go wrong in the story. Juliet drinks the sleeping potion, which makes it look as if she is dead, but she will awake once she is within the family's burial chamber. Word will be sent to her banished lover Romeo who, like a Prince in a fairy story, will be with her when she wakes. They will embrace and escape all their difficulties. But Friar Laurence, though a member of the Church, is human and the reality of the situation proves very different from that in *A Midsummer Night's Dream*.

It is almost as if Shakespeare is using his structure to answer the question 'But what if?' applying it to different scenarios. In this case, what if the fairy tale does not run its true course because circumstances beyond the control of the characters do not allow it to do so? What happens if the fairy-tale prince is ignorant of the friar's plan and thinks that his princess is really dead? Here, Shakespeare is engaged in deconstructing a familiar fairy-tale motif, and refusing to allow the artifice of a dream to provide for reconciliation. As Hamlet is later to note, death and sleep, although at first they may resemble each other, are not the same. In *Romeo and Juliet* we have Shakespeare experimenting with formal alternatives to allow for the creation of tragedy.

Spotlight

In *A Midsummer Night's Dream*, when the antidote is administerd and the victims awake, they do so, as we have seen, with 'parted eye,/When everything seems double' (4.1.188–9). In *Romeo and Juliet*, when the 'meddling friar's' potion wears off, Juliet finds that Romeo has already killed himself. Ironically, his dying words are, 'Thus with a kiss I die.' She awakes and, having kissed Romeo to share his poison, stabs herself with his dagger. Interpret the structure one way and we have a comedy, of the kind when Bottom, as Pyramus, comes back to life after he has stabbed himself; take it the other way and we have, within the mimetic framework of the play, a tragedy. But the structure itself holds both possibilities together, allowing us to conclude that tragedy is the obverse of comedy.

NO FAIRY-TALE SOLUTIONS

Romeo and Juliet concerns itself more explicitly with social political issues; the feud between the Montagues and Capulets sets the scene that leads to the deaths of Mercutio and Tybalt. The search and the expression of the self through love is what takes Romeo, a Montague, into the very home of Juliet, a Capulet, and leads, after the death of Tybalt, to him becoming 'geographically' distanced from Verona. There he hears the news of Juliet's death but not of the plan to unite the lovers because Friar Laurence's messenger is detained in a place where the plague is rife. Romeo's cousin Mercutio's dying curse anticipates this complication: 'A plague o' both your houses' (3.1.107). Earlier in the play, Mercutio has ranted against Queen Mab, 'the fairies' midwife', who 'gallops night by night/Through lovers' brains, and then they dream of love' (1.4.54, 70–71). But as the action develops, the dream turns into a nightmare.

Spotlight

To find its full force and the way Mercutio's famous Queen Mab speech works, you might like to try to declaim it out loud. You will find that it gathers pace to a point almost of incoherence, of getting out of control – forcing Romeo to stop him: 'Peace, peace, Mercutio, peace./Thou talk'st of nothing' (95–6). To this, Mercutio responds:

> True, I talk of dreams,
> Which are the children of an idle brain,
> Begot of nothing but vain fantasy,
> Which is as thin of substance as the air
> And more inconstant than the wind, who woos
> Even now the frozen bosom of the north
> And, being anger'd, puffs away from thence
> Turning his side to the dew-dropping south.
>
> (1.4.96–103)

These dreams of love and the 'madness' that they induce in the lovers are, within the context of the real environment, too innocent, born of fantasy. They are in a sense wish fulfilments that emerge from a Neoplatonic concern with the intangibly spiritual predilections of the lovers, who in the reverie are elevated beyond the physical world. In *Romeo and Juliet* the difficulties of the physical world interfere with the dream, to produce devastating tragic consequences.

In one of Shakespeare's final plays, *The Tempest* (1611), Prospero brings an end to a masque that he has presented to his daughter Miranda and her intended husband, Ferdinand, by admitting that:

> Our revels now are ended. These our actors,
>
> As I foretold you, were all spirits and
>
> Are melted into air, into thin air;

(4.1.148–50)

The revels, the plays, the fairies and the dreams are all metaphors of the way in which art represents the twists and turns of life, leaving in the end nothing behind. They are 'such stuff/As dreams are made on', exposing along the way the conduct, conversations, accidents and ideologies in 'our little life' that underpin the social environment in which we exist, but where we find that it 'is rounded with a sleep' (*The Tempest*, 4.1.156–8).

INNOCENCE AND NAIVETY

In *Romeo and Juliet* there is innocence in the immediacy of the protagonists' love for each other – but also naivety. The lovers wish to transcend the limits of the social world and the responsibilities they have towards their respective families. Romeo tries to prevent the fight between Mercutio and Tybalt, but the former is stabbed under Romeo's arm and killed. The Duke in the play is the embodiment of the law but he cannot control the violence that the historical feud has produced. The lovers try to escape from the feud but they cannot. Even at the end of the play, in their sorrow, Montague and Capulet can only resort to their inanimate wealth to compensate for their grief. Montague promises to erect a statue 'in pure gold' (5.3.299), and Capulet reciprocates in a similar vein.

The friar's meddling is like Puck's; it goes wrong but cannot be corrected because there is no Oberon to rectify the errors of the friar's attempts to effect a solution since the political problem itself is too great, even for the 'innocent' lovers to overcome. This is their naivety, a naivety in a belief that dreams of happiness and reconciliation can overcome and transform reality.

Romeo and Juliet are victims of a social breakdown rather than a social order. In youth and innocence, they believe they can rise above the identities inscribed in their names and the language that determines their being. Juliet asks, 'What's in a name? That which we call a rose / By any other name would smell as sweet' (2.2.43–4). But Tybalt, cousin of Juliet Capulet, kills the Prince's cousin Mercutio, friend of Romeo Montague. Romeo avenges his friend's death, only in turn to be banished by the Prince who has lost his kinsman. The two lovers lack understanding of the full implications of the social determination of identity itself, of peace and concord. Shakespeare, as we will see later, also explores this theme in another, possibly earlier, comedy, *The Taming of the Shrew*.

The social context

The social situation reflected in the quarrel between the Montagues and Capulets and in the protagonists' intense love turns out to be as inanimate as the golden statues to be erected in their memory, as cold and unproductive as death itself. Romeo and Juliet are not characters of high rank of the sort that we find in the later tragedies; they are young and in their youth they refuse to conform; but they also represent the future of society. Juliet refuses to marry Paris in defiance of her father, just as Hermia refuses to marry Demetrius in defiance of Egeus, but here the tragedy is framed within the social context of hatred and ecclesiastical meddling in earthly issues, and by the general political inability to create a sustainable peace in a society that is out of control.

Romeo and Juliet is not an 'innocent' play or a play about 'innocence', as some may be tempted to surmise. It is a play that structurally moves from an early comic narrative to a tragic one, but with a particular care for the details of dramatic form by an exponent of consummate dramatic craftsmanship.

> 'Romeo and Juliet ... is architectonic in layout and design, its
> action punctuated by the three appearances of the Prince,
> always as an authority figure ... The play's characters are
> carefully conceived to complement and contrast with one
> another, the preparations for the Capulets' ball at which
> Romeo first sees Juliet are ironically echoed by those for her
> marriage to Paris, and each of the play's three love duets – one
> in the evening ... the second at night ... and the third at dawn ...
> is interrupted by calls from the Nurse. Before Shakespeare
> started to write ... he must have worked out a ground plan as
> thoroughly as if he had been designing an intricate building.'
>
> Wells, S. (2002: 141), *Shakespeare for All Time*. Basingstoke and
> Oxford: Pan Macmillan

From dream to nightmare

Let us sum up these two plays by returning to the questions at
the beginning of the discussion. What kind of dream is it that
Shakespeare creates in *A Midsummer Night's Dream*? It is a
metaphorical dream charting one of a number of directions
that drama can take, leading in this case to comedy. By
contrast, in *Romeo and Juliet*, what appears at first sight as
a dream that Mercutio claims is a 'vain fantasy' degenerates
into a nightmare of unresolved social tensions and issues that
lead to tragedy. As for whose dream it is, we have to say that,
although the characters of *A Midsummer Night's Dream* are
all part of the dream within the play, and although we who
are watching the play are invited, like Queen Elizabeth, to
think of it as no more than a dream, the play written by the
playwright and acted out by the performers may itself be
the dream. It may be a fantasy reflection of the variety of
experience found in life itself, along with a series of imaginary
resolutions to the problems it raises.

How does Shakespeare achieve all this? The answer is through a
tightly controlled plot held together by an underlying structure
and communicated by language and the action. But, once
performed, the dream ends; it is gone until, of course, it is

time to perform it again, when the environment within which we exist may have changed, imposing different readings and interpretations on the play and creating radically different performances. Shakespeare retains a solid but nonetheless flexible structure beneath his plays, together with tightly constructed narrative lines, and through this combination the dramas are able to withstand and indeed prompt changing interpretations. With this in mind, let us move on to consider one of his principal building materials, language.

Key terms

The Renaissance is a term describing what is now often called the Early Modern period of Western history. It refers to a 'rebirth' of interest in classical writers, myths and ideas, in a period stretching from the late thirteenth century in Italy to the mid-seventeenth century elsewhere in Europe.

The Reformation was a movement of 'reform' in the Church, leading to a break from Rome's control over Church doctrine. It was a rebellion against the excesses of the Catholic Church and a challenge to the authority of the Pope. The protestors were led at first by the German monk Martin Luther, who in 1517 attacked Church practices that he felt needed to be reformed. Those who followed his 'protests' became known as Protestants (see Chapter 24). They believed that Church doctrine should be founded on biblical texts as the only source of truth. The Reformation in England took place during the reign of Henry VIII, with the dissolution of the monasteries and the secession of England from the authority of the Roman Catholic Church.

Mana and *logos* are terms used by the poet and critic William Empson in his explanation of correspondence. During the 1930s the word *mana* became one of intellectual interest, particularly for cultural anthropologists. It is a word found in Polynesia and other South Seas communities, the meaning of which varies slightly. It refers to the power and prestige that in Polynesian culture were attributed to a supernatural force. *Mana* is found within a person. It does not necessarily come just from birth. It can develop within a leader but is not acquired. Empson also uses the term *logos* in his chapter on the double plot in *Some Versions of Pastoral* (2005). The Greek word *logos*, 'word', is from Western culture and particularly the Bible. The opening of St John's Gospel states, 'In the beginning was the Word [*Logos*], and the Word was with God, and the Word was God.' *Logos*, the Word, is the origin of all things. By bringing two heterogeneous terms from different cultures together within his critical perception, Empson points out the incongruous correspondence between the two different words, which each help to explore the other, just as in plays there is a correspondence between various characters in a main plot with characters in a subplot, which helps the audience to explore and elucidate the play as a whole.

Could this have been done if Shakespeare had maintained just a single action as required by the three Unities? Aspects of *The Comedy of Errors* show that correspondence of characters is possible within a play broadly following the Unities. It is more clearly manifested, however, with double-plot structures and their narratives. Empson, in proposing the idea in the 1930s, was decades ahead of his time. I will be talking about correspondence at various times on our journey, with *Hamlet* or with *Troilus and Cressida*, for example, which is a play that Empson discusses as an example of how correspondence works.

For further definitions, see Chapter 24.

Shakespeare's poetic and theatrical language

Shakespeare's plays are written predominantly but not exclusively in verse. He is a poet and, in the twenty-first century, an age relatively unaccustomed to verse speaking or reading poetry, it is his verse that can frighten people. Even without feeling exactly fearful, many people have reservations about the fact that Shakespeare uses verse, but this can be overcome through familiarity with the texts. Once you become more familiar with the language, you will find that the verse form has a simple malleable structure, which allows Shakespeare to paint pictures in words and to inspire imaginations.

At the end of the twentieth century, before the revolution in social networking using modern communication technologies, it could have been argued that the contemporary age was predominantly a visual rather than a verbal one. But new technologies have, to an extent, restored the force and the variety of the written word as well as the need to be concise, as in, for example, the word limitation imposed by Twitter. Ironically, Shakespeare's verse form stems from a similar need for discipline. He uses rhythms of language that imitate speech but in a disciplined way, while still taking advantage of the range of possible forms within that discipline.

The iambic pentameter and the sonnet form

The basic poetic line is the iambic pentameter. This term is used to describe a ten-beat line in which the words are stressed alternately in a soft/hard, soft/hard, soft/hard, soft/hard, soft/hard pattern. Just saying the words 'soft/hard' in this way gives the line rhythm. This rhythm can be changed, as it might be in music, to produce a particular effect. The famous opening line of *Richard III*, 'Now is the winter of our discontent', starts hard/soft, but the speech generally continues on the regular pattern with a few variants. So, for example, Shakespeare elongates line 16, 'I, that am rudely stamp'd, and want love's majesty', where Richard interrupts the regular flow of the lines referring to his own deformity. The change in rhythm thereby mimics his physical deformity by producing a deformity in the poetic line.

In his sonnet sequence, Shakespeare adopted a highly disciplined form, each poem consisting of 14 lines with an internal arrangement of rhymes and rhythms. The sonnet came from Italy and one of its forms is known as the 'Petrarchan', after the Italian poet Francesco Petrarch (1304–74). This sonnet form was constructed as an octave (eight lines) and a sextet (six lines). The eight-line octave has two four-line stanzas, with a repeating rhyme structure in alternate lines. To understand this, we assign a letter to the rhyming word at the end of each line. So the Petrarchan octave rhymes abab abab. This is followed by the sextet, which has its own rhyme scheme; this may be cde cde, or cdc cdc, or cde dce. Generally, the octave presents a proposition or, sometimes, a problem that the sextet reinforces, elaborates or resolves.

Shakespeare uses an innovative alternative to this structure. In his version, the sonnet consists of three distinctive quatrains (four lines), followed by a concluding two-line couplet. For example, the lines would be rhymed as follows: first quatrain abab; second quatrain cdcd; third quatrain efef; and a concluding couplet as gg. The quatrains present the narrative or issue and the final couplet sums it up or pithily comments upon it. This form is usually known as the Shakespearean sonnet. You have already come across one used by the Chorus at the opening of *Romeo and Juliet*, which announces the story of the play through the use of the sonnet form. Have a look at that opening speech again and put letters to the rhyming words; you will be able to see how rhyme is used to bind words together and to suggest issues to the reader or listener. The rhythm of each line is used to direct your attention to important elements of those issues, while the sonnet form itself gives some indication that the substance of the play will be about romantic love.

Key idea

A good tip is to read passages out loud. Only then will you be able to hear the rhythms of the lines and get some idea of how Shakespeare varies his style, sometimes in keeping with different speakers and sometimes mixing verse and prose.

Shakespeare was certainly writing or had written some of his sonnets at the time he wrote many of the early plays. The disciplined structure of the Shakespearean sonnet, and possibly the knowledge of the Petrarchan sonnet, has an affinity at least with the need for the structured discipline discussed in the composition, for example, of the comedies. Whether his sonnet sequence reflects reality and parts of the poet's own autobiography or is a fictional creation by a poet who was also a dramatist has been, and continues to be, a matter for debate (and is discussed in Chapter 26), but you might like to take note of the poet W. H. Auden's view of the critical discussions in his introduction to the sonnets:

'Probably, more nonsense has been talked and written, more intellectual and emotional energy expended in vain, on the sonnets of Shakespeare than on any other literary work in the world. Indeed, they have become the best touchstone I know of for distinguishing the sheep from the goats, those, that is, who love poetry for its own sake and understand its nature, from those who only value poems either as historical documents or because they express feelings or beliefs of which the reader happens to approve.'

Auden, W. H. (1964: Introduction, xviii), *The Sonnets*. New York: The Signet Classic Shakespeare

Spotlight

Successful art is disciplined. It is not haphazard. Sometimes it may appear simple to the point where people will say, 'Well, I could have done that.' But of course they cannot, since beneath the apparent simplicity, or masked complexity, is the experience of trial and error and knowledge of the artistic laws that the skilled artist fashions to his or her purpose. Great artists often show the courage to push such laws to their limits or to develop new ones. Writing can be a journey that the artist has to take, and is sometimes hard and challenging as he or she strives for a finished product. Often, fictional or even real pain and anguish are detected and described by critics in Shakespeare's plays and poems. These may relate to the passing of time, the transience of youth, or mutability and loss. That, however, is matched in some of the plays and the sonnets by a celebration of the progress of human relationships and the sustainability of the art itself.

A muse of fire

Earlier we saw how in Sonnet 55, for example, it was the poem, the art, that is seen to transcend the ravages of time: 'Not marble, nor the gilded monuments/Of princes, shall outlive this powerful rhyme'. The communicative vehicle of the plays is language. Through words, the plays can create images in our minds as well as carry the narrative forward, or build up character, or provide the communication between characters.

In the Prologue to *Henry V*, the figure of the Chorus, the narrator, tells us that the language has to work on our 'imaginary forces'.

The play opens with the actor playing the Chorus calling for 'a muse of fire', so that this historical warrior king might appear like Mars, the god of war, on this stage, which he refers to as a 'cockpit'. (This is because the Elizabethan theatre resembled the arenas where cockfighting took place.) He calls it a 'wooden O', describing the circular architecture of the theatre itself. The poetic rhetoric of the passage draws a picture in the minds of the audience as the Chorus regrets that the action on the stage simply cannot reproduce the glories of this king's triumphs in his war against France and, in particular, his famous victory at Agincourt. By apologizing for the unworthiness of the stage to present such great deeds, the poet dramatically lifts the imagination of the audience. He is saying, in effect, listen to our words, watch the action we present and visualize the past: 'Suppose within the girdle of these walls / Are now confined two mighty monarchies'.

Try reading this speech out loud to see how it modulates; note the break, for example, in line 8 between the word 'employment' and 'But pardon ...' Then note the move to the questions: 'Can this cockpit hold ...?' and 'Or may we cram ...?' After these questions comes the answer, with an explanation: 'O pardon! since ...' He then tells us what the actors are going to do for the audience, leading to the request that the audience imagines the scene of the action and is even persuaded to 'Think, when we talk of horses, that you see them'. Within all of this the Chorus is actually creating the scene, while drawing the audience's attention to what he is doing. As you read it aloud, imagining that there is an audience listening to you, the mastery of the speech's structure will work for itself.

> O for a muse of fire, that would ascend
>
> The brightest heaven of invention,
>
> A kingdom for a stage, princes to act,
>
> And monarchs to behold the swelling scene!
>
> Then should the warlike Harry, like himself,
>
> Assume the port of Mars, and at his heels,

Leashed in like hounds, should famine, sword and fire
Crouch for employment. But pardon, gentles all,
The flat unraised spirits that hath dared
On this unworthy scaffold to bring forth
So great an object. Can this cockpit hold
The vasty fields of France? Or may we cram
Within this wooden O the very casques
That did affright the air at Agincourt?
O pardon, since a crooked figure may
Attest in little place a million,
And let us, ciphers to this great account,
On your imaginary forces work.
Suppose within the girdle of these walls
Are now confined two mighty monarchies,
Whose high upreared and abutting fronts
The perilous narrow ocean parts asunder.
Piece out our imperfections with your thoughts.
Into a thousand parts divide one man
And make imaginary puissance.
Think, when we talk of horses, that you see them
Printing their proud hoofs i'th'receiving earth.
For 'tis your thoughts that now must deck our kings,
Carry them here and there, jumping o'er times,
Turning th'accomplishment of many years
Into an hour-glass: for the which supply,
Admit me Chorus to this history,
Who prologue-like your humble patience pray,
Gently to hear, kindly to judge our play.

                    (*Henry V*, Prologue, 1–34)

The speech sets the historical tone, just as the passage quoted
in Chapter 3 from *A Midsummer Night's Dream*, 'I know
a bank a where the wild thyme blows' (2.1.249f.), creates a

painting in words of natural beauty tinged with magic. Even modern visual technology might find it difficult to present an imaginary picture of the kind that Shakespeare has Oberon deliver in that passage.

'Like all his poetic contemporaries, Shakespeare had a profoundly figurative imagination. Composition was conceived in terms of figures of words, divided into tropes (a word shifted away from its usual context or signification) and schemes (words arranged in expressive patterns), and figures of thought (such as frankness of speech, understatement, vivid description, the structural division of argument, accumulation, refining, dwelling on the point, comparison, exemplification, simile, personification, emphasis, conciseness, ocular demonstration). Tropes and schemes were both a device to assist actors in memorizing their lines and a method of organization to make the words spoken on stage vivid and memorable for the audience.'

Bate, J. (2007: 43), Introduction, *The RSC William Shakespeare: Complete Works*. Basingstoke: Macmillan

Body and stage language

Shakespeare was thinking of his actors when he was writing his plays, but in actual performance oral language (speech) is not the only vehicle of communication. Even as you spoke the lines from *Henry V*, you probably moved, gesticulated, adding physical gestures and facial expressions to accompany the words. As well as conjuring up the imagery of the language, Shakespeare produces a script for the actors who are speaking, moving, sitting, standing and interacting with one another, with the physical elements on the stage itself, the theatre and the audience of which we are members. If you are reading the play, note which characters are on stage since some may not have many lines, or they may not speak at all, but they are all part of the play's action.

Shakespeare realizes the force of this complex process and his art is to use it, bringing the various elements together as well as having to compensate for the fact that in his theatre there was no scenery of the kind we might expect to find in a modern theatre. There was, however, a canopy over the stage, on the underside of which was painted the signs of the zodiac (the heavens). Note, for example, in the tragedy *Hamlet*, how Hamlet, when talking in prose to Rosencrantz and Guildenstern, describes the physical theatrical stage on which he is acting: a stage thrusting out into the auditorium as a 'promontory' with the painted 'canopy' above leading to the sky that can be seen over the open-air part of the theatre. This image of 'the Globe' communicates a further intensity in that it gives the dramatic character a context while at the same time providing opportunities to introduce an element of self-awareness through humorous jibes at the audience's expense. Again, try reading this prose passage out loud. Shakespeare even tells his actor to signal to Rosencrantz and Guildenstern to 'look' up from the 'promontory' that is the stage, to what is above it all:

> ... I have of late, but wherefore I know not, lost all my mirth, forgone all custom of exercises; and indeed it goes so heavily with my disposition that this goodly frame the earth seems to me a sterile promontory, this most excellent canopy the air, look you, this brave o'erhanging firmament, this majestical roof fretted with golden fire, why, it appeareth nothing to me but a foul and pestilent congregation of vapours.
>
> (*Hamlet*, 2.2.297–305)

Shakespeare is here giving his actors stage directions, looking at, or even pointing to, the open air above the groundlings, the canopy over the stage. The audience members themselves are coughing and reeking – a congregation is breathing its 'pestilence' of air, which in time of plague would cause the authorities to close the theatres. The character is thereby reflecting upon himself, instructing Rosencrantz and Guildenstern while at the same time jibing at the audience. How the audience would have reacted to these jibes from the stage we cannot tell, but to have the confidence to work in this way, and with what seems to have been the full cooperation of his audience, demonstrates Shakespeare's command of his medium.

The play communicates its concerns by having the actors move around the physical environment of the stage, addressing each other and sometimes involving the audience directly. Such interactions between the actor and audience may have had a dramatic effect very different from the romantic, empathetic or more sentimental appeal of a passage such as this from *Hamlet*, as interpreted in some conventional literary critical readings. The fact is that we cannot be certain, although we sometimes see in plays by Shakespeare's fellow dramatists the use of banter with the audience as an integral element in the drama. In the famous opening of *Richard III*, as with the later speeches in that play, and as with Iago in *Othello*, for example, we find that Shakespeare allows characters to confide in his spectators by addressing them directly, drawing them into the action and engaging them with the story. The Chorus in both *Romeo and Juliet* and *Henry V*, and as we will see with Gower in *Pericles*, directly addresses the audience in the telling of the story.

'The Elizabethan stage can be anything in this world or the next: a battlefield, the Court, the underworld. The self-enclosed, self-sufficient world of the play is a primary convention. Against that lies a set of conventions ... [which] ... challenge or subvert the autonomy of the play world. They include choric speeches, together with prologue and epilogue. They permit direct address to the audience by clowns (Launce with his dog) and lineal descendants of the Vice (Richard III, Iago). Sometimes the stage draws attention to itself explicitly ... we have learned to be alert to "act", "scene", "play", "perform" ... as they occur in the text of a play. Through them we understand a fundamental premise of Elizabethan dramaturgy, that the stage is also a stage.'

Berry, R. (1985: 1–2), *Shakespeare and the Awareness of the Audience*. London and Basingstoke: Macmillan

Forms of communication

The semiotics of the theatre is a study of the communication system of the play, the world created by dramatist and actors, including oral language. It can be self-referential, deliberately artificial or affected, but going beyond that to encompass all the elements of theatrical representation. In comedy, for example, Shakespeare is not averse to self-referential humour, laughing at his own mastery of poetic language as, for example, in *Love's Labour's Lost*, Act 4, Scene 3, when the male lovers read their sonnets aloud, not to the women they love but directly to the audience (and to each other), to great comic effect in performance. Indeed, in this play the characters persistently fail to communicate with one another.

It is sometimes held that in a number of plays the characters that are of inferior social status speak in prose, and to an extent that is the case – as with the Mechanicals in *A Midsummer Night's Dream*. Bottom, in his 'audition' for the 'Pyramus and Thisbe' play within the play, aspires to speak verse, and the result allows Shakespeare to mimic the bombastic lines of some of his contemporaries and predecessors:

> The raging rocks,
> And shivering shocks,
> Shall break the locks
> Of prison gates;
> And Phibbus' car
> Shall shine from far
> And make and mar
> The foolish fates.

> (1.2.28–35)

Humorously, Shakespeare has Bottom sum up his recitation with the words 'This was lofty', and the character then returns to his usual prose (1.2.36). The distinctions within language, however, vary throughout the plays. Sometimes, for example, prose is used to increase the emotional impact of what a central character is saying, as with Shylock's affirmation of his humanity and his sense of injustice at the way, it is implied, that his nation has been persecuted by the Venetian Christians:

> ... he [Antonio] hath disgrac'd me, and hind'red me half a million, laugh'd at my losses, mock'd at my gains, scorned my nation, thwarted my bargains, cooled my friends, heated mine enemies, – and what's his reason? I am a Jew.
>
> (*The Merchant of Venice*, 3.1.50–54)

Note the accumulation of the short, sharp clauses, rising to an emphasis on the verb 'heated', and then the brief pause before the question.

In *As You Like It*, Rosalind speaks much of her part in prose, perhaps bringing a more immediate realism to what is happening behind her contrived and controlling romantic narrative. It is such variations between poetry and prose and within poetry itself that allow modulations in tone, creating atmosphere and leaving ambiguities hanging in the air for the audience to savour in the richness of the experience, as, for example, in Viola's concealed poetically expressed admission of her love for Orsino in *Twelfth Night:*

VIOLA   My father had a daughter lov'd a man,
          As it might be, perhaps, were I a woman,
          I should your lordship.

ORSINO   And what's her history?

VIOLA   A blank, my lord: She never told her love,
          But let concealment, like a worm i'th' bud
          Feed on her damask cheek: she pin'd in thought,
          And with a green and yellow melancholy
          She sat like Patience on a monument,
          Smiling at grief. Was not this love indeed?

          ...

ORSINO But died thy sister of her love, my boy?

VIOLA   I am all the daughters of my father's house,
        And all the brothers too: and yet I know not.

                                    (2.4.108–16, 120–22)

This rich passage, brimming with images and gentle
ambiguity, permits a softness of empathetic humour for the
audience whose knowledge of what is going on is greater
than that of either character being portrayed: the Duke
doesn't know Viola is a woman; Viola doesn't know her
brother is alive, but the audience does – and, in Shakespeare's
day, it knew moreover that all the actors were male. Viola's
melancholy tone feeds into the warm melancholy of the
play's action.

Music and song

Shakespeare sustains this mood by introducing music and song
to great effect in *Twelfth Night*, reinforcing the play's action
and thereby inviting the audience to share the experience. For
example, Feste sings of the transience of youth:

    O mistress mine, where are you roaming?
    O stay and hear, your true love's coming.
    …
    What is love? 'Tis not hereafter,
    Present mirth hath present laughter:
    What's to come is still unsure.
    In delay there lies no plenty,
    Then come kiss me, sweet and twenty:
    Youth's a stuff will not endure.

                                    (2.3.39–40, 47–52)

The importance of the songs, however, has not always been
perceived through the centuries.

From Shakespeare's script, we understand that music is played in order to complement the poetry and the prose. In *Much Ado About Nothing* (2.3.57–9), Benedick humorously asks: 'Is it not strange that sheep's guts should hale souls out of men's bodies?' but later he is forced to ridicule his own attempt at wooing through song or poetry, reflecting 'No, I was not born under a rhyming planet, nor I cannot woo in festival terms' (5.2.39–41).

Spotlight

It may be that Richard Burbage, the actor who first played Benedick, had no singing voice and was also being gently mocked by the playwright. When the clown Will Kempe left the company in 1598, Robert Armin, a singer, took over the role of clown in the company. The result was that music appears to have been written into the comedies at the same time as the humour of the 'clown' became more sardonic. You might like to consider whether you agree that there is a change in the role of the clown after this date, by comparing the role of Dogberry in *Much Ado About Nothing*, which was played by Will Kempe, and the role of Feste in *Twelfth Night*, which was played by Robert Armin.

The perils of over-analysis

As we have seen, scholarship has tended over the years inadvertently to underplay the performance aspect of the plays in its attempts to evaluate their literary merits. The result has been almost to imprison Shakespeare in an elitist culture. But Shakespeare's profession was far from elitist. He needed a popular audience in order to earn his living, the composition of which continues to be debated. (See Maguire, L. and Smith, E. [2013: 86–93].) However, there are some lines that are now very difficult for us to understand without footnotes and scholarship. The language of *Love's Labour's Lost* is particularly challenging in this respect but it can be understood if, as readers or a theatre audience, we do not get too bogged down in the minutiae of scholarship. We need to remember that the progress, the fluidity and the movement of the whole is greater than the detail of particular words, phrases or lines. We have to let the play run in our reading of it, in order to allow it to work.

In everyday speech we allow the conversation to flow. Few of us can recount every word exactly as it was spoken once a conversation has come to an end, but we are aware of the tenor and nature of what has been said. Poetic language has a degree of intensity that raises it above ordinary everyday speech but, even so, we can begin understanding great art as we would everyday speech. Then we can recall moments of real significance that stand out through the economy, clarity and beauty of their expression.

The more you read, declaim or see Shakespeare in performance, the less inhibited you will become by the language itself.

The rise of the English language

Shakespeare lived in an age of great change. The English language more than doubled its vocabulary during his lifetime. He used many of the new words then in circulation, coining some himself and repeating neologisms coined by others. But generally there was a move from visual to oral communication, for example in the churches, as the iconography of the Catholic Church was replaced by oral and written communication (through sermons and through the growth of printing). In the Catholic Church, where the services were in Latin, frescoes and stained-glass windows told stories through pictures, but after the Reformation the walls were whitewashed over and much of the stained glass destroyed. English became the language of the Reformed Church under Henry VIII, Edward and Elizabeth. Everyone by law had to attend church on Sunday, where the sermon would be preached according to the new, often politically inspired religion.

Shakespeare's language is not something to fear, although if you are not used to poetry it can, as we have noted, cause some initial anxiety. So find a space of your own and take some further major speeches, such as Antony's 'Friends, Romans, countrymen' (*Julius Caesar*, 3.2.74f.), delivered to the Plebeians after the murder of Caesar, or Isabella's soliloquy, 'To whom should I complain? Did I tell this' (*Measure for Measure*, 2.4.170–86), following the indecent proposition made to her by Angelo, or any soliloquy from *Hamlet* and / or *Macbeth*, and try reading them out loud, finding the emphasis and the rhythm of the lines. Soon the language will flow, your fears will be dispelled and your love of Shakespeare and amazement at his achievements will begin to flourish.

Key idea

In today's increasingly materialistic and violent world where spiritual values have been eroded, art, music, poetry, dance and drama can remind us of the qualities as well as the infirmities of the human condition. They cause us to pause, and as a consequence they matter, by affirming the positive nature of art and of being human.

6

Love's Labour's Lost (1595) and The Two Gentlemen of Verona (1591–2)

In the early romantic comedies, including the ones previously discussed, Shakespeare appears to be developing a structure, which will come to fruition in *As You Like It* and *Twelfth Night*. He experimented further in this direction in later plays, and in the process challenged the expectations of his audiences. Here we will examine briefly two relatively early plays, *Love's Labour's Lost* and *The Two Gentlemen of Verona*. The limitation of this approach, however, is that the methodology can only be empirical, derived from actual readings of the plays that form the basis of our evaluations and suppositions.

Understanding the plays' structure

Until now I have suggested that Shakespeare used a formula or underlying structure as the basis for the narratives or plots for some of his plays. That structure deviates significantly from the neoclassical rules of drama, and this allows him to tell a story, usually found in his sources, in a particular way. Whether he was consciously doing this or not it is impossible to say, since our knowledge of the structure is derived primarily from the texts we have. Just as we recognized that we confer meanings on these texts in our reading and performance of Shakespeare's plays, so we derive an understanding of his structure empirically from the plays, assuming an authorial presence without knowing the details of how he constructed them.

Spotlight

This appears to be the formula for the plays we call the romantic comedies:

1   An opening statement of a dilemma or an impossible resolution, often but not always associated with the threat of death

2   A search deriving from the opening statement relating, firstly, to an individual or a number of individuals attempting to find identity or self-knowledge, and secondly to one or more couples seeking to surmount obstacles in their attempts to find some form of relationship

3   The requirement of certain characters, usually lovers, to remove themselves from the society that is responsible for setting up the obstacle to fulfilment, that removal often being signified by geographical relocation or physical disguise, or both

4   Through the adventures under disguise or in the area of relocation, a movement is made towards the resolution of the difficulties, which is usually effected through a contrived recognition scene – Aristotelian anagnorisis – in which misunderstandings of identity are rectified, multiple marriages result and a new revitalized society emerges that looks towards a future in which generations are now reconciled with each other.

In *Love's Labour's Lost* and *The Two Gentlemen of Verona*, we can see the elements of the formula taking shape – the initial problem, the journey and the disguise, the revelation and the reconciliation. However, in both plays the dramatist is already playing with the expectations of his audience, and in such a way that the structure being developed is already under some stress. In *Love's Labour's Lost*, Shakespeare includes topical warm satire within a structure that has a stark conclusion. In *The Two Gentlemen of Verona*, he uses song and an old comic routine as part of the entertainment within a narrative plot that is over-elaborate and which, with an attempted rape, threatens to undermine its comic genre. And yet at the same time this technique points towards complexities that will become more marked in later plays.

We have also already seen how Shakespeare experimented – in 1595 – with both the comic and the tragic genre, moving the fairy world of *A Midsummer Night's Dream* into the poetic extravagance of Mercutio's 'Queen Mab' speech in *Romeo and Juliet*, which presages the movement from comedy to tragedy that follows Mercutio's 'accidental' death.

Key idea

Relatively early in his career as a writer, Shakespeare is not afraid to experiment, pushing the boundaries, as if asking himself, and the narratives with which he is dealing, the question 'What if?' So 'what if' there is no magic potion to put right the mistakes in *A Midsummer Night's Dream*? 'What if' Romeo arrives at the tomb without knowing that Juliet is not dead but only asleep? In *The Two Gentlemen* or *Love's Labour's Lost*, these experiments are pushed even further to suggest a questioning of elements of the very structure that we can detect in his other early comedies. The sudden reformation of the aptly named Proteus in the former is unsettling, while the failure in the formal ending of *Love's Labour's Lost* challenges the convention of a return to an ordered society.

We have also seen that during the 1590s Shakespeare is involved in writing a number of sonnets, at first to a young man and subsequently to a 'dark lady' with whom he (or his fictional persona as the poet) is involved in an affair, only to discover that she is also sexually involved with a young rival. There is also within the sonnets a sense of time passing, of the need to seize the day, a concept known as *carpe diem*. It is dangerous to read autobiography into fictional work but no writer can absolutely escape from him- or herself. The act of writing necessitates, in one form or another, the exposure of the self, although Shakespeare's own 'self' is elusive.

Love's Labour's Lost

In this early comic play, Ferdinand, the King of Navarre, believes he can divorce himself and three of his courtiers from the world and create 'a little academe,/Still and contemplative in living art' (*Love's Labour's Lost*, 1.1.13–14). His plan is to vow to abjure the society of women for three years while he and his companions study together. This turns out to be impossible, since no sooner is the oath made than an emissary from the King of France, his daughter the Princess, accompanied by three ladies, arrives to negotiate with King Ferdinand. Thus the obstacle to resolution is constructed and the resulting comedy arises from the four men humorously trying to find ways, including going in disguise, of breaking their oath in order to woo the ladies, who are forced to remain outside the palace 'gates'.

The breaking of an oath is a serious business in Shakespearean drama, but in this case the attempts to do so drive the King and his companions into the comic world of deception, self-deception and 'merriment', until a messenger, Monsieur Marcade, arrives from France to announce to the Princess the death of 'The King, your father –' (5.2.716). This change of mood, coupled with the failure of the men to reconcile themselves to the women, prepares the audience for an inversion of the customary comic ending.

THE THEME: A PROCESS TO BE TAKEN
Protestations by the men that 'Honest plain words best pierce the ear of grief;' (5.2.749) are rejected by the Princess and her women. Death has produced a different perspective on the

humour of the men's perjury, and no commitment to marriage can take place until each has served a term in which they will be forced to understand the realities of the world. So one of them, the iconoclastic Berowne, known for his disarming comic wit, is told by his new love, Rosaline, to spend a year with the sick, helping them to laugh before she can consider him:

> ROSALINE You shall this twelvemonth term from day to day
> Visit the speechless sick and still converse
> With groaning wretches; and your task shall be
> With all fierce endeavour of your wit
> To enforce the pained impotent to smile.
>
> BEROWNE To move wild laughter in the throat of death?
> It cannot be, it is impossible.
> Mirth cannot move a soul in agony.
>
> (5.2.841–8)

But to his protests she replies (849–59) that until now his laughter has been 'shallow' and that, if he cannot make the sick laugh, he should 'throw away that spirit' as part of his 'reformation'. In other words, he has to go through a process to make him worthy of love. In this, the play comments on the purpose of the formula that Shakespeare is developing to underpin both theme and plot within an innovative aesthetic structure. Shakespeare is signalling, thereby, the seriousness of his comedy – the movement into a world of error, confusion, even death in order to comprehend the realities of the world itself – and our experience of it.

As critics such as Derek Traversi in *An Approach to Shakespeare* (1969) have noted, the sentence the women impose on the men forces them back into a severity that reminds them that vows are not to be made lightly since they are part of the bedrock of language, and hence important in holding society together. There are hints here, in this otherwise frivolous play, of the Shakespearean vision that was later to produce the great tragedy of *King Lear*, which some have called a grotesque comedy. In that play, Lear in old age plays games with his daughters' affections and attempts to elicit vows from them that have disastrous consequences.

TOPICALITY

Love's Labour's Lost also contains a satire on court life, and shows a familiarity with 'local' characters such as Holofernes the pedantic schoolmaster and Nathaniel the curate, both of whom, with the clown Costard and a comic Spaniard, Don Adriano de Armado, present an entertainment of the Four Worthies – Hector, Pompey, Alexander and Judas Maccabeus – at the end of the play. It is a comic sketch within the play, with a Spaniard, described as the Braggart, being reduced to ridicule along with the curate and the schoolmaster. As topical entertainment, the ridiculing of pedantry and the satirizing of Spain after the defeat of the Armada are set pieces that Shakespeare's Elizabethan audience would no doubt have enjoyed.

Spotlight

The construction of the overall plot and themes of *Love's Labour's Lost* have serious implications that are concerned with appropriate conclusions to all things as well as the tribulations of life. The fact is that illness and death often do strike suddenly and unexpectedly. In contemporary society we try to isolate or contain this fact through material insurance and welfare systems. We know that death is unavoidable, but generally we do not see it in quite the same way that the Elizabethans did. Illness, paupers and public executions were part of the fabric of society embedded in the daily consciousness of people such as Holofernes and Sir Nathaniel and, indeed, the aristocracy and the monarchy. As much as the threat from Spain, the Elizabethans faced the continuing threat of widespread sickness, especially outbreaks of plague. They lived with poverty and disease in their streets and their homes, although Elizabeth I's government did introduce taxes to help fund the poor.

'YOU THAT WAY, WE THIS WAY'

Despite Elizabethan London's familiarity with death, however,
comedy is clearly a requirement. Shakespeare therefore
compensates for the unsatisfactory irresolution of the lovers
with a conclusion in which 'This side is Hiems, winter; this Ver,
the spring'. The songs of the two seasons are sung: the spring
with the cuckoo and the winter with the owl. 'The words of
Mercury', the messenger of the gods, we are told, 'are harsh after
the songs of Apollo. You that way, we this way' (5.2.882f.).

In the seasons there is movement between scepticism and
optimism, which give way to each other. Comedy is usually
associated with the spring and with 'rebirth', and although
'love's labour' has been 'lost' on this occasion, there is always
the promise of regeneration in the future, inscribed in that
movement of the seasons. Sadly, perhaps ironically, unless it
was renamed and exists as another play, *Love's Labour's Won*,
recorded by Francis Meres in 1598 as a play by Shakespeare,
remains 'lost' to us.

The Two Gentlemen of Verona

A serious undertone is also present in the earlier play *The Two
Gentlemen of Verona*.

The two gentlemen of the title are close friends Valentine and Proteus. Their names are deliberately appropriate: Valentine after St Valentine, patron saint of lovers, Proteus after the Greek god who could quickly change his shape at will, thereby associating the name with deceit. Proteus stays in Verona because of his love for Julia – the name relating to July signifying 'passionate love' as in, for example, Juliet – when Valentine goes off to Milan. Proteus's father, Antonio, however, instructs his son to follow Valentine to the Duke of Milan's court. Valentine, already there, has fallen in love with the Duke's daughter, Silvia. The Duke wishes her to marry Thurio, whose name denotes a young shoot. So Valentine and Silvia plan to elope.

On seeing Sylvia, Proteus immediately falls in love with her and, learning of the planned elopement, betrays his friend Valentine to the Duke. Valentine is banished into the wilderness where he becomes the leader of a band of outlaws. Julia disguises herself as a boy, Sebastian, and follows Proteus to the court of Milan, where she overhears him declare his love for Silvia. Disguised as Sebastian she serves as a page to Proteus, who sends her with a message to Silvia, who continues to reject Proteus because of her fidelity to Valentine. Silvia escapes to join Valentine in the forest. The Duke and Thurio pursue them, as do Proteus and Julia. Silvia is captured by the outlaws but rescued by Proteus, who attempts to force his love on her in the form of an attempted rape. Valentine appears and Proteus's betrayal of his friend is discovered, but Julia reveals herself in order to facilitate a reconciliation.

This play has something of the sonnets' story about it. Here, the madness of love is a force working within what is otherwise a rambling comedy, renowned for a comic scene (2.3) with Proteus's servant Launce and his dog Crab. This episode is possibly based on a comic routine reworked by Shakespeare for Will Kempe.

Key idea

The convoluted plot has many elements found in other, later comedies – *A Midsummer Night's Dream*, *As You Like It* and *Twelfth Night* – but without the clear structural discipline characterized by those works.

> '[At the time of the formation of the Chamberlain's Men in the early 1590s] one of Shakespeare's first acts was to take an old play and to construct a part in it for Kemp [sic] based on Kemp's routines or "merriments". Kemp's scenes ... are only loosely tied to the narrative, and give him the freedom to improvise if he chooses.'

Wiles, D. (1987: 73), *Shakespeare's Clown: Actor and Text in the Elizabethan Playhouse*. Cambridge: Cambridge University Press

Satire

Critics have noted that the relationship between Launce and his dog Crab – whose name is associated with sexual disease – offers a parallel perspective on issues of loyalty and disloyalty that occur in the main narrative. Satirical comedy abounds, particularly in Act 3, Scene 1 through the interaction of Launce and the clown Speed, possibly played by a boy, which offers a parody of a courtly lover's 'complaint': the praise and evaluation of a courtly lover's mistress – who in Launce's case is a milkmaid. Among her virtues are that she can 'milk', brew 'good ale', 'sew', 'wash and scour' and 'spin' and among her vices are her 'sour breath' and that 'she doth talk in her sleep'. You might like to compare 'greasy Nell' in *The Comedy of Errors* who has a similar comic function. It is a satire on a literary tradition as well as on the upper classes.

BEYOND THE CONVOLUTED CONSTRUCTION

The Two Gentlemen of Verona is written as an entertainment and, as well as the humour, contains the famous song 'Who is Silvia? What is she / That all our swains commend her?' (4.2.38–52). In its variety and convolutions, some might regard it as a 'slight play', overworked in its desire to be successful and therefore overloaded in its comic entertainment, which jars with the violence that Proteus displays.

Nevertheless, despite all this and its strained construction, we can see at a relatively early stage in Shakespeare's career the presence of themes such as 'constancy' and the 'violent' male temperament that will later develop, with more careful handling, in *Twelfth Night* and in the satirical 'tragedy' *Troilus and Cressida*, as well as in *Measure for Measure* and *All's Well That Ends Well*, and, of course, throughout the sonnets.

'Shakespeare seems to have set out to write a play about friendship. The essential quality of friendship, wrote Sir Thomas Elyot, is constancy ... Proteus's inconstancy, his failure in both friendship and love ... could have made him the most interesting character, and perhaps the most sympathetic ... if ... Shakespeare's sympathies hadn't moved elsewhere – to Julia, Launce and Speed. These characters have a charm, a magnetic power that Proteus lacks.

'... Launce takes on himself the blame for his dog's physiological impertinence, and asks the audience "How many masters would do this for his servant?" (4.4.28–9) ... Julia, a mere woman, is able to uphold the standard of constancy to which Proteus merely gives lip service.'

French, M. (1983: 89–90), *Shakespeare's Division of Experience.* London: Abacus, Sphere Books

The idea that Shakespeare is just a 'natural genius' is belied by the fact that in *The Two Gentlemen of Verona* and *Love's Labour's Lost* he is developing his craftsmanship. Signs of this may be more clearly seen in *A Midsummer Night's Dream* and *The Comedy of Errors* but we can also consider his craftsmanship in the context of two further romantic comedies, *As You Like It* and *Twelfth Night*. In these later plays we see his comic formula aligning within his narrative plots, producing complex thematic issues and requiring more sophisticated interpretation. But even so, *Love's Labour's Lost* and the earlier *The Two Gentlemen of Verona* demonstrate his ability to create comic entertainments for a public theatre and they can therefore be evaluated as such. We should, perhaps, follow Shakespeare's example and not become too precious about 'rules' but rather admire and enjoy these comedies for what they are.

Living up to its title: *As You Like It* (1599–1600)

Love's Labour's Lost shows the development of Shakespeare's comic structure and formula, but *As You Like It* exercises it in a much tighter way. This play was written at a time of some anxiety in Shakespeare's own personal life as well as in his career, the affairs of his company and professional practice.

The 'seasonal' patterning of life and death is never far away in *As You Like It* (1599–1600) and *Twelfth Night* (1601), the plays to be considered in this and the next chapter. These plays achieve an almost aesthetic perfection without the need for neoclassical rules. In both, Shakespeare's own formula achieves a maturity that subsequently he will deliberately frustrate or even deconstruct in plays such as *Cymbeline* (1609–10) – which is termed a 'tragedy' in the First Folio – in order to produce differing effects.

In *Love's Labour's Lost*, the Princess of France is prevented from entering Navarre's Court because of his vow. The vow places Navarre in a dilemma, as the Princess points out:

> 'Tis deadly sin to keep that oath, my lord,
> And sin to break it.

(2.1.105–6)

The end of that play and the romantic comedies that were to follow can be regarded, particularly by festive and archetypal forms of criticism, as embodying the seasonal energies of spring combating the 'death' of winter. It is the energy of life, which is to lead ultimately to the festivity of a midsummer night, for example. These critics hold that a seasonal rhythm underpins the way in which civilization and art order their affairs. The King of Navarre and his courtiers are acting unnaturally in taking their vows of celibacy for three years. Sexuality and procreation are fundamental to new life and life itself follows a seasonal pattern.

Pleading for her brother Claudio's life in *Measure for Measure* (1604), Isabella reminds Angelo that even the killing of animals for food is determined by the requirements of the various seasons:

> ... Even for our kitchens
> We kill the fowl of season: shall we serve heaven
> With less respect than we do minister
> To our gross selves?

(2.2.85–8)

And as we will see in *As You Like It,* Jaques observes a seasonal pattern of life going through seven ages, the last being 'mere oblivion,/Sans teeth, sans eyes, sans taste, sans everything' (2.7.165–6).

Troubled times

Recent criticism has been alert to the fact that at the time he was writing *As You Like It* and *Twelfth Night* – along with the tragedy *Hamlet* (1601) – Shakespeare was himself facing deaths in his family. His young son, Hamnet, twin brother of Judith, had died in August 1596. James Burbage, the father of the company and the man who had helped frame his career, had died in 1598 and Shakespeare's own father died in 1601 (and was buried in Stratford on 8 September). It was thus a period of loss. We, of course, have to be wary of reading autobiographical detail into fictional works, and death, as noted earlier, was a more common everyday event in Elizabethan society than in our contemporary, sanitized existence. But, whatever the age, there are few deeper sorrows than the death of a child, a parent, a close friend and/or mentor, and it appears that Shakespeare experienced the loss of all three in a short space of time.

Further, although Shakespeare appears to have been personally financially secure, his company had also been experiencing difficulties. The lease on their playhouse in the north of the city, The Theatre, expired in 1598, and a quarrel broke out between the company and the owner of the lease of the land on which it had been built. The company dismantled the timbers of The Theatre in late December 1598, as their lease allowed, and having acquired land near the sewers on the South Bank of the Thames, had transported the wood and fabric to build a new theatre, the Globe, which opened in 1599.

Almost simultaneously with the opening came adverse publicity. This was in the form of an argument with one of their star actors, the clown Will Kempe, who acrimoniously left the company and made his departure known by dancing a jig from London to Norwich. Further, a young poet, John Marston, who had had his profane and satiric verses publicly burned in 1599, following Bishops Whitgift and Bancroft's ban on the writing of satiric poems and epigrams, had turned to writing plays. He and some other satiric playwrights wrote for the more expensive, small private theatres at St Paul's and Blackfriars. They satirized one another and those writing in the public theatres and also the 'feathered' gentry who would pay for the sixpenny seats to watch, and be seen at, the plays performed in the Globe theatre. Such gallants would be better off, possibly, paying their sixpence to go to the private theatres – although that didn't mean they would not be satirized there – thus reducing the revenues of the Globe. But perhaps the biggest commercial threat of all was the plague. This regularly closed the theatres, leaving theatre companies without a steady income for long periods.

Key idea

Although Shakespeare was personally reasonably wealthy by the time he wrote *As You Like It*, the period between 1599 and 1604 was a critical one for the company, which faced many commercial challenges including the frequent closing of the theatres because of the plague. His plays therefore had to be as audiences 'liked' them. Shakespeare duly produced a series of highly successful plays including *Henry V* (1599), *Julius Caesar* (1599) (two plays that may have been the ones with which the new theatre opened), *As You Like It* (1599–1600), *Twelfth Night* (1601) and *Hamlet* (1600–1601).

Sex and sexual titillation

There is something pertinent about the title of a play such as *As You Like It*, but the same could be said of the subtitle of *Twelfth Night*, which was *or, What You Will*, or even the title *Much Ado About Nothing*; they all have a certain bawdy edge to them. *What You Will* has the pun on 'will', or 'penis', but Twelfth Night itself was also regarded as 'the feast of fools'. *Much Ado About Nothing* has a pun on 'no thing' or 'vagina', while at the same time advertising that the play concerns itself with trivia. *As You Like It*, of course, refers to what audiences like, and at the end of the play Rosalind in the epilogue makes that very point:

> I charge you, O women, for the love you bear to men, to like as much of this play as please you. And I charge you, O men, for the love you bear to women – as I perceive by your simpering none of you hates them – that between you and the women the play may please.

> (Epilogue, 207–12)

Spotlight

Two of the issues that these plays deal with are certainly sex and sexual titillation, although the list of concerns by those opposed to theatres was much longer. In these plays and other comedies, Shakespeare capitalizes on the fact that, as women were not allowed to perform in plays, he had prepubescent boys playing the roles of young women. One of them, Rosalind, then dresses up as a young man and calls herself Ganymede, Jove's errand-boy – a name with homoerotic associations – and under that disguise woos another young man named Orlando, who in the poem *Orlando Furioso* by Ariosto (1532) engages in a number of emotionally charged activities, one of which involves his running through the countryside naked.

But even the names of some of the other characters draw attention to the body or bodily functions. Touchstone, for example, may be a 'touchstone' of reality, but there is a sexual pun on stones, meaning testicles, and the name Jaques may well refer to the 'jakes' or privy, a flushing lavatory that had recently been invented by Sir John Harrington.

Although *As You Like It* is a romantic comedy, within it there is a great deal of banter and punning on sexual matters and on physical desire, as, for example, in 4.1.138f., when Orlando wishes his wife will be faithful 'For ever, and a day', to which Rosalind, disguised as Ganymede, replies 'Say a day, without ever', later explaining 'Make the doors upon a woman's wit, and it will out at the casement; shut that, and 'twill out at the keyhole; stop that, 'twill fly with the smoke out at the chimney'. To get outside is to go 'out of doors', which suggests that given freedom from restraint women will become 'whores', and woman's 'wit' refers both to female anarchic ingenuity (particularly in sexual matters but also in her capacity for subversion generally) and to her apparently insatiable desire. She'll find an opening 'out of doors' and shortly will be found in an adulterous bed with a 'neighbour'. Indeed, there is a possible sexual pun even on each of the ways out of the house. (See Rubinstein, F. [1989, 2nd edn: 181], *A Dictionary of Shakespeare's Sexual Puns and Their Significance*. Basingstoke and London: Macmillan.)

Much of this punning is now lost on a modern audience or reader without the help of footnotes or specific reference books, but it gives an indication of the earthy humour of the play itself and helps performers in their interpretation, as, indeed, it can the reader. But it is not necessary to get sidetracked in trying to recognize all the puns, since in a number of cases the double entendres depend heavily on context.

Today, of course, women usually play the female roles and so another historical dimension is lost to the plays such as *As You Like It*, in which the gender disguises would have played such an important part in the performance. Indeed, Rosalind's final appearance in the Epilogue, now in her woman's attire but with the boy actor, draws attention to the fact that he is still in a woman's role: 'It is not the fashion to see the lady the epilogue;' later saying 'If I were a woman, I would kiss as many of you as had beards that pleased me, complexions that liked me, and breaths that I defied not' (Epilogue 1–2, 212–15). Catherine Belsey calls this the 'comedy of uncertainty', where 'a male actor and a female character is speaking' (Belsey, C., in Drakakis, J. [ed.] [1985: 181], *Alternative Shakespeares*. London and New York: Methuen New Accents).

It is the uncertainty of gender identity that may well have attracted Shakespeare's audience, but Belsey notes that it may also have exposed the way in which that identity was socially constructed, allowing the audience 'to glimpse a possible meaning, an image of being, which is not a-sexual, but which disrupts the system of difference on which sexual stereotyping depends' (Belsey, 1985: 190).

Herein lies the comedy of the play. This isn't a bawdy play, despite the sexual puns and bawdy innuendos which no doubt delighted the original audience. It goes beneath that to produce a humour of the genders, to a point where in the epilogue the boy actor can refer openly to both genders in a single speech.

> 'Conventional or no, the taking of female parts by boy players actually occasioned a good deal of contemporary comment, and created considerable moral uneasiness, even among those who patronized and supported the theatres. Among those who opposed them, transvestism on stage was a main plank in the anti-stage polemic.'
>
> Jardine, L. (1983: 9), *Still Harping on Daughters: Women and Drama in the Age of Shakespeare.* Hemel Hempstead: Harvester Press. (See also Dunsinberre, J. [1975: 231].)

The play in this respect was one that 'took on' the civil authorities with a challenge that could not be criticized. It is a humour on the edge of what was permitted but it simultaneously demonstrated what it is to be human.

> 'Shakespeare is profoundly and continuously interested in sex as a fundamental human instinct and activity, as a source not only of comedy but also of joy, of anguish, of disillusionment and of jealousy, of nausea as well as of ecstasy, as a site of moral and ethical debate, and at its best, as a natural fulfilment of spiritual love.'
>
> Wells, S. (2010: 9–10), *Shakespeare, Sex and Love.* Oxford: Oxford University Press

In the Forest of Arden

Duke Senior has been usurped by his brother and banished. He lives like Robin Hood in the forest but despite his protestations in 2.1.1–17, that 'in exile,/Hath not old custom made this life more sweet', he still conducts himself as an authority figure. Orlando, under the rule of his tyrannical brother, Oliver, escapes into the forest with his father's old retainer Adam, who almost dies from starvation (2.6.1f.). The two are saved by human hospitality rather than by Orlando's aggression in trying to steal the exiled duke's food: entering with sword drawn, he cries

'Forbear, and eat no more', to which the melancholy Jaques sardonically replies 'Why, I have eat none yet' (2.7.88–9). It is a put-down in relation to Orlando's expectations concerning the behaviour of 'outlaw'.

Attention is being drawn to the difference between nature and civilization as well as the differences within humankind inscribed in circumstances and levels of birth. Orlando, Rosalind, Oliver and Celia come from the upper stratum of society and retain that status even in refuge in the forest. Phoebe, Silvius, Audrey and Touchstone are from the lower stratum, although it is their existence at the lower end of society that allows Touchstone the clown to use his urbane knowledge of court behaviour to displace William – a possible reference to the playwright – in love, reducing him to the status of a 'clown':

> TOUCHSTONE [I am] He sir that must marry this woman. Therefore, you clown, abandon – which is in the vulgar leave – the society – which in the boorish is company – of this female – which in the common is woman. Which together is, abandon the society of this female, or clown, thou perishest;

> (5.1.45–50)

Touchstone here assumes a ridiculous linguistic superiority to William, humorously placing himself in a dominant hierarchical position, allying himself in his imagination with a cultural and political superiority. He has found someone, William, whom he can force to relieve him of his position of 'clown', which would allow him to move up the social ladder. In reality, however, he does not progress very far in sophistication, since for him marriage is reduced simply to a means of legitimizing sexual gratification: 'Come sweet Audrey, We must be married or we must live in bawdry' (3.3.87–8).

For her part, Phoebe, who has aspirations above her social status, falls in love with Rosalind disguised as Ganymede, thereby adding a further, audacious dimension to the sexual interest: two boy actors playing two women, one of whom has fallen for the other in her male attire.

Defying the dream

In the midst of this sexual and social melee within the forest is the malcontent, Jaques. Throughout the drama, Jaques demonstrates that he cannot be assimilated into the illusion that the characters are creating for themselves, since he feels compelled to defy their dream by reminding everyone of the frailty of flesh. His vision of a fallen, postlapsarian world is in conflict with the Duke's illusory prelapsarian Edenic vision. Jaques offers his own vision of human progress in the famous Seven Ages of Man speech, in which he goes beyond drawing a parallel between life and the stage to suggest that life is itself a theatrical performance:

> All the world's a stage,
> And all the men and women merely players.
> They have their exits and their entrances,
> And one man in his time plays many parts,
> His acts being seven ages.

(2.7.139f.)

He continues by drawing out the different phases of human life as it declines towards imbecility and death. Society is constant only in its repetition of the mutability of its members, with the result that the process of living is also an inescapable part of a process of dying.

Key idea

In this context the comic plot builds on the foundation of a Shakespearean formulaic structure, and may be seen as a mating game in a world of birth, copulation and death, where rebirth and an investment in youth are Nature's way of compensating for the rise and decline of existence.

The structure of the play

Within the structure, the obstacle with which this play begins is twofold: firstly, the usurpation of Duke Senior by his brother Ferdinand leads to the rejection of Rosalind; and secondly,

Oliver's dislike of his younger brother leads to him trying to have him killed in a wrestling match. Within that first stage of the play, not only are the issues set out but Shakespeare includes a wrestling bout which in itself has entertainment value – as have, of course, the songs performed in the forest setting.

In keeping with the formula of escape from a threat, subsequent lovers escape to the forest. There, the various re-articulations of the problem and the finding of a resolution take place under a pretence, a fantasy of the sort that constitutes 'theatre', to where the point of teasing and pretending are no longer enough. In 5.2.50–51 Rosalind's lover Orlando declares, 'I can live no longer by thinking' and she replies, 'I will weary you then no longer with idle talking.' Their playing must come to an end, as must the play itself. Of course, that will be the point when the lovers' true identities are discovered.

Rosalind subsequently uses Hymen's masque, another 'entertainment', as a recognition scene, revealing who she is and thereby bringing each of the couples together. In this, Phoebe's dream is shattered as she realizes that the man she loves (Ganymede) is a woman (Rosalind), and that she should be satisfied with the lover she has rejected (Silvius). But structurally there remain many unanswered questions. What about the original problem of the usurpation of the Duke? While a means has been found to bring Oliver into the wood and for him to fall in love, almost magically, with Celia, a device outside the harmony of the structural formula has to be created by the dramatist in order to allow for a reconciliation between the two dukes.

With only a brief prior reference (1.1.5–6), 'My brother Jaques he keeps at school, and report speaks goldenly of his profit …', Sir Rowland de Boys's second son, confusingly named Jaques (or Jacques in the Arden stage direction), appears on the stage for the first time to convey the news of Duke Frederick's conversion (5.4.149f.). The audience can scarcely be expected to recall the brief reference to him so early in the play, and so his introduction into the action comes as a surprise. It is a creaky dramatic solution that usually causes the audience to laugh and to forgive the dramatist for its implausibility. Yet, in its artifice, the second son's appearance draws attention to the construct of the play as much as Hymen's masque.

Its artificiality proclaims the self-referential nature of the artefact, in an attempt to alleviate the implausibility of the usurping Duke Frederick's meeting 'with an old religious man' (5.4.158) and subsequent departure into a religious life. This also cleverly allows an exit for the malcontent Jaques, who has been left isolated by the plot and who elects to go to the converted Duke Frederick, commenting, 'Out of these convertites,/There is much to be heard and learned' (5.4.182–3). The resolution for him neatly suits his character as Shakespeare has him follow Duke Frederick's fortunes now, as before he had followed Duke Senior in his banishment.

All that is left to do is for Rosalind, as we've seen, to close the play with that expression of the comic ambiguity of gender, allowing the audience a completeness and understanding of their place as a necessary component of the total performance. In all of this, however, there is still something highly satisfactory about *As You Like It*: it is a play that lives up to its name.

Twelfth Night; or, What You Will (1601)

Twelfth Night, to my mind, despite charges of being formulaic, is one of the finest comedies ever written. Only perhaps Anton Chekhov and Samuel Beckett come as close to gaining the kind of aesthetic perfection that underpins this comedy, fusing the elements of structure, plot, humour and pathos into a satisfying creative whole. Aesthetic roundness is not, of course, the only determinant of quality but this play has a modulation and movement deep within it that are both inspiring and satisfying.

Each element of the play is interconnected in a more sophisticated way than those set pieces of comedy found, for example, in *The Two Gentlemen of Verona*, in the depiction of constancy and loyalty in the episode with Launce and his dog Crab, or the comic masques and sonnet readings of the male lovers in *Love's Labour's Lost*. These are great comic episodes, but *Twelfth Night* takes the elegance of the structure underpinning *As You Like It* one step further and does so adventurously through pursuing a correspondence motif, in which comedy is haunted by the threat of death.

Carpe diem

Shakespeare shows an interest in doubles: the two pairs of twins in *The Comedy of Errors*; the double set of lovers in *A Midsummer Night's Dream*; the two women in *As You Like It* with Rosalind taller than Celia; and Beatrice and Hero in *Much Ado About Nothing*. In his personal life Shakespeare had twins of his own, Hamnet and Judith, separated by the death of Hamnet in 1596.

Spotlight

In the late 1590s and early 1600s Shakespeare's company clearly had two boy actors of real quality playing the roles of Rosalind and Celia in *As You Like It* and Viola and Olivia in *Twelfth Night*. Shakespeare used this resource cleverly and fully until, presumably, one or both of the actors' voices broke. Some boy actors may have continued to play more mature women's roles well into their careers but, once the voice had broken, it is doubtful that they played the younger romantic females.

Four years after Hamnet's death, Shakespeare, perhaps bravely, returns to the portrayal of twins, only this time they are a boy and a girl (as he himself had) named Viola and Sebastian. In this play there are correspondences between a number of characters that share the letters of their names: Viola, Olivia, Malvolio. It is also a comedy haunted by the knowledge of death and the need to appreciate and value life.

Viola survives a shipwreck but fears her brother is drowned. Her brother also survives the shipwreck but fears his sister is drowned. Shakespeare appears on the surface to have returned to the plot territory of *The Comedy of Errors*, but with a difference. It may be to do with his growth in maturity as a dramatist but, with due caution, we have to note that Hamnet's death occurred between the writing of *The Comedy of Errors* and *Twelfth Night*, and might have influenced his artistic perception.

Death is present throughout the play, not just as a framing device – as in *The Comedy of Errors*, where Egeon is sentenced to death unless he can find redemption within the hours of daylight – but permeating the fabric of the play with a gentle melancholy, as exemplified in the Fool's song:

Come away, come away death,

And in sad cypress let me be laid.

Fie away, fie away breath,

I am slain by a fair cruel maid:

My shroud of white, stuck all with yew,

O prepare it.

My part of death no one so true

Did share it.

(2.4.51–8)

The *carpe diem* ('seize the day') motif represents a balance between the energy of life and the finality of death.

Spotlight

The play's title, *Twelfth Night; or, What You Will*, has attracted the attention of scholars over the years. In the 1950s Northrop Frye (1957) identified archetypal similarities between the comedies in which the action moves into a green world and returns. C. L. Barber (1959) linked *Twelfth Night*, as he did *A Midsummer Night's Dream* and other comedies, with festive traditions in an interpretation that was further explored by other critics such as Anne Righter (1962), whose husband John Barton produced the play for the RSC in 1969–72.

Barber observes that 'The title tells us that the play is like holiday misrule – though not just like it, for it adds "or what you will"' (Barber, C. L. [1959: 241], *Shakespeare's Festive Comedy*. Princeton: Princeton University Press). Towards the end of the century Barber's views, although still respected, were challenged by post-structuralist critics such as Malcolm Evans and by the new historicist critic Stephen Greenblatt. Greenblatt questions Barber's claim that in the play there is a 'basic security' which 'explains why there is so little that is queasy in all Shakespeare's handling of boy actors playing women, and playing women pretending to be men' (Barber, 1959: 245). Such a critical position prompts Greenblatt to call for a different kind of reading that seeks to place these categories within their historical and historicizing context.

'... how can we unsettle the secure relation between the normal and the aberrant? How can we question the nature that like a weighted bowl so providentially draws to her bias and resolves the comic predicaments? I propose that ... we must historicize Shakespearean sexual nature, restoring it to its relation of negotiation and exchange with other social discourses of the body.'

Greenblatt, S. (1992: 72), *Shakespearean Negotiations: The Circulation of Social Energy in Renaissance England.* Oxford: Clarendon Press

Greenblatt argues that the play has to be considered not in isolation but by 'swerving' into historical contextual narratives. He subsequently elaborates this view by extending his research into historical medical transsexual accounts of the period. Although this is a somewhat strained, if not obscure, correspondence of interest in relation to the play itself, it nevertheless offers a critical corrective and an alternative reading to Barber.

There is some validity in both viewpoints. Barber was writing at a time when the 'sexual revolution' of the last decades of the twentieth century that questioned the notion of 'basic security' in assumptions, description, articulation or judgement of 'norms' was in its infancy. But Greenblatt's position isn't beyond question, either. Kiernan Ryan (Ryan [2002: 25], *Shakespeare*), challenging the new historicist approach, suggests that we go back to the text itself as an active element in an historical process. With *Twelfth Night* you may wish to take this suggestion further by investigating the structural foundation that makes the play work dramatically.

Shakespeare's structural formula in this play not only allows the development of a good story, as the audience likes it, but offers an even more complex depiction of character development, and also of emotion, social satire, sexual humour and ambiguity, while the audience is encouraged to make of it what they want or 'what you will'. So the subtitle of the play is drawn to our attention. Interestingly, John Marston also wrote a play called *What You Will*, possibly in the same year, almost as if the two dramatists were shadowing one another.

'What if?'

Let us experiment, using 'what you will' in the context of 'what if?' We can imagine a scenario in which a playwright, knowing his sources, which are various, and mapping out his play, asked himself: what if we have a duke who is infatuated with self-love and who professes love for a wealthy woman of a slightly lower social status than himself? What if she rejects him, just as Elizabeth I rejected Philip of Spain? What would he do? A man of self-love – let me (Shakespeare) call him Orsino (a foreign dignitary of that name had recently visited London) – and, given the attribution of the name, a 'young cub', how would he react?

But let me (Shakespeare), having encountered a number of narratives of this kind, complicate it further. What if, at the time of this rejection, a young woman is shipwrecked on a land that I will call Illyria, as it sounds like, but is not, Elysium (Heaven)? What if she thinks her brother, who could be her twin, has drowned and gone to Elysium, but unknown to her has also survived? What would she do to survive in this strange land? What if we call the two women by similar names, making a connection between the two, even in the letters of their name, providing within the narrative parallels a thematic element that suggests a relationship? The first could be Olivia, as in the olive tree, with its connection to the Christian tradition of sadness manifest in relation to the death of Christ. The second woman, the shipwrecked one, we call Viola, a violet being the pure flower of tranquillity, now saddened by death and believing herself to be in danger in an alien land.

By asking 'What if?' we may develop an understanding, not of the way Shakespeare actually created his play, but of the narrative itself. At its centre there are two women who are both sad and in mourning, but whose names interact by a kind of metathesis with each other, thus providing a correspondence between the two.

We can, of course, introduce further complications into this speculative model. What if there is another potential lover? Just as Olivia is not equal in status to Duke Orsino but rejects him, what if the chief steward of her household, not someone of her station, also believes that she can love him but, like the Duke, is vain and deluded in his desire? Let him even have the letters of her name, Olivia, embedded within his own, 'Malvolio', rendered incongruous by the prefix 'Mal' (bad). He can be a Puritan who manipulates her mourning in an attempt to become indispensable to her but is frustrated by her anarchic relative Sir Toby Belch and members of her household who are temperamentally and diametrically opposed to him: frivolous, easy-going, self-indulgent, fun-loving. One of these can be a visitor, a ridiculous figure desperate to woo Olivia – Sir Andrew Aguecheek – who is manipulated by her uncle, Sir Toby, an archetypal self-indulgent corpulent Falstaffian figure.

Complications and conflict

These 'what ifs' provide a recipe for the conflict, which is the essential ingredient of good drama. But the playwright includes a few more ingredients: a fool who stands apart and yet simultaneously can engage with every level of the society that the play depicts, and who comments on what he sees, while at the same time willingly participating in the events. Shipwrecked Viola can dress in similar clothes to her apparently dead brother and she calls herself Cesario ('little Caesar') because she was ripped from the sea as if new born (caesarean). Her brother can be named Sebastian, after the saint who, according to Christian tradition, was shot with arrows for his love of God and left for dead, only to be revived to health by Irene. Sebastian is also the same name that the faithfully passionate Julia takes in her disguise in *The Two Gentlemen of Verona*. His name, of faithful love, is a foil to those of the others: Toby, Malvolio and Toby's gull Sir Andrew Aguecheek, who, in trying to profess his love to Olivia, is simply ignored. Sir Andrew can even be made to pick a fight with the girl pretending to be the man Cesario, with whom Olivia has fallen in love. The boy actor, feigning female reticence but pitted against a cowardly adversary, raises expectations of a future encounter, which makes for farcical, appealing comedy.

Creating and animating a tableau

Now we have the ingredients of the play but, reader, you might like to try an experiment. Go back over the above discussion again and create a tableau in which each image is frozen in juxtaposition with the others as if in a painting. In your mind's eye, just look for a moment at that painting, which can be called 'What You Will', 'Twelfth Night' perhaps. After considering the image for a while, animate those frozen figures and we have the play in action in accordance with the Shakespearean formula.

We start with the problem relating to the threat of multiple deaths. We have a geographical relocation, in that Viola is washed up on a strange shore and is motivated, for her own protection, to disguise herself as a man who gains service in Orsino's court. In the search for her own identity, she tries to teach Orsino what love is, and in the process she falls in love with him. He, for his part, begins to depend on her, thinking her a man, and sends her to woo Olivia on his behalf. Olivia instantly falls in love with the cross-dressed Viola/Cesario. Confusion reigns; the Fool acts as a commentator on the various events; a trick is played on the other aspiring lover, the Puritan Malvolio, by Sir Toby and the maid Maria who is named after the revered Mother of God.

All either delude themselves or struggle to find out who they really are. Sebastian, the twin brother, meanwhile, is saved from the sea and, like Antipholus of Syracuse in *The Comedy of Errors*, is mistaken for his twin but this time it is a twin sister (who in her disguise looks like her brother). In the errors of *Twelfth Night* and the topsy-turvy world that it depicts, humour and sadness, love and injustice, redemption and aggression all mingle.

All these issues are resolved in the end by the exposure of all the errors in a single concluding scene. Secretly, Olivia has persuaded Sebastian to marry her, thinking him to be Cesario. The Duke himself now arrives to try to court Olivia, but this time in his own person. Cesario is with him and Olivia, thinking Cesario is her newly wedded husband, reveals to Orsino that she is married to his servant. He responds by turning on her and on Cesario with the violence of the adolescent whose character has been threatened with exposure throughout the play. The concept of accepting all these images together, as you might do with a complex painting, may help you to grasp the totality of this intricately designed play, where one image, and even each reflection, reflects another. So the play progresses, drawing you towards its 'most wonderful' (5.2.210) self-reflective discovery.

Meanwhile, Sebastian, a faithful agent of true love, has fought with Sir Toby and now appears on stage at the same time as Viola. It is one of the great recognition scenes in Renaissance drama, a moment of quiet anagnorisis, and its emotional power affects audience and dramatic characters alike, as Sebastian recognizes his lost twin sister:

> Do I stand there? I never had a brother;
> Nor can there be that deity in my nature
> Of here and everywhere. I had a sister,
> Whom the blind waves and surges have devour'd:
> Of charity, what kin are you to me?
> What countryman? What name? What parentage?

Viola replies simply:

> Of Messaline: Sebastian was my father;
> Such a Sebastian was my brother too:
> So went he suited to his watery tomb.
> …
> If nothing lets to make us happy both,
> But this my masculine usurp'd attire,
> Do not embrace me, till each circumstance
> Of place, time, fortune, do cohere and jump
> That I am Viola …

> > (5.1.222–7, 228–30, 245–9)

Within this lengthy recognition scene, which the above quotation draws out a little, we see the traditional elements of classical anagnorisis, including, for example (as in the later play *Cymbeline*), a physical identifier used to substantiate the characters' claims – (VIOLA) 'My father had a mole upon his brow./ (SEBASTIAN) And so had mine' (lines 238–9). But there is also added a Christian reference to resurrection, though in this case it is secularized. As after death, the resurrected Christ forbids those who first see him from touching him, so here, Viola, unlike Rosalind in *As You Like It*, instructs Sebastian not to embrace her until the truth of what has happened has been finally confirmed.

Key idea

Anagnorisis is being gently fused with a secularized expression of the deepest Christian 'mystery': resurrection. The impact on the original audiences, consciously or unconsciously, must have been immense and, despite the greater secularization of our own society, this conclusion still retains its emotional power.

'This is I'

The mature Shakespearean plays, whether comedy or tragedy, insist on exploring the identity of the self – something that, as we have already seen, Shakespeare began to address in *The Comedy of Errors*. In *Hamlet*, written possibly in the same year as *Twelfth Night*, the prince returning to Elsinore reveals himself at the graveside of his love, Ophelia: 'This is I,/Hamlet the Dane' (5.1.255–6). In the comedy of *Twelfth Night*, the twin sister who discovers that her brother is not dead leads to the proof of her own identity: 'That I am Viola' (5.1.249). These statements of the substance of the name are confirmations of sanity, self-reconciliation and of community and knowledge. Yet how does the actor or actress playing the respective parts rehearse themselves into an understanding of the fictional character they are portraying?

They do so, of course, by their training, their technique and accomplishment as professional actors. The directors, in assisting them in any given performance, usually try to find a 'through-line' for the play as a whole, an interpretative logic that will provide a consistency in communication. For example, Sir Peter Hall, founding director of the Royal Shakespeare Company, summed up *Twelfth Night* for his 1958 production by telling his actors that the play 'like all the comedies, is about growing up'. It is a typical all-embracing simple statement by a director who has to engage his cast with a dominant idea that will provide the glue, the consistency that will cement the various elements of the production together.

For his 1970 production of *A Midsummer Night's Dream*, Peter Brook similarly held to the unifying idea of the play's 'rough magic', a phrase coined by Shakespeare himself in *The Tempest*. As with Brook in 1970, so Hall in 1958 felt he needed to break away from stereotypical productions, presenting a challenge to the cast and ultimately to the audience. John Barton attempted to do the same thing with his famous production 11 years later, where – quietly, softly, magically, with a cadence of joy in her throat – Judi Dench's Viola finally acknowledged her name, in what proved to be an almost Chekhovian interpretation of the play with its comic blend of outrage and subtlety.

As these examples show, characterization comes from the text but it is created through the actor, who is a product of his or her own age, charged with reinterpreting a centuries-old malleable text. Hall's and Barton's productions today would not hold the same force as they did in 1958 or 1969, largely because the tastes and expectations of modern audiences have changed. So let me refer you to a more recent stage interpretation.

Spotlight

The 2012 RSC production directed by David Farr, with Jonathan Slinger as Malvolio, revealed a cruder, though still effective, bawdy humour in a more explicitly dangerous environment in which Viola literally came out of a reservoir of water. A director might advise the actor playing Malvolio that, while the characters of Viola and Olivia are experiencing the tribulations of youth, his harsh Puritanism is the result of a persistent victimization that makes it difficult for him to learn from experience. It was this that David Farr may have felt was what the characterization needed to communicate to an audience. In the text, Malvolio is imprisoned, a Puritan duped to the point of madness by a Saturnalian. But he is no less 'human' in characterization than the Saturnalian himself. Jonathan Slinger's bawdy exposure in the yellow stockings scene was reflective of a character 'caught out' by his own sexual desire – a comically modern Priapus.

'That that is, is'

In the text, Sir Toby engineers a bitter revenge on Malvolio by manipulating the authority to which his own superior social statues entitles him, to destroy a servile aspiring inferior. Ironically, however, Malvolio is depicted as someone who believes in the superiority of the very social order that humiliates him. The steward's self-deception has led him to misunderstand the cruel nature of society itself. 'That that is, is' (4.2.14) may be a tautology in the play, as claimed by Malcolm Evans, but it is portrayed as a reality of conduct. One should not get above oneself in a hierarchical society and Malvolio's 'I'll be reveng'd on the whole pack of you!' (5.1.370) may indicate that at the conclusion he is still delusional about himself, but it also points forward to the prospect of a much more serious social upheaval that was to unfold. We might conjecture that, just as in the early twentieth century Anton Chekhov wrote the comedy *Uncle Vanya*, which looked towards the Russian Revolution, so in *Twelfth Night* there is a prophetic glance of what will occur after the feasting and comedy is over: the English Revolution and execution of the King in 1649.

By being imprisoned, Malvolio has been deliberately kept away from the recognition scene. However, in the final scene, Olivia goes as far as her society will allow in promising him that he can be 'both the plaintiff and judge/ Of thine own cause' (5.1.347–8). His humiliation is too great and for a moment threatens to destroy the comic resolution. Trevor Nunn's 1996 film version of the play sees him, luggage in hand, leaving the household. It is a justifiable interpretation.

In the end, Sir Toby conforms to the values of the society by marrying Maria and the Fool remains, just as Malvolio had accurately depicted him, an outsider within the household, an important parasitic commentator who can easily outlive his comic or nuisance value. The Fool knows that 'the rain it raineth every day' and that 'truth' is less attractive than fantasy but, unlike Malvolio, the appropriately named Feste does not delude himself into thinking that he is other than what he is.

This is a comically melancholic play, in which the comedy is used to counterbalance, by means of an anarchic festivity, the seriousness of some of the issues raised.

Key idea

In *Twelfth Night* there is no place for looking back – what is dead is gone – but the present still has to define itself according to the prevailing political and social forces and the demands of social and religious conformity that control it. This leaves a modern audience with questions emanating from the nature of both structure and plot.

We will never know how Shakespeare reacted as a father to the death of his son. This biographical 'fact' may or may not haunt this play. But behind this story something lingers. We are born, we cry, we laugh, we endure and we die – sometimes in youth but certainly in old age. It is a view of life and humanity that *King Lear* will later confirm. In this comedy, Shakespeare's play confronts both life and death, bringing characters 'back to life' to an Illyria where self-absorption finally gives way to a recognition of the mutuality of love. The dramatic structure of Shakespeare's play determines that this is so.

We may ask whether he offers us a timeless or a trans-historical truth by offering hope as part of the very process of a self-recognition that gives way to love as the foundation of the social order. We may find critical help in understanding what Shakespeare attempted to do by fictionalizing a 'what if', but in the end he still leaves us to make of it 'what you will'.

9

Critical perspectives 2: Theatrical influences on Shakespeare in performance and interpretation

Conventional literary critical interpretations of Shakespeare's plays focus largely on the texts, but through the twentieth century and into the twenty-first a greater interest has developed in actual performance and the meanings that it generates. During the early twentieth century two main acting styles emerged, each producing contrasting theatrical perspectives that continue into the present century. The first of these was Stanislavskian, the second Brechtian, but there has also been a movement that aims to present the plays in a manner close to the way the Elizabethans might themselves have performed them.

The empty space

Some modern scholarship has challenged the primacy of traditional literary textual criticism as the dominant interpretative authority of Shakespeare in performance. The actor Sam Wanamaker's recreation of Shakespeare's Globe Theatre in London (1997), and the performances that have been staged there, have awakened a further understanding that we cannot comprehend the plays, even historically, from the printed text alone. Critics have noted how the environment of the theatre itself affects the performance and the variety of ways in which the actors at those early performances may have delivered the lines.

Shakespeare references the physical theatre of performance in many of the plays and in doing so perhaps assists in the redefinition of some of our perspectives. An awareness of this theatrical self-consciousness pushes us further to consider the historically and culturally specific contexts within which the plays are performed generally. Theatre director Peter Brook's seminal work *The Empty Space* (first published in 1968) directed our attention to the very effect of the playing space as part of the language of the drama, influencing both contemporary performance and the critical evaluation of Shakespeare.

'... the early modern playhouse seems to have repeatedly been used as a way of interpreting and heightening the words and, sometimes, as a way of querying or undercutting them. Against this, Shakespeare's calls for imagination need to be reconceptualized. True, there are moments when Shakespeare wants not to be constrained either by the overarching metaphors of his stage, or its crude realism. But a look at the way he locates a poet's imagination in A Midsummer Night's Dream (5.1.12–17) shows just how fundamentally organized it was by and around the stage ... Imagination seems, for Shakespeare, to be scarcely distinguishable from its theatrical home and ultimately located there.'

Stern, T. (2014: 31–2), '"This Wide and Universal Theatre": The Theatre as Prop in Shakespeare's Metadrama', in Karim-Cooper, F. and Stern, T., *Shakespeare's Theatres and the Effects of Performance*. London and New York: Bloomsbury Arden Shakespeare

You may recall that earlier I noted how in *Hamlet* the often-quoted speech 'I have of late, but wherefore I know not, lost all my mirth ... ' (2.2.297–8) worked in the theatre by reference to the stage canopy, the sky and the bad breath of the audience around the thrust stage. Similarly, in the passage from *A Midsummer Night's Dream* referred to by Tiffany Stern above, the point is that the environment of Shakespeare's stage as a physical image is designed not only to complement his words, 'The poet's eye, in a fine frenzy rolling, / Doth glance from heaven to earth, from earth to heaven;' (5.1.12–13), but to embody the dramatic poet creating his art in the theatre, 'And as imagination bodies forth / The forms of things unknown, the poet's pen / Turns them to shapes, and gives to airy nothing / A local habitation and a name' (5.1.14–17).

Artistry and the theatrical experience

The overt presence of the dramatist's artistry, as a poet and as a writer for the theatre in which his plays are being performed, is a hallmark of Shakespeare's drama. It is never far away from his writing. It is exemplified in one of his last plays, *The Tempest* (4.1.146–58), but is found throughout his career. His self-referencing of theatre art, is, therefore, an important element of the plays in which it is found. It is an example of what is termed 'metatheatre' in action. It works as part of the 'sign system' of a play or, indeed, a poem. In the *Sonnets*, Shakespeare consciously refers to the fact that he is writing a poem that will last for generations to come. But in theatre his language, within this environment, provides something more than words. It is the theatrical experience itself, beyond just the specific playhouse for which Shakespeare was writing, but looking also to playhouses of the future that will interpret and present these plays according to their own age, culture, ideology and circumstances.

> *'Shakespeare's drama bears out better than the work of any other author the truth of Shelley's belief that the poet "not only beholds intensely the present as it is, and discovers those laws according to which present things ought to be ordered, but he beholds the future in the present".'*
>
> Ryan, K. (2001), 'Shakespeare and the Future' (quoting Reiman, D.H. and Powers, S.B. [eds] [1977: 482–3], *Shelley's Poetry and Prose*. New York: W.W. Norton), in Cartmell, D. and Scott, M. (2001: 192), *Talking Shakespeare*. Basingstoke: Palgrave

Acting style

The idea that there was a uniform acting style in the Elizabethan theatre has been challenged in recent years by, for example, Paul Manzer, as a textually devised concept. He notes that historically Shakespeare's actors were literally given their parts as rolls, 'Parts were made of strips of paper that were then joined top-to-tail and rolled around a wooden baton, requiring motion. A "roll" takes its name from the action it demands in its use. You "read" a book, but you "roll" a roll' (Menzer, P. [2014: 164], 'Character Acting', in Karim Cooper, F. and Stern, T., *Shakespeare's Theatres and the Effects of Performance*). The claim is that the dramatic character's part was given to the actor along with his cues as one long joined roll, and that this – naturally confined – produced a homogeneity of role for that actor, obscuring the wider context of the play as a complete action. This in turn would have affected the way in which an actor approached and performed the part as a contribution to the play as a whole. Some actors would, no doubt, have bought a complete text, once published, but this was not their *modus operandi* in the day-to-day performance of the play, although there is no hard evidence to suggest that they did not have a general grasp of the play as a whole. Indeed, as a dramatist who also acted in his and other dramatist's plays, Shakespeare would certainly have had an outline of the larger context of the play.

Just as with literary criticism, so with performance criticism: we find ourselves confronted by a variety of theoretical models and concepts. Some of the valid issues raised, however, can still leave questions unanswered. There is no evidence, for example, that the actors disappeared during the rehearsals of the play or that they were not briefed in one way or another about the context of the play as a whole and the location of their role within it. So we have to take care that we do not impose conjectural models on an historical process of which we do not have an undisputed model. We have to weigh one conjecture against another or even amalgamate ideas to imagine how the plays were first performed. John Drakakis, in an unpublished note to me, comments, 'I think that the best we can say is that the acting was more stylized though some of the realistic dialogue departed from this model occasionally.'

Spotlight

Modern Shakespearean performance, however, relies usually on the 'book'; this contains the text of the play as a whole, infused by textually based interpretation. So the actor Simon Russell Beale has referred to acting as 'three-dimensional literary criticism'. In *Hamlet*, Shakespeare famously tells his actors, in the scene where Hamlet instructs the players, not to be over-flamboyant in gesture, and with some exceptions – Launce and his dog or perhaps the Porter's scene in *Macbeth* – he appears to show an irritation with the clowns' extempore interpolations for comic effect.

In tragedy this may unbalance the overall conception that the dramatist may have had in mind. Indeed, speculation holds that this is what may have led to the argument with Will Kempe and his subsequent departure from the company. However, in the original 1600 text of *Much Ado About Nothing* explicit reference is made to the actor Will Kempe who played the role of Dogberry, suggesting that, even in scripting the Clown's part, Shakespeare had a particular actor and his distinctive style of acting in mind.

In *A Midsummer Night's Dream*, as we have seen, Shakespeare may ridicule amateur acting or indeed the acting of a rival company. For example, the Mechanicals' rehearsal in Act 1, Scene 2 parodies a humorous description of the ways in which various roles might be played. Bottom's imitation of 'Ercles' vein, a tyrant's vein' (1.2.26–38) may be a warm satiric jibe at Shakespeare's competitor company the Admiral's Men and their principal actor Edward Alleyn (1566–1626), with whom some of Shakespeare's colleagues – Kempe, Pope, Heminges, Phillips and maybe Shakespeare himself – had once acted, and as such is another 'in-joke' of the theatre which no doubt would have been understood and appreciated by his audiences.

Film and television

Today the complexity of interpretative styles becomes more taxing through film and television. It is useful to compare, for example, a recording of the 2011 production of *Much Ado About Nothing* at the reconstructed Shakespeare's Globe in London with the 1993 film version made by Kenneth Branagh. The Dogberry and Verges scenes in the latter, to my mind, just do not work at all. In fact, they are somewhat embarrassing when set against the clever cinematic portrayal of the main narrative by Branagh. But even the new Globe version, purporting to offer some kind of imitation of how these scenes might have originally been performed, is similarly disappointing. In both, there appears too great an externality of acting imposed on the scenes rather than an interpretation confident that the comic lines can work effectively. One mantra might be that, instead of trying to make the lines funny, we should allow them to be funny!

Key idea

The actor's belief in the dramatic power of the script is not always essential but it certainly helps in creating successful productions, even though the script may have been adapted for a particular theatre. 'Metatheatre' works when there is confidence in it as part of the whole rather than something extraneous to the whole. It is both exterior to and intrinsic to the play's design. I sometimes wonder whether in performance we should trust Shakespeare a little more. He was a professional. He knew what he was doing.

Film and, indeed, modern technology, however, add a further dimension to the study of Shakespeare. Modern media have generated a criticism and history of their own in which Shakespeare becomes located. (See, for example, Cartmell, D.

[2000], *Interpreting Shakespeare on Screen*. Basingstoke: Macmillan, for an incisive balanced discussion of Shakespeare on film in relation to gender, sexuality, race and nationalism as well as references to film history itself, and also see the work of Graham Holderness [2003], *Visual Shakespeare Essays in Film and Television*. Hatfield: University of Hertfordshire Press.)

Spotlight

With film there is always the opportunity and the temptation to take what is implied even on the stage and making it sexually or violently explicit, to the point where it adds gratuitously to the work itself. You may decide for yourself if this is so in, for example, Ralph Fiennes' 2010 film version of *Coriolanus* with its violently graphic and bloody contemporary depiction of modern war, or Justin Kurzel's graphically violent *Macbeth* (2015), with Michael Fassbender and Marion Cotillard. Compare these productions, however, with the nationalism displayed by Laurence Olivier's *Henry V* made in 1944 as an avowed contribution to the war effort, which, as Cartmell notes, 'appropriates Shakespeare in order to glorify war in a morale-boosting exercise' (p. 95), and we see how interpretation becomes a record not of the play but of the ideologically motivated investments imposed on it.

Kenneth Branagh's cinematic film version of *Henry V* (1989) deliberately takes a different approach from Olivier's version, paying 'homage to its predecessor while seemingly recovering the history for a 1980s audience' (Cartmell: 101). It also grew out of a new awareness and an increasingly graphic depiction on screen of the realities of warfare. But it would be misleading to think that performance-related criticism is a phenomenon of the late twentieth or early twenty-first centuries. Critics since Shakespeare have consistently referred to the plays in performance and actors themselves have written through the centuries about the plays, but in the early decades of the twentieth century detailed performance-led studies began to appear, with the work of directors such as Harley Granville-Barker's *Prefaces to Shakespeare* and G. Wilson-Knight's *Principles of Shakespearian Production*, later published as *Shakespearian Production*.

The multi-conscious apprehension of the audience

In 1944 S. L. Bethell, in *Shakespeare and the Popular Dramatic Tradition*, referred to what we realize to be the multi-conscious apprehension of the audience. Spectators at a play are not only aware of the performance action but of their surroundings. This includes the type of theatre – open air, proscenium-arched, thrust stage, large, small, intimate – and whether it is hot or cold. If in the open air is it going to rain, or is the sun too hot? Are they standing or sitting? Are the seats comfortable or hard? They are also conscious of other things; will the play end in time for me to catch the last train or bus? Did I lock the car?

It goes further than this, since the spectators will also bring their own receptivity: their differences in attitude, gender, ideologies, education, class, problems, perplexities, desires and wishes. There will also be concerns regarding those around them – local or visitors, talking, whispering, laughing, coughing or silent; restless or engaged; bored or concentrating. All of these and other audience issues have an effect on an individual's perception of what is happening on stage and can have a communal effect within the theatre about which the actors become aware. They might see an individual who distracts them, in a positive or a negative way, or discern an atmosphere, for example, of encouragement or frustration with the performance. Communication in a live performance is a highly complex matter and every performance is consequently unique.

Recreating the Shakespearean stage

In 1894 William Poel founded the Elizabethan Stage Society, in which he attempted to recreate the staging of Elizabethan plays within the context of what he considered to be something approaching the original Shakespearean theatre. Poel was reacting against the lavish stage productions of the late nineteenth century and was looking forward, perhaps, to the re-creation of Shakespeare's Globe in London, just over a hundred years later (1997) by Sam Wanamaker. Wanamaker drew on the rich tradition of twentieth-century research and scholarship in the construction of the theatres of Shakespeare's day and the manner of performance. In this the actor Mark Rylance, as the first artistic director of the new Shakespeare's Globe, had a major influence, not only on our understanding of how the plays might have originally been performed but how they could still be effective within that performance tradition.

Acting traditions cited earlier – Stanislavskian and Brechtian – nevertheless have had, and still retain, a strong influence. They are not the only interpretative ways of staging Shakespeare, as Rylance, for example, has demonstrated, but understanding something about them will enable you to locate productions you may see or interpretations you read. Let us begin with the Russian director Stanislavsky.

STANISLAVSKY

At the end of the nineteenth and the beginning of the twentieth century, the Moscow-based director Constantin Stanislavsky (1863–1938) developed a realistic form of acting, ostensibly to deal with the naturalistic plays of the Russian dramatist Anton Chekhov. This was later developed by Lee Strasberg (1901–82) at the Actors' Studio in New York into what is known as 'method acting'. It influenced a range of theatre and later film actors of the twentieth century such as Marlon Brando and Rod Steiger.

Theatrical realism, in Stanislavsky's system, depended on what he termed 'emotion memory'. Through a range of exercises and rehearsal techniques in realistic settings, the actor has to find within his/her emotional memory an affinity with the part he/she is acting, so that a relationship develops between the role and the actor and they almost become one. This technique works well within a style in which verbal language is not the only (or indeed the primary) means of communication. Indeed, as the late John Russell Brown demonstrated in *Shakespeare in Performance* (1969), Stanislavsky's technique explored those areas of experience that exist underneath the text, and that various non-verbal means of communication, such as gesture, body language and paralinguistic expression (such as stutters), seek to present to an audience.

Key idea

The phrase 'they almost become one' is important, since Stanislavsky stressed that the actors should never totally lose a consciousness of their true identities as actors on a stage, but should speak in their own self as the person in the role.

'When a real artist is speaking the soliloquy "To be or not to be", is he merely putting before us the thoughts of the author and executing the business indicated by his director? No, he puts into his lines much of his own conception of life.

'Such an artist is not speaking in the person of an imaginary Hamlet. He speaks in his own right as one placed in the circumstances created by the play. The thoughts, feelings, conceptions, reasoning of the author are transformed into his own. And it is not his sole purpose to render the lines so that they shall be understood. For him it is necessary that the spectators feel his inner relationship to what he is saying. They must follow his own creative will and desires. Here the motive forces of his psychic life are united in action and interdependent. This combined power is of utmost importance to us actors and we should be gravely mistaken not to use it for our practical ends.'

Stanislavsky, C. (1937: 248–9), *An Actor Prepares*. London: Geoffrey Bles

Stanislavsky's views might have been an anathema to traditional literary critics, but he was actually taking the 'realism' found in the nineteenth- and early twentieth-century character criticism to a logical conclusion on the stage. But Stanislavsky's 'realism' was questioned from the start. Anton Chekhov (1860–1904), made famous by Stanislavsky's realistic productions of his plays, complained that the director ruined them by turning what he had written as comedies into naturalistic tragedies. He disliked Stanislavsky having frogs croaking or the sound of trains passing in some productions. He pointed to paintings. If you take a portrait of a person created by a great artist and cut out the nose and insert a real one, he commented, you would have realism but not art. Indeed, you would have ruined the painting!

Stanislavsky's influence on RSC productions of Shakespeare in the late twentieth century was marked, but subject to similar criticism as those made by Chekhov, as Janice Wardle's discussion of John Barton's influential 1969 production of *Twelfth Night* makes apparent:

> 'Barton's application of Stanislavskian-based techniques led him to implant detailed character analysis within accepted anthropological structures, derived from Frye and Barber, which had primarily displayed the social, and not the individual's function in comedy. Arguably, tensions would inevitably result and, as in the case of Stanislavsky's exploration of Chekhov's individual trapped within a limiting social system, the prevailing mood would be melancholic.'
>
> Wardle, J. (2001: 116), '*Twelfth Night*: "One face, one voice, one habit and two persons!"', in Cartmell, D. and Scott, M., *Talking Shakespeare.* Basingstoke: Palgrave

BRECHT AND EPIC THEATRE

One of Stanislavsky's main actors, Vsevolod Meyerhold (1874–1940), left the company and developed an expressionist form of acting at a time when Russia was experiencing its communist revolution and its aftermath. Art was becoming more politicized and Meyerhold's theatre became constructivist with an explicitly political dimension, later developed by the German communist director Erwin Piscator (1893–1966).

Meyerhold and Piscator heralded the development in Germany of what became known as Epic Theatre – a term first used by Piscator – or the theatre of alienation. This was developed by Bertolt Brecht (1898–1956), who drew a distinction between Dramatic Theatre in a realistic tradition and the episodic approach of Epic Theatre. The first exploited the emotional impact of drama on stage, which, as we will see later, evolves from the early Greek drama and its range and purpose as defined by Aristotle in the *Poetics*. By contrast, Epic Theatre exposed the mechanisms, theatrical and political, through which drama was constructed, thereby recontextualizing performance and exposing the flaws in the Aristotelian conception of drama. This was a theatre that downplayed bourgeois notions of 'emotion' by appealing to a more analytical frame of mind. Brecht regarded the Elizabethan theatre as instructive in its meta-dramatic disclosures of its own practical methodologies, but he was also influenced heavily by the stylized plays of the Japanese Noh theatre tradition. From this, radical political interpretations and readings of Shakespeare's plays were to evolve. So, for example, Brecht rejects in his poem 'On Shakespeare's Play *Hamlet*' (*c*.1940) the romantic and realistic interpretations of the Prince and his 'tragedy' *Hamlet*. Such interpretations do not challenge the spectators but rather confirm their own bourgeois prejudices. For Brecht, Shakespeare's plays needed to be performed as dialectical in the context of the anti-bourgeois philosophy.

'Here is the body, puffy and inert
Where we can trace the virus of the mind.
How lost he seems among his steel-clad kind
This introspective sponger in a shirt!
Till they bring drums to wake him up again
As Fortinbras and all the fools he's found
March off to win that little patch of ground
Which is not tomb enough ... to hide the slain.

...

So we can nod when the last Act is done
And they pronounce that he was of the stuff
To prove most royally, had he been put on.'

Brecht, B., 'On Shakespeare's Play *Hamlet*', c.1940 (1959), quoted in
Willett, J. (1977, p/b ed: 120–21), *The Theatre of Bertolt Brecht*. London:
Eyre Methuen

Key idea

In considering Shakespeare, the performances and the construction of the plays in general, Brecht holds that realistic Dramatic Theatre implicates the audience in the action of the plot, whereas Epic Theatre, by concentrating on narrative, allows the spectators to be observers of the action, distancing them to encourage an intellectual engagement with the issues of the play rather than in an uncritical acceptance of its conclusion. The Brechtian *Verfremdungseffekt*, 'alienation' or 'A-effect', was designed to produce this distance from the action as a means of helping the audience to take a critical view of what was being represented on stage. This debate between Dramatic Theatre and Epic Theatre continues to have an influence on how we perceive Shakespeare today.

We will consider the Brechtian approach in more detail in Chapter 16, as it informs or coincides with the radical literary critical readings of Shakespeare that gradually emerged through the twentieth century, to the point of challenging, for example, conventional Aristotelian views of 'tragedy' rooted in classical theatre and adopted by the Christian and humanist traditions. But, before doing so, having planted the thought in your mind, let us continue our journey with an examination of some further Shakespearean comedies which in both criticism and production tend to spark significant critical debate: *Much Ado About Nothing*, *The Taming of the Shrew* and *The Merchant of Venice*.

10

Much Ado About Nothing (1598–9) and *The Taming of the Shrew* (1589–92?)

In this chapter we will look at two further comedies that raise certain challenges for the audience. These two plays are comedies about love but they differ from the romantic comedies so far considered. They explicitly raise social issues, testing the audience's reactions and sensibilities, and they employ different perspectives from those we have so far examined. They are not being considered in their probable chronological order of composition because I want to introduce you first to the concept of structural confrontation and alienation, as contained in *Much Ado About Nothing*, before discussing the social and gender issues raised in *The Taming of the Shrew*.

Spotlight

In the romantic comedies, the dramatist presents various levels of reality. Through the range of his plays across genres, Shakespeare appears to suggest a variety of perceptions:

1 The perceived reality around us in nature and society, including political reality

2 A reality that can be created in our imaginations in order to make sense of the first: fairies, transformations, sexual fantasies, grotesque or harmonious experiences, heroic, desolate or discordant elements and endings

3 A suggested or speculated reality of something beyond death that can only be the subject of contemplation, even though ghosts may appear from the grave to give an assurance of its validity – as Hamlet says to his friend, 'There are more things in heaven and earth, Horatio,/Than are dreamt of in your philosophy' (Hamlet, 2.1.174–5).

We'll explore the third speculative reality described above in the later discussion of the tragedies but it is always useful in considering the comedies to keep your mind open to the reflective nature of the issues being raised in one genre compared with other genres. We have seen, for example, that *Twelfth Night* is haunted by images, songs and references to death and was written at around the same time as *Hamlet*.

Much Ado About Nothing does not exactly follow the traditional structure of the Shakespearean romance comedies, although some important elements of that structure, including death, or a threat of death, are important ingredients within it. These, however, make their appearance at the centre of the narrative rather than the beginning, although in *Much Ado About Nothing* the soldiers are returning from a victorious war, and the threat of death is now over with 'few of any sort, and none of name' having been killed (1.1.7). We learn from Leonato that the bastard Don John has been 'reconciled to the

Prince your brother' (1.1.149), although as he replies with what could be curt politeness, as a man 'not of many words', we might have our suspicions about him.

Shakespeare appears to be experimenting again with dramatic structure, as he had done with *Romeo and Juliet*, where comedy moves into tragedy. In *Much Ado About Nothing*, the comedy takes a potentially serious turn but this is temporary and tragedy is ultimately averted, allowing the play to end harmoniously, although the potential for the tragic does not disappear entirely from the audience's minds. In this, *Much Ado About Nothing* points towards plays such as *Measure for Measure* (1604), which critics in the past termed a 'problem play', *Othello* (1604), where the 'love' interest is demeaned, and *The Winter's Tale* (1611), variously categorized as a 'romance' or a 'last play', and which combines elements of *Much Ado* and *Othello* in order to produce a hybrid genre, which some term a 'tragicomedy'.

The Taming of the Shrew, although the date of it is uncertain, is an earlier play than *Much Ado About Nothing* but it raises social issues that are equally if not more confrontational, certainly for a modern audience, in its exposure and possible exploitation of gender issues. It may help you by linking it to the ensuing chapter on *The Merchant of Venice* and the controversies that play has generated. With these three plays Shakespearean criticism follows Shakespeare into some challenging political and social territory.

'Shakespeare did not choose one of the several patterns in common use, but modified and supplemented whatever he borrowed. And having once pleased his audience, he was not content to repeat a single pattern but continued to modify his basic structure, adding or rejecting certain elements, and sometimes rejecting one for a time only to return to it later.'

Brown, J.R. (1968: 27), *Shakespeare and His Comedies*. London: Methuen

Much Ado About Nothing

Much Ado About Nothing was written sometime before 1600 when its first publication in quarto noted that it had been 'sundry times publicly acted'. There is speculation, as there is about *As You Like It*, that it may be the 'lost play' *Love's Labour's Won*, as the RSC surprisingly and disingenuously described it in their 2015 production. The case, however, remains unproven.

As mentioned in Chapter 7, *Much Ado About Nothing* as a title has an affinity with *What You Will* (*Twelfth Night*) and *As You Like It*, in being designed to appeal through sexual innuendo and suggestion. The title *Much Ado About Nothing* can also point to a great deal of fuss about issues that prove to be of no lasting consequence. That, indeed, is what the play appears, on one level, to proclaim since, despite all the machinations that occur, in the end all is reconciled through the exposure of Don John's deception. The sexual quibble on the word 'nothing' that some critics have pointed to suggests a much more bawdy meaning, which indicates that, contrary to its manifest meaning, this play is about an issue central to Elizabethan patriarchal culture.

NOTHING OR NOTING

This critical line also leads to a consideration that the play contains various instances of characters 'noting' the perceived actions of others and making judgements thereby. It has been suggested that Elizabethan pronounced the words 'noting' and 'nothing' in the same way. Or it may be allowing a parallel with the 'notes' of music, leading us to regard it as being like a musical composition. The title of a play, of course, like the opening scenes, is important in setting the tone of what is to follow.

Deborah Cartmell gives an instructive insight on how the opening sequence of Kenneth Branagh's 1993 film version draws on artistic symbols and cinematic history to reinforce the work's sexual force.

'In the first half of the film Beatrice is frequently seen with fruit in her hand, underlining her ripeness. The sexuality of the opening sequence is hard to miss: the men arrive on horseback, charging into the women's domain in deliberate imitation of The Magnificent Seven (1960; directed by John Sturges); this is followed with the parties rushing to the bathhouse, stripping off and washing, culminating in the men thrusting towards the women in a phallic "V" formation. In the opening moments of the film we move from the words of the song "Sigh no more" represented as a page of text, to Beatrice's voice speaking the words (significantly prefacing the film with her knowledge that "men are deceivers ever" ...).'

Cartmell, D. (2000: 50), *Interpreting Shakespeare on Screen*.
Basingstoke: Macmillan

'WHAT IF?'

Like *Twelfth Night*, *Much Ado About Nothing* is a comedy that also explores the 'what if?' of a story, just as it appears that Shakespeare explored 'what if?' in placing the early part of *Romeo and Juliet* in a comic vein that was to be reversed. The 'what if?' question can prompt different courses of action to take place or to be suggested, which appear to take the play beyond an easy or harmonious encounter with comedy. This combination of tones allows the seriousness underlying the comedy to be foregrounded.

Don John and Don Pedro

At the heart of this play is a deceit by Don Pedro's bastard brother, Don John, which leads to another deception, the supposed death of Hero, and an invitation to revenge which, if accepted, will lead to a 'further death' – Claudio's by Benedick. This is demanded by Hero's cousin Beatrice, with whom Benedick has been engineered into thinking that he is in love. Don John's malign deceit has a parallel benign and intentionally benevolent one: Don Pedro's deceit of Benedick and Beatrice to get them to recognize their love for each other and to persuade them to marry. It could be argued that Don Pedro's deception is framed as legitimate while Don John's deceit, like himself, is illegitimate and that the play works through the mirror image of the one with the other, based on historically accepted Renaissance social cultural attitudes about legitimacy and illegitimacy.

CHALLENGING CONVENTION

Much Ado About Nothing unfolds as a critique of male conduct within a particular social structure that, though different from our own, still has modern resonance. In this, the play may be seen to challenge some aspects of its generic allegiance to the romance genre. Shakespeare moves away somewhat from his usual formula for romance, gently challenging some audience expectations while nevertheless maintaining dramatic integrity.

In the early seventeenth century, through the work particularly of the French man of letters Michel de Montaigne (1533–92), an understanding of male cultural attitudes in relation to sexual dominance was beginning to be gained and the dramatists of the period began to expose its various perspectives within their drama; see, for example, John Marston's *The Dutch Courtesan* (1603–4). The idea of a different sexual morality pertaining to men and women – men even in marriage being able to be promiscuous but women, in and before marriage, expected to remain chaste and faithful in accordance with patriarchal social convention – came under satiric scrutiny.

In his essay on sexual attitudes and conventions, 'Upon Some Verses of Virgil', Montaigne wrote, '... Women are not altogether in the wrong, when they refuse the rules of life prescribed to the World, forsomuch as only men have established them without their consent' (pp. 77–8), and he concluded with the statement: 'I say, that both male and female, are cast in one same moulde; instruction and custome excepted, there is no great difference between them' (p. 128). His essays, published variously in 1580 and in a complete edition in 1595, were not translated into English until 1603 by John Florio, after *Much Ado About Nothing* was published. Florio, however, was the tutor of the Earl of Southampton and someone possibly known to Shakespeare. Whether this is so or not, Shakespeare deals in the play with issues that were probably circulating during the late 1590s, prior to Florio's translation. (Quotations come from the Everyman edition, 1910, of the Florio translation of *Montaigne's Essays*, Vol. 3, 1965. Lechworth: J. M. Dent, Everyman's Library.)

Shakespeare, Marston, Jonson, Middleton and other Elizabethan and Jacobean dramatists were at the beginning of a long movement that brought about a gradual re-evaluation of sexual conduct and the exposure of patriarchal social conventions. It is too easy, from a twenty-first-century viewpoint, to become focused exclusively on a debate prompted by the evil of Don John because of our modern understanding of gender roles, expecting more from the play than it presents.

You might like to note further that Shakespeare is drawing on certain dramatic conventions in the play. The character Don John, for example, is to an extent a bridge between the stock Vice figure who leads mankind astray in the old medieval morality plays and the more rounded complex characters found in some of Shakespeare's later plays. In *Othello*, for example, Iago's possible 'motiveless malignity', as we will see later, is what is considered by some to destroy the tragic protagonist, Othello. In *Much Ado About Nothing*, Don John (1.3.25f.) declares that he would rather be a 'canker in a hedge than a rose' in his brother's 'grace' and continues by proclaiming that it cannot be said that he is a 'flattering honest man'. Iago in the later *Othello* is portrayed as the supposedly 'honest' man who wreaks havoc on all with whom he comes into contact. Don John continues, '… I have decreed not to sing in my cage. If I had my mouth I would bite; if I had my liberty I would do my liking: in the meantime, let me be that I am, and seek not to alter me' (1.3.25–34).

Don John's wish to 'be that I am' is taken a step further by Iago's single-minded, almost blasphemous statement, 'I am not what I am' (*Othello*, 1.1.64), while the image of singing in a cage is given great poignancy towards the tragic end of *King Lear*, where the captured Lear says to the defeated Cordelia, 'Come, let's away to prison;/We two alone will sing like birds i'the cage./When thou dost ask me blessing I'll kneel down/And ask of thee forgiveness' (5.3.8–11).

Although Don John in his discontentment is solely looking 'to build mischief' (1.3.42), he is not as developed a character as Iago; but the potential for development is present. His design against Claudio and Hero also exploits accepted social practice such as the aristocratic protocol whereby Claudio asks Don Pedro to woo Hero on his behalf. In the Elizabethan court, the monarch had a significant role to play in who married whom.

In the later Jacobean court, King James involved himself even in the marriage bedroom and sometimes the wedding bed. The danger of wooing by proxy is also something that Don John can exploit, so that Claudio can be made to believe that 'the Prince woos for himself./Friendship is constant in all other things/Save in the office and affairs of love' (2.1.153–5).

Key idea

Shakespeare in this play creates dramatic tension by building up the viability of realities based on perceptions that are underscored by contemporary patriarchal political structures. It is possible that someone like Don Pedro would deceive Claudio and that Claudio would have no recourse against it. The Elizabethan audience would have understood the significance of this possibly far more readily than we do.

DECEPTION AND CRUELTY

In contrast to the Don John narrative, Beatrice and Benedick are endowed with a competitive dislike for each other that has a history. In the play, their mutual dislike is so fierce that the audience is able to perceive that they are, deep down, in love with each other. They are attracted by their witty antagonism. Shakespeare builds this antagonism by having other characters play tricks on them in order to bring them together. The result is that the audience is presented with some hilariously comic scenes, in which protestations of love, one for the other, are falsely reported but that bring them actually into an admission of their love for each other, although initially they do not come to this realization simultaneously. This deception allows for comedy but it is balanced by a much more sinister deception in which one of the perpetrators, Hero, is herself unwittingly subjected to a cruel and potentially deadly falsehood.

Don John instigates the perception that Hero is unfaithful and unchaste even before marriage. A visual proof is given that she has been with another man the night before her wedding with Claudio. The audience knows that it was not Hero but Margaret, with Borachio, two 'attendants' on those of a higher social standing who are part of a charade, the full significance of which is unknown. Moral perplexities abound in the course of exposure of this deliberate distraction. But the focus is on the 'deceit' itself. What is perceived to be reality is not necessarily the case in human affairs. Your senses can be tricked and manipulated into making false judgements. This makes for a good drama and, in comedy, one that can end in narrative harmony.

Yet the conclusion is not all that there is to a play. Claudio's public humiliation of Hero, in the church and at the altar, is violently extreme, exposing both masculine cruelty and the threat it poses to the sacrament of marriage. Take this into other, later plays such as *Othello* and such cruelty will lead to Desdemona's death or, in *The Winter's Tale*, it will cause the death of the child prince Mamillius, leading to penance and years of heartache before forgiveness and reconciliation. As we will see in *Measure for Measure*, hypocritical deception challenges the very stability of the structure of comedy. In *Much Ado About Nothing*, however, the deception is revealed, allowing for an alternative reading of the shocked Hero's blushes.

'KILL CLAUDIO!'
The resolution of the problem is not forthcoming before a twist in the narrative takes place. This twist takes the emphasis away from the cruelty displayed at the altar by Claudio and Don Pedro. It also distracts the audience from that cruelty, allowing them to accept that forgiveness may be possible within the framework of the fiction. So what is it that Shakespeare introduces to allow the comedy to remain a comedy?

With the love of Benedick and Beatrice becoming a revelation to each other, Beatrice, out of loyalty to the wronged Hero, challenges Benedick to prove his love. She demands that he should 'Kill Claudio!' (4.1.287). The woman here says to the man, 'Kill your best friend for the love of me, because I am enraged at the treatment of my dearest cousin and friend. Not to do so means that you are not in love with me.' There is no deception here. Beatrice is characterized as being in earnest, and for the moment it threatens to take the play into another realm – that of revenge.

It is interesting to watch the 2010 Shakespeare's Globe Theatre production, widely available, because when Beatrice makes her demand, the audience laughs at Benedick's response but then quietens as she expands upon it and Benedick finally agrees to the challenge.

Spotlight

The play here takes an unexpected turn; the seriousness beneath the comedy has started to dominate and as an audience we are suddenly not sure of our bearings. Is this Eve asking Adam to eat the forbidden fruit, or Lady Macbeth goading Macbeth to kill King Duncan? The request is contrary to comic expectations. With Don John's deceit known to the audience, we are confident that it will be exposed eventually, but this scene threatens something different. Structurally, it relieves the concerns the audience might have about the injustice of Hero's condemnation, but this still leaves unresolved the behaviour of Claudio.

The truth of the deception rests with the linguistically eccentric 'Watch', Dogberry. Once Don John's evil deed is revealed, Beatrice's injunction for Benedick to kill his friend Claudio falls away, but Claudio must now learn 'trust' by accepting whoever Leonato prescribes for him to marry. The partner is, of course, Hero, who only died 'whilst her slander lived'. The escaped Don John is recaptured, cruelties are forgotten and attention can finally be turned to uniting Beatrice and Benedick, so that all can end happily. Beatrice's loquacity is silenced – usually in performance by a kiss from Benedick, but in the 1600 quarto by the injunction from Leonato: 'Peace, I will stop your mouth.' For all her female feistiness, Beatrice must agree to be the quiet wife, the silent woman of Elizabethan patriarchal fantasy.

This is confident, professional, masterly writing by Shakespeare who here is moving away from his own earlier formula of comedy and demonstrating the courage of measured experimentation in making a play work. He manipulates the audience's reaction and emotion as its perceptions, as well as those of the characters, are challenged through the narrative process.

The Taming of the Shrew

In a post-feminist world, *The Taming of the Shrew* might be seen as a problematic play in the way that Kate, the so-called 'shrew', is treated by society, and by Petruchio in particular. But some feminists have seen the play as more of an exposure of a variety of issues and thereby a play of commitment, cleverly developed by Shakespeare.

> 'The Taming of the Shrew *concludes with a harmonious synthesis of unabused masculine and inlaw feminine principles, but it celebrates the outlaw aspect, defiance and rebellion.*'
>
> French, M. (1992: 85), *Shakespeare's Division of Experience.*
> London: Abacus

THE SHREW AND *A* SHREW

Ideas do not just come from a single mind – even Montaigne's or Shakespeare's – but emerge from everything that is circulating within society itself. Plays can feed off one another. It is possible that *The Taming of the Shrew* may have grown out of an earlier play, *The Taming of a Shrew.* This requires some consideration, especially as the anonymous *A Shrew* provides a framing device that is only partially used in Shakespeare's play. *A Shrew*'s structure is dependent upon Christopher Sly's dream that he awakes from at the end of the play and confesses that he has had 'The bravest dream tonight, that ever thou / Hardest in all thy life ...'

Shakespeare may or may not have been involved in some way in the creation of *The Taming of a Shrew.* Scholars debate that at length. But the fact remains that in his *The Taming of the Shrew*, although the opening frame portrays Sly in a drunken stupor transformed into a 'Lord' and, subsequently watching a play being presented, the drama ends without Shakespeare closing the frame; Sly seems to be forgotten. Some modern directors resort to *The Taming of a Shrew*'s ending in order to round off Shakespeare's play in production, while other directors are content with the ending of the play as it was published in the 1623 Folio, without a closing frame.

THE INITIAL 'PROBLEM'

The following discussion focuses on the Shakespearean version. Underlying the play is the traditional structure of romantic comedy: a problem, a geographical relocation, a discovery, a celebration. The nature of the initial problem, however, is what may attract your interest. Bianca, 'all white' as her name perhaps ironically implies, in the end is the cause of her husband Lucentio losing a wager made between him and Kate's husband Petruchio concerning which of their wives is more 'obedient'. Petruchio's departing comment to Lucentio rubs in the loser's failure: "Twas I won the wager, though you hit the white,/ And being a winner, God give you good night!' (5.2.187–8). The idea of this wager brings us back to the problem at the beginning of the play where we find that, until a husband can be found for Baptista Minola's shrewish elder daughter, Katherina, known as Kate, the father will not allow his younger daughter, Bianca, who guards carefully her own shrewishness, to marry.

To solve the problem, it appears that a larger force than Baptista – or any eligible man in Padua – has to be found: a husband who can 'tame' Kate. The apparently eccentric Petruchio from Verona is that force. His successful courtship of Kate, however idiosyncratic or cruel, solves the Paduan's problem. But what is the cost? At the end of the play, Kate and Petruchio are the ones who triumph; Bianca, Baptista's favourite, and Lucentio are the ones humiliated. Kate may have been tamed but in being so grows stronger in her marriage than the Paduans thought possible. They wager on it and lose but the question arises over the manner in which this is done. Petruchio, in his eccentricity and his studied poverty, exercises cruelty over Kate by acting as a mirror image of her own shrewishness. He does this in an attempt to force her to channel her frustrations and to accept her role in the patriarchal society against whose values she rebels. He demands that she behaves in accordance with the requirements of a reality that he creates and that he then invites her to share. She does so because it is the only way in this male-dominated society that she can survive.

In putting it this way, I wonder if you might see within it a general ethical problem in which people, or indeed nations, deal with each other. Bringing a larger force than yourself to help solve a problem can leave you without control over the process and, indeed, the consequences of your decisions.

Some critics, rather than considering social, even political, issues, have tended to debate whether Kate is subdued at the end of the play. Has she succumbed to Petruchio's brainwashing or has she found a more subtle way to undermine his authority? The absence of the ending present in the anonymous play suggests that what happens is more than a wishful male fantasy: that tension between husband and wife will always be an issue, and each is charged with the task of working out the relationship to their own advantage. Shakespeare, wisely perhaps, does not come to a firm conclusion on this matter.

MOON, OR SUN, OR WHAT YOU PLEASE

A key scene is Act 4, Scene 5, when Petruchio decides to call the sun the moon. He is imposing an alternative name on the sun and thereby forcing upon Kate, through language, an alternative universe. Once Kate has accepted that in Petruchio's use of language the sun can be called the moon and the moon the sun, and that if she doesn't accede she will be penalized, then she is seen, superficially at least, to accept the alternative world that Petruchio forces upon her. This is an alternative 'reality' that is more extreme even than the one from which she has come. They meet someone on the road as they return to Padua, which allows the question of the perception of reality to be foregrounded. Is the person they meet a beautiful young woman or an old man? How do you differentiate between the different elements of reality, and how do you represent reality?

Spotlight

In this scene Shakespeare is asking about the relationship between words and actuality. Are words the instruments of will, and is dominant will determined in the end by those with most power, by a tyrannical individual, or more subtly? And is that power something that can be imposed upon one human being by another, violently, or does power work through persuasion and agreement between members of a society? In a complex social organization, how can an individual survive or even overcome the obstacles placed in their way? If the play asks such questions, we may have to look beyond the plot of the play itself to what it signifies, almost in the manner of a humanist parable.

In her own interest and for her own preservation, Kate is forced to acquiesce, accepting the new reality of Petruchio's alternative world. She has, in other words, been 'tamed', or at least gives him the impression that she has:

> Forward, I pray, since we have come so far,
>
> And be it moon, or sun, or what you please.
>
> And if you please to call it a rush-candle,
>
> Henceforth I vow it shall be so for me.

(4.5.12–15)

Her answer can be read ambivalently: call it what you want, even a 'rush-candle' if you like: whatever, it doesn't matter what I say as long as I get what I want. This is one possible interpretation. The question remains about the extent to which she has acquiesced in the process and found a way to neutralize the force of Petruchio's power.

Key idea

At the opening of the story, Petruchio and Kate had both been portrayed as rebels in their different attitudes to the prevailing social order, Kate behaving in an uncooperative manner ('shrewishly') and Petruchio willing to violate social decorum. But by the end they appear to be in harmony with each other, to such an extent that they triumph, exposing the hollowness of their fellow characters' relationships. In fact, at the end of the play, it is Bianca and the newly married Widow who display, from within the institution of marriage, the characteristics of shrewishness about which, at the beginning, the dominant order had disapproved.

UNCERTAINTY IN THE DETERMINING OF SOCIAL VALUES

In this early play, Shakespeare is posing, through its structure and narrative, questions concerning the constructions of reality that depend on who gains power. As we will see, this is to become a significant area of exploration in Shakespeare's early history plays, which he was writing possibly at around the same time. The question here isn't so much 'What if?' as 'How does?'

in the sense of how does power operate, construct, develop or destroy particular conceptions of reality.

In this play Shakespeare explores the question by deploying a 'Punch and Judy' type of humour, and some productions (for example Jonathan Miller's for the Royal Shakespeare Company in 1987) have set it as a *commedia dell'arte* entertainment – *commedia dell'arte* being an Italian Renaissance form of stereotypical comic drama from which the Punch and Judy routine developed.

In the history plays, as we will see, Shakespeare later uses the comic character Falstaff, and his tavern companions, to expose the issue of the uncertainty in the determination of social values. The action of those plays similarly displays the uncertainty of moral values, which are challenged and/or constructed both by those in power or those seeking power.

The Taming of the Shrew *cannot in the twenty-first century be looked on as a domestic, marital comedy, with an erring wife rightly and meekly subjecting herself to the will of her husband, wrapped up in comedy and fun as in the Burton and Taylor film. It has to be viewed as the ruthless subduing of a woman by a man in a violent excess of male savagery, couched in the form of a class wish-fulfilment dream of revenge.'*

Bogdanov, M. (2013: 173), *Shakespeare: The Director's Cut.* Edinburgh: Capercaillie Books

You may, of course, agree with Michael Bogdanov, who directed *The Taming of the Shrew* for the RSC in 1978, and decide that *The Taming of the Shrew* asks the 'How does?' question in a way that is socially unacceptable today, but there may be a danger that in doing so the critical focus is narrowed. But is that a good or a bad thing? Shakespeare doesn't answer the questions he raises in *Much Ado About Nothing* or in *The Taming of the Shrew*. Both these plays are sufficiently open-ended to suggest that his conclusions are provisional and leave answers for us to consider and debate.

11

The Merchant of Venice (1596–8)

Since the Jewish Holocaust of the Second World War, *The Merchant of Venice* has provoked much debate about how it can be read or performed without causing unease. This is because it contains what some regard as overt anti-Semitism. The question many critics ask is whether in this play Shakespeare is confronting or pandering to the anti-Semitic prejudices of his audience or readers, both historical and contemporary.

While this complex play is often considered controversial because of its treatment of the Jew, Christians do not entirely escape without blame. The play has three interwoven themes, each of which depends on the structure for comedy that Shakespeare had developed.

Confronting or pandering to anti-Semitic prejudices?

Much has been written on the historical existence of Jews in Elizabethan London and reference is frequently made to the execution in 1594 of Dr Roderigo Lopez, Elizabeth I's Portuguese physician, who was thought to have been a Jew, and who was accused of trying to murder her. Lopez's trial and execution stoked a degree of anti-Semitism. Julia Briggs points to the fact that Jews in London, like Roman Catholics, could not profess their faith openly and notes that many of them were European 'converts', or *converses,* who had come from Spain.

> 'There may have been as many as 200 Jewish converts in England, working as doctors and in other professional or advisory capacities. Socially and physically they were virtually invisible, and this, along with their (usually) Spanish origins further contributed to the anxiety their presence aroused.'
>
> Briggs, J. (1977: 100), *This Stage-play World: Texts and Contexts, 1580–1625.* Oxford: Oxford University Press

To be a Jew from Catholic Spain, the bitter enemy of Protestant England, was probably not something many desired to publicize, but it raised the possibility of dramatic conflict that was ripe for theatre. The Jew in Shakespeare's play, set in Catholic Venice rather than Spain, dislikes the Christians as much as the Christians demonstrate that they dislike the Jews. This is how Shylock refers to Antonio:

> How like a fawning publican he looks!
>
> I hate him for he is a Christian:
>
> But more, for that in low simplicity
>
> He lends out money gratis, and brings down
>
> The rate of usance here with us in Venice.

(1.3.39–43)

He accuses Antonio of spitting on 'my Jewish gaberdine' and calling him 'misbeliever, cut-throat dog', to which the Christian churlishly replies:

I am as like to call thee so again,

To spit on thee again, to spurn thee too.

If thou wilt lend this money, lend it not

As to thy friends, ...

But lend it rather to thine enemy.

(1.3.128f.)

And this is exactly what Shylock does, encouraging his 'enemy' Antonio into an agreement which, when taken seriously and enacted, will endanger the merchant's life. The equity demanded is a pound of Antonio's flesh, should he default on a loan he takes out to fund his friend Bassanio's quest to gain 'In Belmont' Portia, '... a lady richly left,/...fair, and (fairer than that word),/ Of wondrous virtues' (1.1.161–3). Antonio defaults on the loan and the matter goes to trial where, disguised as a lawyer, Portia – now won by Bassanio – pleads Antonio's case. In the famous trial scene (Act 4, Scene 1), the Jew's demand for justice is counterbalanced by Portia's often-quoted Christian appeal for mercy, beginning:

The quality of mercy is not strain'd,

It droppeth as the gentle rain from heaven

Upon the place beneath:

(4.1.182f.)

Shylock's reply is one of cruel rejection, 'My deeds upon my head! I crave the law,' (4.1.204), a statement that is a faint echo of the curse that, according to St Matthew's Gospel, the Jews called down upon themselves and their children in demanding Christ's blood: 'His blood be on us and on our children!' (Matthew 27.25). Portia allows him his bond according to justice but warns that there is no mention of the spilling of blood in the deed. So Shylock may cut out exactly a pound of flesh, no more, no less, but in doing so he must not shed a drop of blood. The Jew is defeated but then finds himself frustrated by the law as the Christians taunt him, exposing the limits of their mercy. He is forced to bequeath part of his wealth to his daughter, who has rejected him and eloped with a Christian, and the remainder is confiscated by the State. Further, he is forced to convert to Christianity, just as historically some

Spanish Jews in Elizabethan London may have been forced to do, although firm evidence of this is scarce. Shylock leaves the court a broken man.

Spotlight

But why, an actor of the part might ask, does Shylock behave as he does, bringing about his own downfall? In the concluding lines of Act 3, Scene 1, Shylock tells Tubal that, by exercising his revenge on Antonio, he will profit. 'I will have the heart of him if he forfeit, for were he out of Venice I can make what merchandise I will:' (3.1.118–20). He has a further motive than revenge: he can make money out of Antonio's death because he will have eliminated someone who opposes him on the Rialto, frustrating his business dealings. He is shown to be premeditating a murder. Bassanio (1.3.178) suspected the bond, 'I like not fair terms, and a villain's mind', a view dismissed by Antonio, '… there can be no dismay,/My ships come home a month before the day' (179–80). For any seafarers in Shakespeare's audience, such an assurance would have been seen as tenuous to say the least.

Shakespeare in that scene provides options for playing Antonio, which, of course, he might have discussed with the very first actor playing the role. Does Antonio really believe, after all that has reportedly passed between Shylock and himself, that Shylock is a 'gentle Jew./… he grows kind'? (1.3.176–7). Is he really confident that this is 'a merry sport' (144), as Shylock depicts it? What an actor has to decide is Antonio's motivation. Does it go back to the opening line of the play where he says 'In sooth I know not why I am so sad'? Shakespeare makes none of this absolutely clear. His actors, through the ages, have to make their decisions on how to play the role, helped in modern productions by their directors.

Flesh and blood

So it is still for the modern actor playing Shylock to decide on the interpretation to be created in performance. Shakespeare shows Shylock to be a villain but also to be a father deeply hurt by his daughter Jessica's elopement and her theft of some of his money and valued possessions, including a ring given to him by his wife Leah before they married: 'I had it of Leah when I was a bachelor:' (3.1.113–14). In Act 3, Scene 1, Shylock refers to his daughter in his description of what has happened as 'My own flesh and blood to rebel!' and is taunted by the Christian Salerio, to whom he insists, 'I say my daughter is my flesh and blood' (3.1.31,34). Here, Shakespeare is clearly providing the actor with the opportunity to characterize Shylock's humanity as well as to expose the elements of 'flesh' and 'blood' which will be the Jew's undoing.

Shylock continues with the great speech in which he defends his decision to take revenge, by making Antonio 'look to his bond!' (3.1.45). In some interpretations this can be delivered as an affirmation of his humanity. In others it can be expressed as his vicious determination to be revenged. The actor has to decide where and how on that spectrum he delivers this famous speech in the context of the overall interpretation of the play:

> ... I am a Jew. Hath not a Jew eyes? hath not a Jew hands, organs, dimensions, senses, affections, passions? ... – if you prick us, do we not bleed? if you tickle us do we not laugh? if you poison us do we not die? and if you wrong us shall we not revenge?

> (3.1.54f.)

Try speaking the whole passage yourself in different ways, to bring out various interpretations.

This passage, however, raises a number of other issues. The pricking of the thumb without bloodshed was an Elizabethan proof of witchcraft, so this Jew claims to be without that taint. The opening line of the extract might remind a Christian audience of the difference between the Old Testament 'an eye for an eye' mode of justice and the Christian teaching of love and mercy. But Shylock also plans to imitate the Christians in their demand for revenge. The very thought of 'bleeding' presages the eventual predicament of the Jew in that his bond will demand the bleeding of Antonio, who is thereby placed in a position similar to Christ before the Crucifixion. If you prick or pierce human flesh, then blood will flow. So what will happen when you cut a pound of flesh from near a man's heart? Dr Lopez, of course, had been hung and then bled at his execution and those present would have seen that he was no different from any English Christian executed at Tyburn.

Shylock's 'blood' makes him a 'stranger' within the Venetian community; the carnal blood of youth is constrained by Portia's dead father's 'will', but it also prompts Shylock's daughter's elopement with the Christian Lorenzo, and is a betrayal of her Jewish blood. This in turn, as Drakakis argues, allows the word 'flesh' to open a series of conflicting meanings that reveal a struggle between a socially approved method of generation and a hellish aberration that biologically and fiscally perverts an accepted natural order. Salerio comments to Shylock:

> There is more difference between thy flesh and hers, than
> between jet and ivory, more between your bloods, than
> there is between red wine and Rhenish:
>
> (3.1.35–8)

Spotlight

Such flesh-and-blood images expose many of the preconceptions of the play and prefigure the trial scene in which Christian and Jew face each other as representatives of opposing cultures. Flesh-and-blood imagery and Christian tradition and argument coalesce as the Antonio / Shylock narrative develops through the play.

In Roman Catholic teaching, at the moment of consecration in the communion service, or Mass, the bread and wine are believed to be transformed into Christ's body and blood through a mystical process termed 'transubstantiation'. It was not necessary, however, for the congregation to receive both the bread (body) and the wine (blood) since it was argued that to receive the bread alone necessarily meant that the blood was also being received – since with flesh there would always be blood. The Protestant Reformation questioned the whole notion of transubstantiation but Shakespeare's setting of the play is Catholic Venice. Shakespeare's 'Catholic' Portia from Belmont may in her defence of Antonio be drawing on Catholic doctrine as well as medical fact to triumph over the Jew.

The Christian context

This Christian religious context, however, can be seen to go further in secularizing another theological point. In *The Stripping of the Altars* (2005: 94), Eamon Duffy reminds us that the sacrament of Holy Communion was 'an image of forgiveness and grace, not of judgement'. He points out that the Catholic faithful took communion only at Easter, when it was called 'taking one's right', a revealing phrase, indicating that to take communion was to claim one's place in the adult community.

It can be argued that Shylock's insistence on his taking his 'bond' or 'taking his own right' in law may have fed off past cultural/religious contexts in a negative way. In this instance it is not a communicant who is 'taking his own right', claiming his place through forgiveness and grace within the community. Rather a character is being drawn who is hostile to Christian Venice – and therefore Catholic society. He wishes to take the flesh and therefore the blood of a member of the community to 'bait fish withal', and 'feed my revenge' (3.1.49–50). The fish is one of the earliest symbols of Christianity and of Christ himself. Shylock is not only the outsider in a Christian/Catholic community, foregrounding 'judgement' over 'forgiveness and grace' by a crude parody of the Mass, but also a Jew deliberately trying to destroy the merchant Antonio because he is a Christian.

Antonio, as the play emphasizes from the opening scene (1.1.138f.) to the last scene (5.1.249–53), is prepared to sacrifice all he has, even his life, for the love of his friend. In Christianity, no man has greater love than he who lays down his life for his friend in imitation of Christ, who laid down his life in his love for all humanity. So Shylock is frustrated in his 'baiting of fish' by the courtroom's secularized expression of Christian theology as well as the physical reality that, if you cut the flesh, the body will bleed.

Shakespeare's conclusion of this critically controversial trial scene, however, goes further in not fully condoning the Christian triumph. Holy Communion is not an image of judgement but of forgiveness and grace. At the end of this scene the Christians are exposed in the cruelty of their judgement and triumph, since they demand of Shylock his very identity. He is forced to lose not only his possessions but also the creed by which he lives and his identity as a Jew.

Spotlight

Attending the 2015 production of the play at the Royal Shakespeare Theatre, I was sitting close to some members of the Jewish community, who apparently did not know the play. At the point where the Christians demanded in their revenge that Shylock must become a Christian, one of the Jews near me indignantly commented, 'That's not fair.' Nor, perhaps, did Shakespeare think so since in the final humiliation of Shylock he exposes the Venetians not only as bad Christians but bad Venetians, since Venice was known to consider itself to be a welcoming, hospitable place. Shakespeare's Christians show, through the reports of their taunting and in the execution of their 'justice', that their hospitality, like the Christian virtues of grace, forgiveness and mercy, did not extend to Jews.

The mercantile currency

The story concerning Shylock demands attention in performance and criticism but the character appears only five times (1.3, 2.5, 3.1, 3.3, 4.1) in the whole play, and not at all in the final act. As with other comedies, the title of the play should not go unnoticed, since it foregrounds the 'merchant' Antonio. Consequently, a significant aspect of the play is to do with the mercantile currency of trade: commodities and money.

Bassanio's description of Portia, as we have seen, points not only to her beauty and virtue but also first to her wealth.

According to her father's 'will', suitors have to choose one of three caskets: gold, silver and lead. On opening it, he will find whether he can claim Portia in marriage. The Prince of Morocco, another 'outsider' supposedly welcomed by an Italianate Christian society, soon learns that 'All that glisters is not gold' (2.7.65). Frustrated in choosing the wrong casket, the Moroccan prince departs, leaving Portia to remark, 'Let all of his complexion choose me so' (2.7.79). Similarly, another suitor, the Spanish Prince of Arragon, is ripe for dismissal for an Elizabethan society whose country had recently defeated the Spanish Armada, and whose Queen, the daughter of Anne Boleyn, not Catherine of Aragon, had rejected an earlier proposal of marriage from the Spanish King. He chooses silver. Bassanio has the good sense to choose dull lead, thereby winning Portia's hand.

At the heart of the casket scene is the question of the appearance of wealth as opposed to the dignity of the human being. Portia has been placed at the centre of a dangerous wager that will determine her future. Those who take on the wager and fail will suffer, but what would have happened to Portia if they had triumphed? In the later play *Othello*, part of this question is answered in the elopement of Desdemona with the Moor Othello.

Money, love and betrayal

Money, money, money imbues the three plots of the play: the first relating to Antonio and Bassanio; the second to Portia; the third to Jessica. In each, love is set alongside currency. Antonio and Portia on their first appearances are portrayed as 'weary'. We are uncertain about the initial cause of Antonio's weariness, though some critics and some performances have suggested that it is because of his 'love' for Bassanio, which, converted into a monetary gift, will result in Bassanio leaving him for another. Portia has enough money to be able to help Bassanio's friend but all the money in the world is not as important as the ring, the symbol of her intended marriage that she gives to her new husband as a sign of their faithful love for each other. Under her disguise as the lawyer she tricks him into parting with this ring.

Jessica steals her father's wealth to secure her love Lorenzo, but does he love her? In the intensely poetic opening scene of Act 5, Jessica and Lorenzo recall a number of famous lovers. But they were all victims of tragedy: Troilus and Cressida, Thisbe and Pyramus, Dido and Aeneas, and finally Medea who, though she helped her lover Jason's father Aeson, betrayed her own father in her elopement exactly as Jessica has done in betraying her father. There is an undercurrent of some poignancy, in that these are references to the fragility of love and relationships as a consequence of error or betrayal.

Deception and structure

Set alongside these three plots is a comic subplot involving the clown – variously named Launcelot Gobbo in the 1998–2011 *Shakespeare Complete Works*, Arden Edition, or Lancelet Giobbe in the latest single Arden Edition, Arden 3 (2010–13) – leaving his master Shylock's service for that of Bassanio. In Act 2, Scene 2, the clown inadvertently deceives his blind father (Gobbo/Giobbe), leading him to believe his son 'is indeed deceased, or as you would say in plain terms, gone to heaven' (2.2.61–2).

Deception in other plays – from *Romeo and Juliet* and *Much Ado About Nothing* to *The Winter's Tale* – is used by Shakespeare in a much more significant way but here is applied as a comic interlude, testing and commenting on the emotional aspect of relationships. The interlude gives an insight into what life is like in the Jew's house and about the relationship of a father and son, as the father tries to help improve his son's lot and, no doubt, thereby his own. It is a father–son relationship in a play that concerns a number of close relationships: Antonio and Bassanio; Portia and, through the will, her father; Bassanio and Portia; Shylock (as husband) and Leah; Shylock (as father) and Jessica; Jessica and Lorenzo; Nerissa and Gratiano.

Key idea

The structure underpinning each of the three plots includes an initial problem, a journey, disguise, identity and self-knowledge, all interconnected and coming together in Act 4 with the exposure of Shylock and the Christian community. But this is not the end of the play, since not all of the issues have been resolved. Portia, having saved Antonio, has won back her ring from Bassanio. In Act 5 there is a further process of 'learning' about oneself, about society, about love and identity, which encompasses the recognition of Portia as the lawyer and Nerissa as the clerk. The ring is the symbol of that which shouldn't be given away, the truth of a married relationship.

The Merchant of Venice uses the three interwoven plots and the comic episodes, thereby, to produce a drama that exposes issues of race and religion, of conduct and belief, of trust and oaths, mercy and justice, love, identity, lack of grace and faithfulness, of sacrifice, pain and compensation, of promise and fidelity. It is not a play to be reduced to stark judgements but it does expose the plight of the outsider. Maybe it is a play that tries to do too much, leaving certain issues to perplex the actor, audience or reader. But however complex and however controversial it proves to be, *The Merchant of Venice* is one of Shakespeare's greatest plays, moving and manipulating his comic formula to great dramatic effect.

It is with *The Merchant of Venice* and its complex use of Shakespeare's comic structure that, for the moment, we will leave our discussion of comedy and look at a parallel concern that from the 1590s Shakespeare developed in his dramatic writing: the English history plays, all of which raise a number of critical perspectives for a modern reader or audience.

Critical perspectives 3: Reading history, writing history and the English history plays

We read or watch Shakespeare through our twenty-first century eyes. Shakespeare read history through his Tudor and, later, Stuart eyes and presented what he read as significant drama, creating popular plays from a range of historical sources. When we consider Shakespeare's history plays, we are looking at successful plays designed to entertain audiences (and readers).

We know that Shakespeare used the historical sources available to him at the time, and each generation since then has come to appreciate the history plays almost as a means of providing an historical education about the turmoil and internecine strife of medieval and Early Modern England. However, we might like to consider the plays he created not as 'histories' but as plays for his time and for future times, both in interpretation and performance.

The Elizabethan fashion for history plays

The fashion for history plays had been stimulated in the 1580s by the Elizabethan government, and with the Queen's Men in particular, who put on plays that reinforced the Protestant ethic at a time of increasing fear over Spanish invasion and Catholic 'treachery'. The Government saw an opportunity to press home its championing of the reformed English Church and its Supreme Governor, the Queen. Such propagandist plays, however, were initially somewhat tedious in comparison with what was to come. It is speculated, for example by Katherine Duncan-Jones – but there is no firm evidence – that Shakespeare, as a young man wishing to enter the theatre, may, in the 1580s, have been a member of the Queen's Men. If so, this could have inspired him to write plays on historical themes, in the 1590s, in which he amended and reduced the scale of the political polemic. Instead of it, he chose to explore character, theme and plot to produce an epic theatrical sequence of entertainments that spanned the last decade of the sixteenth century.

Shakespeare sticks fairly close to his sources. From Thomas More's account of Richard III, for example, he would have found and accepted, perhaps, a Tudor, dynastic reading of history which depicts Richard as the murderer of the innocent princes in the Tower. He seems to have exploited the image of the crookbacked man whose physical appearance was popularly seen to be reflecting an evil Machiavellian mind. Modern historical research has questioned whether this reading of history was correct. The discovery in September 2012 of Richard's bones, buried beneath a Leicester City car park in the remains of an old abbey, testify to Richard being deformed but also to the brutal manner of his death. Other historical research points towards a short reign that might not have justified the hostility against him. Also, historians continue to argue about whether the historical Richard was the instigator of the deaths of the young princes.

Key idea

History is a complex matter. Periodically, plays or films on historical subjects are roundly criticized as travesties of the truth. This occurred, for example, with the 2011 film on the authorship of Shakespeare's plays, *Anonymous*, and the 1984 film about Mozart, *Amadeus*.

In some cases, Shakespeare deliberately changed history or, perhaps, chose and manipulated his sources for specific dramatic effect. In terms of particular detail, he would have known from some of his sources, for example, that in *1 Henry IV* Harry Hotspur, son of Northumberland, was not the same age as Prince Hal but significantly older. Shakespeare, however, follows Samuel Daniel (1562–1619) in his *Civil Wars*, who makes them contemporaries.

King Henry's wish that Hal (young Harry) and Hotspur had been exchanged in their cradles is an anathema, even if you did believe in fairies!

> Of my young Harry. O that it could be prov'd
>
> That some night-tripping fairy had exchang'd
>
> In cradle-clothes our children where they lay,
>
> And call'd mine Percy, his Plantagenet!
>
> Then would I have his Harry, and he mine:

> (1 Henry IV, 1.1.85–9)

Kenneth Muir, referring to Daniel's *Civil Wars*, records that:

> *'Hal saves the King's life and fights with Hotspur in single combat, two points in which Daniel and Shakespeare improve on the chroniclers, although the dramatist might well have decided, without Daniel's example, to end the rivalry between Hal and Hotspur foreshadowed in* Richard II, *with such combat. The historical Hotspur was 39 at the time of his death; Daniel and Shakespeare make him the same age as the prince.'*
>
> Muir, K. (1977: 93–4), *The Sources of Shakespeare's Plays*. London: Methuen

But, theatrically, to make them of similar age produces entertaining rivalry and an important thematic conflict to which an audience can respond.

King John (1595–7) was not for much of the twentieth century generally regarded as one of Shakespeare's most entertaining plays, although in earlier times it proved popular. It is based on an earlier Protestant polemical play, *The Troublesome Raigne of King John* (published 1591). Shakespeare still creates very much a Protestant-influenced play but he reduces the polemic in order to produce a more complex drama than its source would suggest, which, as the Shakespeare Globe Theatre production in 2015, for example, demonstrated, can engage, amuse and enthral a twenty-first-century audience.

While the King in *Henry V* can be seen as a heroic character, there are, as we will see, elements of that popular portrayal that are challenged by the dramatist. In *1* and *2 Henry IV*, Falstaff is modelled on the historical figure Sir John Oldcastle but his name had to be changed to address the concerns of the Oldcastle family's claim that the character had been unjustly defamed. Sir John Oldcastle, who had been a friend of Henry V, was hanged in 1417, having led a revolt against the King.

Shakespeare's creation of Falstaff gives an alternative perspective on the world, in which he uses him to satirize established political conventions and yet maintain a relationship with them. His portrayal of an Elizabethan underworld was so well received that the character of Falstaff was later recreated in a comic play, *The Merry Wives of Windsor*, in which the satire emanates from and encompasses the Saturnalian figure. In resurrecting him for *The Merry Wives*, Shakespeare was writing possibly to the Queen's demand and certainly to the market's.

History or tragedy?

What is the difference between a history play and a tragedy? Why is *Macbeth* a tragedy when clearly it is based on historical figures? Why does the frontispiece to the Second Quarto of *Hamlet* refer to the play as 'tragical history'? What of *Julius Caesar*, *Antony and Cleopatra* and *Coriolanus* (which for the purpose of this book I've grouped as Roman plays, placing my consideration of *Titus Andronicus* elsewhere)? The generalized boxes in which Shakespeare's plays are placed are somewhat arbitrary. Is, for example, *Cymbeline* a tragedy, as claimed in the plays in the First Folio edition of 1623, or actually an experiment by the dramatist in tragicomic form? Is the term 'tragicomedy' a helpful one or merely the creation of another pigeonhole? Let us start by asking: what do we make of the English history plays as histories?

Kiernan Ryan, in tackling Shakespeare and history, asks:

'What is the relationship between the reality of history and its creative representation, between the world of the past and the work's account of it? What is the political role of the work in its own world: to shore up or shake the foundations of power? Can the literature of the past speak only of the past, or has it secrets to reveal to the present and appointments to keep with the future?'

Ryan, K. (2002: 38), *Shakespeare.* Basingstoke: Palgrave Macmillan

Critical questioning

In questioning notions of history as drama and drama within the history of its inception, we come to certain fundamental issues about how we read or understand Shakespeare. Until the later decades of the twentieth century, Shakespeare's English history plays were seen by mid-twentieth-century critics as two tetralogies, based on what E. M. W. Tillyard termed 'the Elizabethan world picture' in his book of that title (1943) and discussed in his book *Shakespeare's History Plays* (1944). In this interpretation, the plays, taken together as part of one continuous narrative, represented the stability of an Elizabethan philosophy that allowed Shakespeare to work towards the presentation of a perfect King, Henry V, followed by the disruption of civil war that followed his death.

The tetralogies, however, were in this respect written in the wrong order as Shakespeare wrote the *Henry VI* plays before *Richard II* and the three remaining plays within the second tetralogy, starting with *1 Henry IV*. Further, he probably wrote *2 Henry VI* and *3 Henry*

VI before *1 Henry VI* with the title of *3 Henry VI* originally being *The True Tragedy of Richard Duke of York* and the original title of *2 Henry VI* being *The First Part of the Contention betwixt the two Famous Houses of York and Lancaster*. With all three, it is probable that there were varying degrees of limited collaborative authorship. Consequently, any idea that he set out to write a theatrical dissertation on monarchy does not neatly square with the facts as we have them. It is more likely that Shakespeare realized the demands and market opportunities that these plays offered, and he responded to popular demand to keep the momentum going by writing in this genre through the 1590s. He wrote these plays in parallel with other plays, such as the Seneca-influenced tragedy *Titus Andronicus*, the experimental tragedy *Romeo and Juliet* and the Roman historical tragedy *Julius Caesar*, as well as a number of comedies.

The Tillyardian view, however, was understandable in the context of the mid-twentieth century when, for a time, Britain had stood alone against the might of Nazism. The plays can be read in such a way as to display a historic viewpoint that emphasized a prevailing ideology that Tillyard identified as being part of an English tradition and that influenced his own critical viewpoint. He transported into his own ethos a series of his ideological meanings whose efficacy, he claimed, might provide some comfort in the face of external attack. By the 1980s young left-wing intellectuals found Tillyard's approach inadequate because it was inaccurate in that it represented only a part of a larger, much more complex historical narrative, and that it was itself ideologically distorted.

'Tillyard's world picture, to the extent that it did exist (in Shakespeare's day), was not shared by all; it was an ideological legitimation of an existing social order, one rendered more necessary by the apparent instability, actual and imagined, of that order.'

Dollimore, J. and Sinfield, A. (eds) (1985, 1996, 2nd edn: 5), *Political Shakespeare: Essays in Cultural Materialism*. Manchester: Manchester University Press

Within literary studies, new historicism, led by the American scholar Stephen Greenblatt, developed one of a number of correctives to the Tillyardian approach. Greenblatt (1985), in an influential essay entitled 'Invisible Bullets: Renaissance Authority and Its Subversion, *Henry IV* and *Henry V* Plays', sought to construct an historical context that 'swerved' from the text by drawing attention to historical material outside the text that exerted an influence on the text itself. This essay, published under the shorter title 'Invisible Bullets' in his book *Shakespearean Negotiations* (1988), was included in a seminal collection of cultural materialist and new historicist essays brought together by Alan Sinfield and Jonathan Dollimore in 1985 under the title *Political Shakespeare*. Like Dollimore's influential book *Radical Tragedy* (1989), this book openly declared a series of materialist renderings of the Shakespearean texts.

The critical question, then, was whether being open about your ideology, or using historical texts that were at best tangential to Shakespeare's work and at worst embarrassingly irrelevant, made radical critics more incisive or reliable than those who subscribed to a different ideology. In the arguments that followed, even Dollimore's term 'radical' came under attack:

'Evidence is bypassed. Or, to put it another way, conclusions are generated theoretically and not empirically. It is difficult to call such a procedure history ... to do history means to follow certain rules for generating conclusions from evidence – above all, it means following procedures that allow for the testing of theories and concepts. New historicism systematically evades such procedures.'

Burgess, G. (1996: 14), 'Shakespeare's Political Context', in Klein, H. and Wymer, R., *Shakespeare and History*. New York: Edwin Mellen Press

Sharp diffractions of light in Shakespearean studies

Other critics – including Graham Bradshaw (1993), Brian Vickers (1995) and Kiernan Ryan (2002) – pointed out what they considered the fallacies of the avowedly politically oriented cultural materialists and new historicists, with Rowland

Wymer, for example, claiming that their desire to 'return to history' deviated from 'the main currents of contemporary historical debate about the Tudor and Stuart periods' (Klein and Wymer [1996: 1]).

What had occurred was an apparent fracturing of Shakespearean studies between traditional liberal humanist approaches to literature and what John Drakakis termed 'Alternative Shakespeares', proposed initially in an influential collection of essays published in 1985 and subsequently reissued, and which inaugurated further volumes that have since appeared under that title.

On both sides of the critical divide, a richness of interpretation developed and continues today. There are in Shakespearean studies sharp diffractions of light, but they reflect the richness of debate about Shakespeare's texts and their history. Chapter 24 provides definitions for various critical and historical movements, which you may find useful.

At both conscious and unconscious levels, our own ideologies lead us to see Shakespeare's texts with the 'part'd eye', but in doing so we need empirically to recognize that the history plays are dramas, not objective historical accounts, and the society for which they were first written was very different from the one in which we now live. However much we may strive to recreate the Shakespearean text in Elizabethan/Jacobean performance or replicate the responses of their first audiences, we cannot succeed. We are not, and we cannot become, Elizabethans or Jacobeans, nor is enjoyment of Shakespeare confined to the 'English', even though he may have helped to cultivate an 'English identity' under Elizabeth. But even that claim, as James Shapiro has demonstrated (*1606: William Shakespeare and the Year of Lear*), changes in Shakespeare's plays to one of being 'British' in line with the political and cultural changes that took place following King James's desire for the union of Scotland, Ireland, Wales and England. Today, however, Shakespeare is recognized as a global author, attracting audiences across the world.

History and politics

The name of the father of the academic subject of history, a Greek, Herodotus (c.480–425 BCE), was one synonymous with enquiry into the events of the past. Whereas Greek historians saw a relationship between literature and factual history, the Roman historians were more politically inclined, influencing the later Italian Renaissance humanist historians such as Machiavelli and Guicciardini, who were read by the Elizabethan dramatists and who influenced their work.

In England, chroniclers such as Raphael Holinshed and Edward Hall, alongside Scottish political theorists such as George Buchanan, also provided material for Shakespeare, and throughout their work we can find critiques – sometimes implicit and sometimes explicit – of monarchical authority through Elizabethan/Jacobean eyes. This appears to have led to a political satire found, for example, in the plays by John Marston (1575?–1634), but present also in Shakespeare who some believe may have influenced Marston's writing.

Further, through the Reformation the theological principle of a divine purpose that contrasted with the disjointed political and social actualities of human history created a tension that, as we will see, is displayed in Shakespeare's history plays. The depiction of Bolingbroke, for example, in contrast to Richard II, may be indicative of the shift in political, social and religious perception during a Tudor dynasty when Protestants were brutally executed by Queen Mary or Roman Catholics by Queen Elizabeth. Both monarchs were uncertain of the stability of their authority, especially the way the Divine Purpose was interpreted. Henry VIII's break with Rome sent out ripples across the sixteenth and early seventeenth centuries that could overwhelm individuals, including even his own Chancellor Thomas More, beheaded because of his loyalty to Catholic Christian authority. This humanist was caught between loyalties to his King and to the Divine: 'I die the King's good servant, but God's first.'

Shakespeare's court of Richard II has to be considered primarily through the prism of Tudor history, but we bring our current perspectives to bear on Shakespeare's play, as is the case also with regard to Marlowe's much more controversial study of monarchy and its inadequacies in *Edward II* (*c.*1590). Both these kings are shown by their respective playwrights to be influenced by homosexuality. When Tillyard was writing his critiques of the English history plays, homosexuality was still a criminal offence in the United Kingdom. A sexual revolution has now taken place and, in a Western world freed from prejudice against same-sex love, we may perceive these plays or Shakespeare's sonnets in different ways from critics of earlier times, although we should note along the way that homosexuality was a criminal offence in Elizabeth I's reign, punishable by death.

Self-fashioning

New historicism attempts to understand Shakespearean literature through a variety of non-literary historical texts, such as birth and death records, graveyard inscriptions, financial affairs and accounts. But the one aspect of the historical prism that seems to be of the utmost importance is the public playhouses – the theatre for the people – in which the dramas were performed. Shakespeare's English history plays present a world in torment, turned inside out by internecine warfare over hundreds of years. For the Elizabethans and Jacobeans this was their immediate history. Shakespeare himself had been born only a few years after the death of Henry VIII, Bosworth field was not in the distant past, and only 33 years after Shakespeare's death Charles I would be executed. This was a period when authority and people had to 'fashion' themselves within an ever-changing society where so little appeared to be permanent. It is, perhaps, fortuitous that Shakespeare's texts have survived, and we can now evaluate them both speculatively from within his own time, but also from within our time.

> *'Self-fashioning is in effect the Renaissance version of ... control mechanisms, the cultural system of meanings that creates specific individuals by governing the passage from abstract potential to concrete historical embodiment. Literature functions within this system in three interlocking ways: as a manifestation of the concrete behavior of its particular author, as itself the expression of the codes by which behavior is shaped, and as a reflection upon those codes.'*
>
> Greenblatt, S. (1980: 3–4), *Renaissance Self-Fashioning: From More to Shakespeare.* Chicago: University of Chicago Press

Shakespeare lived in a critical period in which human nature itself was being questioned by Renaissance and reformation writers and artists. The whole nature of society, its actions, practices and traditions were in flux. Mutability and change were ironically a constant, a living oxymoron, through which what Greenblatt calls 'self-fashioning' became the norm. These history plays are part of that process, written to entertain Shakespeare's audiences with stories of great moments from the past, while at the same time demonstrating how 'self-fashioning' took place. Historical accuracy could take second place to entertainment value and the plays themselves were very successful over a number of years.

The English history plays 1: The *Henry VI* plays (1591–2); *Richard III* (1592–4); *King John* (1595–7)

The Wars of the Roses were not so distant a period of English history for Shakespeare as for us. Though they ended in 1485 with the death of Richard III on the battlefield of Bosworth, they had shaped much of the consciousness of Tudor England. Henry VII, the victor of Bosworth who died in 1509, was the grandfather of the reigning queen, Elizabeth I, who had come to the throne on the death of her half-sister Queen Mary in 1558, just six years before the birth of Shakespeare in 1564.

To us, Shakespeare's *Henry VI* and *Richard III* concern a history of over 500 years ago, but for Shakespeare, starting his writing career in the late 1580s, the Battle of Bosworth was only 100 years in the past. It was as if a young writer in 2015 were to have chosen the First World War for the subject of his or her first plays.

The history plays written in the 1590s were set in a period distant enough for Shakespeare to consider writing without causing offence to Elizabeth I. These plays kept a respectable and politically sensible distance from the century of Elizabeth's birth, Elizabeth's reign and the tumultuous reign of her father. Shakespeare, perhaps wisely, didn't write a play about Elizabeth's father, Henry VIII, until approximately ten years after her death in 1603 when, in 1612–13, he wrote one in collaboration with John Fletcher, as discussed in Chapter 27. He also made some minor contributions to a collaborative play, *Sir Thomas More* (Henry VIII's Chancellor), in around 1600.

Nevertheless, the *Henry VI* and *Richard III* plays concerned a history that brought the Tudors, including eventually, in 1558, Elizabeth, to power and as such had a topicality for Elizabethan audiences that Shakespeare was glad to exploit. They were a huge success at attracting audiences for a dramatist who was starting to make his fame as a playwright.

Key idea

To us, unfamiliar mostly with the characters except through his plays, it can become confusing as to which are the Lancastrians, which the Yorkists and who is who and is on whose side at whatever time in the history. Many texts of the plays, including the *Arden Shakespeare*, which I am using, have a chronology, a royal family tree and explanations of who is who. Similarly, when the plays are performed, the programmes usually include such material. It is useful to keep these aids at your side as you go through the plays. You may also find Appendix 3 in this book, listing the historical dates of the English monarchs, useful.

Shakespeare's sources for the history plays

Shakespeare's sources for the English history plays are largely a set of chronicles published or translated throughout the sixteenth century. The principal ones are those by Froissart (translated by Bernes in 1523–5), Edward Hall (1548) and Ralph Holinshed (1587). There was also Samuel Daniel's epic poem on the history of the Civil Wars (1595?); Thomas More's Tudor-biased historical account of Richard III (c.1513); and

A Mirror for Magistrates, a historical poem sequence published in 1559 and with additional material in 1563. Edward Hall's *The Union of the Two Noble Illustre Famelies of Lancastre and Yorke* places the *Henry VI* plays within their historical chronological structure from which Shakespeare develops a dramatic art of counterpointing, which is employed throughout the history plays. Also, although the first tetralogy deals with a single stretch of time, it is probable that Shakespeare completed *2 Henry VI* and *3 Henry VI* before he wrote, probably in collaboration with Thomas Nashe (1567–1601) and others, *1 Henry VI*. (See Chapter 12.)

King Henry VI parts 1–3

The *Henry VI* plays have demonstrated, through modern performance and adaptation, that they are theatrically adept and engrossing in production. Despite each part having its own integrity, they can together tell a good story in a series of episodes which modern audiences, familiar with box-set series perhaps on television or DVD, enjoy.

In the early 1960s, at the time of the Cold War in which the USA and the Soviet Union were squaring up to each other, Peter Hall and John Barton adapted the three *Henry VI* plays into two and added *Richard III* as a sequence entitled *The Wars of the Roses*. They saw the plays as involving polar opposites, inevitably attracting and colliding with one another. Everything stemmed back, however, to the deposition of Richard II:

'Underlying these plays is the curse on the House of Lancaster. Bolingbroke deposed Richard II to become Henry IV. Richard II was a weak and sometimes bad king, unbalanced; he could not order the body politic. Yet for Shakespeare his deposition is a wound in the body politic that festers through reign after reign, a sin which can only be expiated by the letting of quantities of blood. The bloody totalitarianism of Richard III is the expiation of England.'

Hall, P. (1970: xiii), *The Wars of the Roses*. London: BBC Books, 1970

In a letter to John Barton concerning the 'first play' in the adaptation, Peter Hall writes of exposing a movement found 'from the opposition between two principles, one patriotic and constructive, but *misguided*, the other destructive and selfish. There's a feeling of growing disaster. There's the antithesis and interplay between strife and concord, peace and war, at home and abroad' (Hall, P. [1970: xx]).

Later interpretations of *Henry VI* at Shakespeare's Globe in London as well as at the RSC have either placed the plays in a historical context or emphasized elements of subversion contained in their representation of the growing inefficacy and instability of monarchical ritual. In the decade following the turn of the millennium, Michael Boyd, then Artistic Director of the RSC, embarked on an adventurous panoramic, if perhaps controversial, view of Shakespeare's English history plays, rehearsing and producing both cycles 'in the order that they were written and in the order in which Shakespeare's audience would have seen them, thus giving us an insight into Shakespeare's journey as a writer, and a deeper understanding of his developing view of England and its history' (programme note, 2007–8 season).

This was somewhat in contrast to Adrian Noble's 1988 adaptation of *Henry VI, Parts 1, 2, 3* and *Richard III* into *The Plantagenets*, in which he noted the 'apparently cavalier way' in which Shakespeare as 'a writer of fiction ... refused to worship at the shrine of actuality'. For Noble, 'Shakespeare's primary purpose in the plays is moral', especially in being 'explicit in its condemnation of civil war' (Noble, A. [1989: viii–ix], Introduction, *The Plantagenets*. London and Boston: Faber & Faber).

In 1994 Katie Mitchell produced another adaptation for the RSC: *Henry VI: The Battle for the Throne*. In 1977, however, Terry Hands had bravely directed the *Henry VI* plays without adaptation, in a sequential production that demonstrated how a short space of time can change interpretations. Whereas in the 1960s Hall and Barton's work had been influenced by big power oppositional politics, Hands in the 1970s saw his characters as self-aggrandizing, petty people squabbling over and with power at the cost of ordinary people. In 2013

Henry VI, as *Harry the Sixth; The House of York and Lancaster* and *The True Tragedy of the Duke of York,* was produced by Shakespeare's Globe in London and on tour in productions of the three plays as individual units, the programme noting that their original titles 'make it clear that they are not a trilogy' but they were conveniently placed as such by Heminges and Condell in the First Folio. As noted above, the order of composition is uncertain, especially in relation to Part 1. So it was only fitting that Shakespeare's Globe, with some strong productions of the individual plays, raised the issue of historical sequencing through performance.

The character of Henry VI overall, as Julia Briggs has pointed out, 'recalls Erasmus's gentle, passive and unworldly ruler', in contrast with Machiavelli's view that an effective ruler is required to be able to address the world of 'tough, competitive power politics' (Briggs, J. [1977: 207–8]).

1 Henry VI deals with England's loss of its overseas territory and with the downfall of its national hero the Earl of Talbot. In *2 Henry VI*, where the emphasis is more on domestic politics, we witness the comic yet pertinent uprising of Jack Cade, which presages some of the issues that occur in *King John* (1595–7), over the authenticity of inheritance, succession and authority. In a humorous scene, Jack Cade claims to be a Plantagenet and that his wife is 'descended of the Lacies'. These claims are comically undermined by Dick the Butcher, who in a series of asides mocks the rebel leader as in, for example, the claim for his wife: 'She was indeed a pedlar's daughter and sold many laces' (4.2.42f.). It is Jack the Butcher who also gets unfailing predictable laughs from the audience for his suggestion 'The first thing we do, let's kill all the lawyers' (4.2.72). But all this is expressed comically, and seen as such by the audience, even though the poor Clerk, after examination by Cade, is led away to be hanged because he confesses that he can read and write.

The scene, though a pantomime expression of discontent and the dangers of civil disturbance, presaged perhaps the episode in *Julius Caesar* (Act 3, Scene 3) where, with a greater touch of sombre realism, Cinna the Poet is mistaken by the rabble as one of the conspirators and murdered. In both cases, popular unruliness is offered as a symptom of a larger disorder. The plight of the common man, however, is put in a more pertinent perspective in *3 Henry VI* (Act 2, Scene 5), where the weak King Henry VI enters the stage alone and ruminates on the fortunes of the battle and how the thrones of York and Lancaster seem to be of equal strength.

Counterpointing and juxtapositioning

Sitting on a 'molehill', the King wishes to be no more than a 'homely swain' (*3 Henry VI*, 2.5.22), someone not involved in politics and responsibility but rather a man able to count the hours and plan out his quiet life: 'Ah, what a life were this! how sweet! how lovely!' (2.5.41).

As he meditates on this comforting domesticity, a young man enters, dragging the body of a soldier he has just killed in battle. The young man rifles the body for booty and as he does so he uncovers the face:

> Who's this? O God! it is my father's face,
>
> Whom in this conflict I unwares have kill'd.
>
> O heavy times, begetting such events!
>
> From London by the King was I press'd forth;
>
> My father, being the Earl of Warwick's man,
>
> Came on the part of York, press'd by his master;
>
> And I, who at his hands receiv'd my life,
>
> Have by my hands of life bereaved him.
>
> Pardon me, God, I knew not what I did:
>
> (2.5.61–9)

The son grieves, as does the King witnessing his distress:

> O piteous spectacle! O bloody times!
>
> …
>
> Weep, wretched man; I'll aid thee tear for tear;
>
> And let our hearts and eyes, like civil war,
>
> Be blind with tears, and break o'ercharg'd with grief.
>
> (2.5.73, 76–8)

As the King weeps, an older man enters carrying the body of a soldier and, rifling the body, similarly uncovers the face:

> Is this our foeman's face?
>
> Ah, no, no, no; it is mine only son!
>
> Ah, boy, if any life be left in thee,
>
> Throw up thine eye!
>
> …
>
> O, pity, God, this miserable age!
>
> What stratagems, how fell, how butcherly,
>
> Erroneous, mutinous and unnatural,
>
> This deadly quarrel daily doth beget!
>
> (2.5.82–5, 88–91)

Again, the King grieves and wishes that his own death might stop the warring factions. It appears a fatuous desire.

Spotlight

Shakespeare, with this scene – and, as we will see later with Falstaff's diatribe against honour (*1 Henry IV*, 5.1.127–41) and with the soldier Michael Williams' warning (*Henry V*, 4.1.132–44) of the King's responsibility for the souls of those killed in battle – expresses something of the common man caught up in the power games of kings. Counterpointing by the juxtaposition of experiences and attitudes reveals, thereby, an understanding of the social condition of ordinary people. So in *Henry V* the King's heroic call to battle, 'Once more unto the breach, dear friends, once more', ending 'Cry "God for Harry! England and Saint George!"' (*Henry V*, 3.1.1–34), is immediately parodied in the following scene by Bardolph, Nym, Pistol and the Boy.

BARDOLPH   On, on, on, on, on, to the breach, to the breach!

NYM   Pray thee, Corporal, stay; the knocks are too hot, and for mine own part I have not a case of lives. The humour of it is too hot, that is the very plain-song of it.

PISTOL   The plain-song is most just, for humours do abound,
Knocks go and come, God's vassals drop and die,

> And sword and shield
>
> In bloody field
>
> Doth win immortal fame.

BOY   Would I were in an alehouse in London! I would give all my fame for a pot of ale and safety.

                                                          (Henry V, 3.2.1–11)

Note here the comical fivefold repetition of 'On', and the fact that Shakespeare moves from verse into prose and then doggerel of the kind that Bottom uses in *A Midsummer Night's Dream*. The simple, naively honest expression of the Boy's desire is indicative of the way in which Shakespeare invests the history plays with a human viewpoint in the face of the miseries and tragedies that are unfolding. Civil war in the *Henry VI* plays is not just about the aristocratic classes, political ineptitude or ambition, since decisions made affect everyone whether or not they are educated or have access to power.

Richard III

Historically, Richard the crookback, having been defeated at the Battle of Bosworth (1485) by Henry VII, became the butt of Tudor propaganda. His deformity symbolizes and caricatures evil, which from the opening of the play allows for virtuoso acting that has attracted the greatest actors of successive generations.

ADDRESSING THE AUDIENCE

Uniquely for Shakespeare, the play opens with the protagonist acting as a chorus – which is also a commentator on his own intrigue and evil – entering the stage alone to confide in his audience:

> Now is the winter of our discontent
>
> Made glorious summer by this son of York;

                                                             (1.1.1f.)

Richard's soliloquy sets the framework for the play, taking the audience into the character's confidence as he plays and toys with them as he reveals what he is and what he intends to do:

And therefore, since I cannot prove a lover
To entertain these fair well-spoken days,
I am determined to prove a villain,
And hate the idle pleasures of these days.
Plots have I laid, inductions dangerous,
By drunken prophecies, libels, and dreams,
To set my brother Clarence and the King
In deadly hate, the one against the other:

(1.1.28–35)

To this extent Richard is in control of the narrative for the first four acts of the play.

Reminiscent of Iago in the later play *Othello*, Richard audaciously proclaims to the audience at the end of the scene that he'll 'marry Warwick's youngest daughter–/What though I kill'd her husband and her father?' In the next scene he proceeds to woo Lady Anne successfully, despite her condemning him as a 'dreadful minister of hell!', a 'lump of foul deformity', a 'Villain (that) … know'st no law of God nor man' (1.2.46, 57, 70). He keeps her talking, perseveres, offers her his sword to kill him, or offers to kill himself, and persuades her to agree. Once she has left the stage, he turns and confides in the audience with incredulous, humorous relish:

Was ever woman in this humour woo'd?
Was ever woman in this humour won?
I'll have her, but I will not keep her long.
What, I that kill'd her husband and his father:
To take her in her heart's extremest hate,
With curses in her mouth, tears in her eyes,
The bleeding witness of her hatred by,
Having God, her conscience, and those bars against me –

(1.2.232–9f.)

Spotlight

Shakespeare creates this character's outrageous impudence through his direct interaction with the audience, which draws us into the character's confidence, relishing with him the arrogance of his self-proclaimed enjoyment and pride in his evil – 'I'll have her, but I will not keep her long.' The audience recognizes this as a disgraceful statement and yet unfailingly laughs at it. We appreciate and enjoy Richard's outrageous manipulation, but we are also being manipulated by Shakespeare. This is not Richard's art but the art of the dramatist.

There is little sympathy for Lady Anne at this point, in contrast to Katherine of Aragon's predicament in the later collaborative play *Henry VIII* (1613), because here Shakespeare's focus is on the dexterity of the evil villain. Some critics, for example Bernard Spivak, see Richard in this respect as a secularized adaptation of the medieval Vice figure from the medieval morality plays. Other critical perspectives have challenged this view, but the old Vice figure was comic in his audacious declaration and sought to establish a close bond with audiences, all of which Richard, Duke of Gloucester does.

'His weeping and laughter do not by themselves establish the archaic source of Richard's performance, but they confirm it, alongside his other unmistakable tricks of language and behavior. The dominant trait in his descent appears in the unnaturalistic dimension of his role, in the repetitious and gratuitous deceit surviving out of the old Christian metaphor, in the homiletic method of the timeless personification. It is the inspirational force of the method itself that gives birth to Richard's wooing of Lady Anne, for which there is no hint in the chronicles (Shakespeare's sources). That scene has its origin in theatrical convention, not in history, and its dramatic caliber sufficiently explains the playwright's recourse to the old dramaturgy. His caliber explains the great energy and brilliance we discover in this flashing version of the transformed Vice.'

Spivak, B. (1958: 406–7), *Shakespeare and the Allegory of Evil*. New York and London: Columbia University Press

DE CASIBUS TRAGEDY

Richard III is not just a history play in the sense of the chronicle history plays that preceded it. Some might argue that it is part of Tudor propaganda, reinforcing the Tudors' legitimacy and authority. There is little doubt that Shakespeare was influenced by Sir Thomas More's historical account of Richard III, written during the reign of Henry VIII. The play, however, although it has historically determined the perception of Richard III for generations, also provides an opportunity for the actor playing the protagonist. Within the context of what is termed *de casibus* tragedy (see Chapter 16), *Richard III* demonstrates the rise and fall of the protagonist.

Through the course of the play, Richard moves from the role of manipulative, intimidating and insinuating villain assisted by Buckingham, into that of the King practised in the art of counterfeit. Indeed, he is the consummate actor, who inadvertently exposes the ways in which power invests heavily in theatrical performance. He encourages Buckingham to do likewise, saying:

> Come, cousin, canst thou quake and change thy colour,
>
> Murder thy breath in middle of a word,
>
> And then again begin, and stop again,
>
> As if thou were distraught and mad with terror?

To which Buckingham replies:

> Tut, I can counterfeit the deep tragedian,
>
> Speak, and look back, and pry on every side,
>
> Tremble and start at wagging of a straw,
>
> Intending deep suspicion.

(3.5.1–8)

But once he gains the crown, Richard loses control of the narrative and the wheel of fortune turns. The play now takes a different course until, haunted by the ghosts of those he's murdered (including Buckingham), Richard is brought to despair on the eve of the Battle of Bosworth, where he ends on the battlefield famously crying out, 'A horse! A horse! My kingdom for a horse!' (5.4.7).

King John

Whether *King John* was written before or after *Richard III* is not entirely certain but it, too, has a comic side that comes through in performance. There is, however, a difference in that Shakespeare's focus in *King John* is not mainly on the King, to create a virtuoso acting role, as in *Richard III*, but on the surrounding events. Here it is the bastard Falconbridge who takes on the role of the protagonist, as the King had in *Richard III,* and in addition to the decrying of 'commodity' Falconbridge is tolerated because he is part of the opposition to the power of the Pope.

King John appears to have been a successful play in Elizabethan England and certainly it proved popular in the nineteenth century. In the twentieth century, however, it did not greatly appeal. For mid-twentieth-century production it had neither the heroism of *Henry V* nor the comic villainy of *Richard III*. 'What a bad play this is! All about a war in which it is not possible to take the slightest interest', wrote the theatre critic James Agate in 1941. In 1924 he had written, 'One does not pretend that the play has no good bits. There are one or two exquisite bits.'

'*King John is a character at once odious and weak... Shakespeare... had little taste for the spineless, and therefore wrote this play, not about, but round King John, whom he leaves mum in the middle of the stage whilst everybody else, including that old bore, Pandalph, talks his head off. And when John does talk it is all wind... One of the reasons why this play is so seldom acted is the difficulty of doing much with the title role.*'

Agate, J. (1943: 89, 86), *Brief Chronicles: A Survey of the Plays of Shakespeare and the Elizabethans in Actual Performance*. London: Cape

INFIGHTING

Historically, and particularly since the nineteenth century, the reign of King John is known in the Western world for the signing of the Magna Carta. Although historically it was an agreement between the King and his barons, it has become indicative of the start of an evolution towards democratic governance, which extends centuries later to include the creation of the USA. Ironically, however, the Magna Carta does not figure in the play, although some modern productions insert some reference to it.

King John's reign, historically, stands apart from the English history plays. To some extent, Shakespeare emphasizes the theatrical element rather than the political polemics, but does not, as in *Richard III*, exploit this in the context of *de casibus* tragedy. Rather he explores, as in the *Henry VI* plays, the infighting over power and questions of 'truth' and 'authority'.

Whereas in *2 Henry VI*, Jack Cade absurdly claims his royal heritage, in *King John* the issue of claims and reality becomes a major focus. Where in the history of King John is the truth behind the claims to the English throne? John's proclamation of his right is that he is the one who occupies the throne. His nephew Arthur's claim is that he is really the first in line. So whom do the people follow? The character of Hubert stands on the walls of the French town of Angiers, being besieged by the forces of the rival claimants, and he proclaims '... we are the king of England's subjects:/For him, and in his right, we hold this town.' John replies: 'Acknowledge then the king, and let me in.' But in reply Hubert demands proof of authority:

> That can we not; but he that proves the king,
>
> To him will we prove loyal: till that time
>
> Have we ramm'd up our gates against the world.

(2.1.269–72)

So the town of Angiers watches as men fight and die to prove legitimacy and, again, they are similarly asked '... who's your king?' to receive the reply 'The King of England, when we know the King' (2.1.362–3).

LEGITIMACY AND AUTHORITY; TRUTH AND THE LAW

The issue is over the legitimacy and authority of the rival claims; John's coronation hasn't persuaded them that he is king; nor has France's argument in favour of Arthur. So where is the proof of legitimate authority? It is then that the bastard son of Richard Coeur de Lion, who sees through the various claims and what motivates them, pragmatically advises the rival forces to unite and take the town. Arguments of legitimacy can be put to one side and authority is demonstrated by force when townspeople quibble.

The Bastard's authority is like the Alexandrian order to cut the Gordian knot. Truth is irrelevant in the face of brute force or pragmatic politics. In the opening scene, the Bastard claims possession of his father's lands that have been given to the second son, Robert, on the basis of a deathbed revelation that the elder boy 'was none of his' (1.1.111), but that is challenged by King John telling Robert '… your brother is legitimate;/ Your father's wife did after wedlock bear him …' (116–17), but the Bastard, on being recognized to have the features of a possible illegitimate son of Coeur de Lion, gives up his inheritance to follow John. Opportunism, pragmatism and ambition win the day, no matter whose son he is.

Spotlight

When is the truth law? Is it with the word of the king? Is it with the word of God? John is excommunicated by the Pope, through the words of Cardinal Pandulph. Who has the greater authority, the reigning King or the Pope? John proclaims himself to be supreme head of the Church in defiance of Rome and orders that the monasteries should give up their wealth. So John's history presages Henry VIII's revolt against Rome, the dissolution of the monasteries and his declaration of ecclesiastical independence.

RELEVANCE TO TUDOR ENGLAND

Although more historically distant from Shakespeare in time than either the subject of *Henry VI* or *Richard III*, *King John* is nevertheless concerned with issues close to the Tudor England in which Shakespeare lived, and he constructs a series of parallels with which his Queen would no doubt have concurred.

> 'Nineteenth-century readers first noticed the plot's correspondence to events in the 1580s; the problem is whether the Elizabethans noticed it. Elizabeth I's right to the throne was challenged, as John's is in the play. She inherited from a sister, he from a brother. Her legitimacy was questioned, and she was under papal excommunication, so that the Armada of 1588 was under the same sanction as the Dauphin's forces in the play. Mary, Queen of Scots, like Arthur, was a legitimate claimant to the throne, supported by France and the Church. Like John, Elizabeth issued a kind of indirect death warrant, and she disowned the state servant who carried it out as John disowns Hubert. Shortly after Mary's death, the Catholic powers tried to invade England and depose Elizabeth; as in the play, the attack was beaten off by English valour, and finally scattered by violent storms.'
>
> Brownlow, F. W. (1977: 93), *Two Shakespearean Sequences*.
> London and Basingstoke: Macmillan

Critical debates, however, continue about how much weight to place on the historical parallels found in the play with the Elizabethan political situation immediately prior to and contemporaneous with its composition, but to my mind these connections are quite evident. Shakespeare may have diluted the overt Protestant polemic of his source play but the conflict with papal authority is manifest. Interestingly, in 2015 the Shakespeare's Globe production of the play began with incense and ritual.

ENGAGING THE MODERN AUDIENCE

King John is not a tragedy but an exploration of chronicle history with much humour, even farce, some terror and diplomacy. It is an entertainment and, remarkably, one that in its historicity still has the power of narrative to engage with modern audiences, who also enjoy modern works such as Hilary Mantel's *Wolf Hall* both as a novel and as a television adaptation. Over the last decades of the twentieth century and into the twenty-first, the play has had number of contemporary revivals, often emphasizing its comic elements. It is a play that comes in and out of fashion as the appetite for social humour lessens or heightens, in contrast with the virtuoso acting tradition of a play such as *Richard III*, but it is a play that deserves more attention than it usually receives.

The English history plays 2: *Richard II* (1595–6)

Drama depends on conflict. In *Richard II* we have a conflict of the transition from one culture enshrined in ritual and ceremony to a new one of political expediency and opportunism.

To understand what is happening in *Richard II*, it is useful to know about the institution of monarchy as it was understood by many at the time of Shakespeare. Whether that is exactly the same as at the time of Richard II himself (King of England 1377–99) is a matter for historians to debate, though certain common elements may well have been present.

The anointed king

In Act 3 of *Richard II* the discomforted king states:

> Not all the water in the rough rude sea
> Can wash the balm off from an anointed king;
> The breath of worldly men cannot depose
> The deputy elected by the Lord.

(3.2.54–7)

An anointed king, at his coronation, shares an affinity with the identity of a priest, who is similarly anointed at his ordination. The relationship between the two can be traced back to the Old Testament of the Bible, and particularly to the account of the Jewish Priest-King Melchisideck. In Christianity a priest, once ordained with holy oils, is regarded as a member of the order of Melchisideck 'for ever'. The oils used at a king's coronation, like those at a priest's ordination, cannot be removed. Such anointing cannot be reversed for a priest of God or for the king, who is 'the deputy elected by the Lord', that is, God's deputy on earth.

In 1957 E. H. Kantorowicz published *The King's Two Bodies: A Study in Mediaeval Political Theology*, which was reissued in 1998. It is a book that has been harshly contested by new historicists such as Richard Wilson, who, in his consideration of *Julius Caesar* (2002: 11), discusses it as 'manufactured medievalism' of 'mystic kingship', which 'infiltrated English Studies ... to become an ersatz reference for spiritualizing critics' (see Chapter 23). Ironically for one of the new historicists, who have themselves been criticized for the tangential nature of some of their evidence, Wilson adds that there is 'no proof that, except for a few lawyers, Elizabethans had ever heard of the fantasy of "the king's two bodies"' (Wilson, R. N. [2002: 11]).

The theory of the king's two bodies, 'a Body natural, and a Body politic' comes from Plowden's Elizabethan *Commentaries and Reports* quoted by Kantorowicz as 'collected and written under Queen Elizabeth'. Within this, Kantorowicz holds, is 'the first clear elaboration of that mystical talk with which the English crown jurists enveloped and trimmed their definitions of kingship and royal capacities'. The theory is that the king's natural body is mortal, as with other people, and just as subject to illness, imbecility, old age and death. But the king's 'Body politic is a Body that cannot be seen or handled, consisting of Policy and Government, and constituted for the Direction of the People, and the Management of the public weal'. This body is 'utterly void' of the 'defects and Imbecilities' of the body natural, and it passes from one ruler to the next in what should be orderly succession (Kantorowicz, E. H. [1957, p/b 1981: 7]).

It may well be that the general populace was not acquainted with the detailed legalistic argument of the jurists, but kingship then and until the present day has been based on at least one of three aspects: victory in arms; justification through sacramental anointing as God's deputy; and the stability of a nation through heritage and custom. When the monarch dies, the phrase 'the King/Queen is dead, long live the King/Queen' is invoked. Whether it is fantasy, mysticism or ersatz reference, the concept of the God's anointed was – and in some quarters still is – a basis of belief for which some Elizabethan jurists appear to have given an explanation. This is part of the 'discourse' of kingship, and while it can be criticized as an ideology in the way that cultural materialists like Alan Sinfield and Jonathan Dollimore do, its effects in the sense that it shaped people's thinking were material. It is clear that kingship was promoted by the Tudors and Stuarts as being an eternal living entity. At the anointing of the king at his coronation the abstract body of the institution of kingship and the actual mortal body of the king become one and could not be separated except through death.

Queen Elizabeth and Shakespeare's *Richard II*

Shakespeare wrote *Richard II* at the time when there was no king, but a queen. Elizabeth, however, modelled herself on Christ's mother, the Virgin Mary, who in the New Testament is reported to have conceived her son, Jesus Christ, by the power of the Holy Ghost, the third person of the Holy Trinity accepted by Catholic and most Protestant Christianity. In one sense, the Virgin Mary had served a priest-like function. The Virgin Mary intercedes on behalf of sinners in the way that saints were supposed to act as intermediaries.

Elizabeth fabricated a similar identity, suggesting that she saw herself as interceding between her subjects and God. The doctrine of the Virgin Mary holds that she had been miraculously conceived by the Holy Ghost and thereby remained the 'Virgin Mother of God', and the 'Virgin Queen of Heaven' to whom people prayed for protection. This was exactly the identification that Elizabeth encouraged. She was anointed at her coronation just as a king would have been, and she regarded and promoted herself as the 'Virgin Queen', while at the same time images of the Virgin Mary were being burned by the radical Protestant converts.

Elizabeth accepted the title of the Supreme Governor of the Church rather than Supreme Head of the Church and, like her father, Henry VIII, she refused to be subjected to the authority of the Papacy. Through encouraging her image of the Virgin Queen, however, we can surmise that Elizabeth sought to capitalize on residual Catholic beliefs in order to assert her political control over the state and the Church. Through her coronation and anointing she retained her link with the king-priest historical association. Julia Briggs (1997: 223) notes that contemporary paintings of Elizabeth imitated those of the Virgin Mary crowned with the stars of heaven; that in 1600 in Dowland's *Second Book of Songs* it was proposed that 'Vivat Eliza' should replace 'Ave Maria'; and that 'memorial poems described her ascent to heaven and coronation there'.

William Tyndale (1494?–1536), the translator of the New Testament and the Pentateuch, the opening books of the Old Testament, who was executed by Emperor Charles V acting as proxy for Henry VIII, upheld ironically a relationship between God and monarch:

> 'The powers that be are ordained of God. Whosoever, therefore, resisteth the power, resisteth the ordinance of God. They that shall resist shall receive unto themselves damnation ... God ... hath given laws unto all nations, and in all lands hath put kings, governors and rulers in His own stead to rule the world through them.'
>
> Tyndale, W, 1528 (2000), *The Obedience of a Christian Man*. London: Penguin

Not everyone agreed with this doctrine. The Protestant John Ponet (*c.*1514–56), for example, in *A Shorte Treatise on Politik Power* (1556), made a case for justified opposition to what he considered to be secular rulers. Sensibly, he had gone into exile in 1553 on the accession of Mary I, where he died in 1556, the same year that his Protestant friend Thomas Cranmer (1489–1556), Archbishop of Canterbury, was burned at the stake for heresy by the Catholic Queen 'Bloody Mary'. So writing or performing plays depicting the deposition of monarchs was, to put it mildly, a little dangerous to pull off.

On 6 February 1601 Shakespeare's company accepted 40 silver pieces from Gilly Megrick, a friend of Robert Devereux, Earl of Essex, to perform *Richard II*, in which the anointed king is deposed and killed. Two days later, Essex led his abortive rebellion against the Queen. Shakespeare, Burbage and the company were consequently in serious trouble. One of their number, Augustine Phillips, argued their way out of the problem. He maintained that they didn't want to revive the play as some of the original cast were no longer available and, therefore, parts had to be learned quickly but nevertheless, it was a good sum of money being offered and they were a commercial theatre. Some critics have associated the Queen's remark 'I am Richard II. Know ye not that?' with this performance but in fact she said this some six months later on another occasion.

Politically, the company, whether knowingly or not, was being asked to stage a deposition of a monarch who was God's anointed, even though in *Richard II* there are speeches which uphold the basis of that authority, and even though the so-called 'deposition scene' (that was not usually performed) is framed in such a way that Richard effectively abdicates. That the monarch, God's anointed deputy – even if guilty of wrongdoing – cannot be deposed is made explicit by John of Gaunt in Act 1, Scene 2, even though it is implied that King Richard has been involved in the death of Gaunt's brother, Thomas of Woodstock, the first Duke of Gloucester. Gaunt tells the widowed Duchess:

> God's is the quarrel – for God's substitute,
>
> His deputy anointed is His sight,
>
> Hath caus'd his [Woodstock's] death; the which if wrongfully,
>
> Let heaven revenge, for I may never lift
>
> An angry arm against His minister.

(1.2.37–41)

Richard and kingship

In this play Richard is depicted as someone careless of the realities and obligations of kingship. In the famous passage 2.1.31f., the dying Gaunt mourns the fact that England '... this seat of Mars, /This other Eden, demi-paradise ... This blessed plot, this earth, this realm, this England' is being 'leas'd out', or mortgaged, by its monarch to pay for the King's extravagances and expeditions. Gaunt can but plead to the King, who does not listen and who after Gaunt's death confiscates his possessions and wealth to pay for the Irish wars, thus dispossessing Bolingbroke of his rightful inheritance.

This will become an issue when the banished Bolingbroke returns to reclaim his lands. With Bolingbroke there is no divine right but pragmatic argument and force, and his rebellion, initially justified by involving his rights of inheritance, signals the end of Richard's particular ritualistic way of conducting affairs. At the beginning of the play Richard had shown his commitment to staged ceremony, as shown by the tournament, which he curtails by throwing his 'warder' down. Like Protestantism, Bolingbroke in this play is of a new order. The deposition of Richard is supposed by Bolingbroke to be of that new order, but becomes through Richard's histrionics an expression of the tension between two opposing cultures, one of ceremony (Richard) and one of pragmatism (Bolingbroke/Northumberland).

TWO OPPOSING WORLDS

Richard's mindset, as presented by the dramatist, is focused on ceremony and ritual as the nature of his authority. Bolingbroke's is one that looks towards political realism and military force. So the play works by dramatizing two opposing worlds that appear to collide, with neither giving way to the other, just as, in the context of the Reformation, liturgical ritualistic Catholicism sought to resist the advance of text-based Protestant reform. The biblically, textually based assertions of Protestantism encapsulated in the play, therefore, are core elements of that political and religious struggle which was to lead to the execution of an anointed king, Charles I, in 1649.

Key idea

Richard II is a play of its age, reflecting some of the political and religious tensions building through Elizabeth's reign and presaging a collision of two conflicting forms of belief and faith, which ultimately led to the radical questioning of the monarch's authority and to the English Civil War.

On Richard's return from Ireland to quell Bolingbroke's rebellion, the King's response (3.2.36f.) is to describe himself as 'the searching eye of heaven', the sun, which has been hidden and which will now illuminate the evils of Bolingbroke, embarrass him and make him 'tremble at his sin'. It is a fantasy, since Bolingbroke's antecedent materialism and opportunism constitute too great a force for Richard, who descends into a self-indulgent melancholy about the mortality of kings:

> ... – for within the hollow crown
> That rounds the mortal temples of a king
> Keeps Death his court, and there the antic sits,
> Scoffing his state and grinning at his pomp,
> Allowing him a breath, a little scene,
> To monarchize, be fear'd, and kill with looks;
> ...
>
>   ... and, humour'd thus,

Comes at the last, and with a little pin

Bores thorough his castle wall, and farewell king!

(3.2. 160–65, 168–70)

This whole passage (3.2.144f.) portrays the King still in theatrical mode, expressing the material reality of death that he now believes will be his fate. The language is extravagant, self-indulgent and ritualistic. For the now self-obsessed Richard, this is what happens to great men and it is something he will have to accept; indeed, the concluding lines of the speech are self-gratifying in their defeat, as Richard now describes himself as a 'subject':

… – subjected thus,

How can you say to me, I am King?

(176–7)

The speech is indicative of his capacity for self-fashioning, even in a defeat, as Richard's political status changes. It is presented histrionically as an imitation of Christ's agony in the Garden of Gethsemane the night before his crucifixion, but here being assumed by God's deputy on earth whose own sins have led to his downfall. Later in the deposition scene (Act 4, Scene 1), he is to call those around him 'Judas' (Christ's betrayer, 4.1.170) and equate others with Pontius Pilate who sentenced Christ to death:

… yet you Pilates

Have here deliver'd me to my sour cross,

And water cannot wash away your sin.

(4.1.240–42)

You may note the contrast here between the washing away of the oils of coronation with Pontius Pilate's abrogation of the responsibility for the sentencing of Christ. In an extravagant, self-dramatizing gesture, Richard equates the permanence of his anointment with the impossibility of the erasing of Bolingbroke's 'sin'. While all his self-analysis is being made in Act 4, Scene 1, Northumberland on behalf of Bolingbroke remains doggedly politically pragmatic, demanding that Richard read the articles of accusation and confess his 'grievous crimes' (4.1.223), because unless he does, 'The commons will not then be satisfi'd' (4.1.272). In this way, Shakespeare builds up levels of confrontation, all of which makes for good drama.

Spotlight

Richard insists upon his identity and derives some fortitude from the knowledge of what it is that supports that identity. Northumberland, by demanding Richard confess his crimes, forces the King back into Bolingbroke's world. But Richard cannot easily enter such a world since his whole being is linked to the concept of ceremonial consecrated kingship. As Northumberland continues to use the term 'My lord', Richard turns on him:

> No lord of thine, thou haught insulting man;
>
> Nor no man's lord. I have no name, no title;
>
> No, not that name was given me at the font,
>
> But 'tis usurp'd.
>
> (4.1.254–7)

To take away his regal title is to sever him from his very identity. It is to separate the body mortal from the body politic, which can only be divided in death. It is, therefore, to kill the King, because, without his title, he has no name, no identity, no life.

In the preceding scene in which Richard, devoid of earthly help, is captured at Barkloughly Castle, Shakespeare stages the King high above the thrust stage, where he talks of 'God omnipotent, … mustering in his clouds, on our behalf, / Armies of pestilence, …' (3.3.85–7) to avenge his downfall. There, too, he enters into a mood of self-pity, histrionically dramatizing his fall from a position associated with his ceremonial apprehension of himself, to the lowly status when his 'sovereign's head' will be trampled upon by his 'subjects' feet':

> … a little grave,
>
> A little little grave, an obscure grave,
>
> Or I'll be buried in the king's highway,
>
> … where subjects' feet
>
> May hourly trample on their sovereign's head;
>
> (3.3.153–7)

By placing him up on high, Shakespeare is able to depict his descent into the court beneath, where Bolingbroke holds sway. It is as if he is coming from heaven down into hell, though the imagery used is classical:

> Down, down I come, like glist'ring Phaeton,
>
> Wanting the manage of unruly jades.
>
> In the base court? Base court, where kings grow base,
>
> To come at traitors' calls, and do them grace!

> (3.3.178–81)

In the trial scene he calls for a mirror to look at his usurped self, commenting, 'How soon my sorrow hath destroy'd my face.' To which Bolingbroke replies, being perfectly aware of Richard's capacity for self-dramatization, 'The shadow of your sorrow hath destroy'd/The shadow of your face.' (4.1.291–3). For Bolingbroke, Richard's world is one of illusion, of shadows, with no understanding of the reality of what he is, of what he has done. But Richard has already smashed the glass in which he sees that illusion.

Key idea

Subtle though the deposition scene (Act 4, Scene 1) is, even before 1599 it appears that the Elizabethan authorities possibly regarded it as too controversial to be staged or published, since the first edition of the play, the quarto of 1597, omits it.

Whether or not Shakespeare and his colleagues were implicitly supporting the Essex Rebellion is still a matter of debate. The historian Michael Wood notes that 'it seems hard to avoid the conclusion that Shakespeare and his company were sympathetic to Essex, who we know had long loved the play's "conceit"' (Wood, M. [2005: 255]) but Jonathan Bate challenges a similar view by Greenblatt (2004) and others:

> '... how can the strategy of those who commissioned the performance have been to plant the idea of a successful rebellion in the minds of the London crowd when they had not themselves planned the rebellion? The trigger for Essex's march into the streets came only after the show ... [The authorities led by Cecil] in the subsequent investigations [give no indication that this was] how they regarded the performance.'
>
> Bate, J. (2009: 255)

Clearly, with or without the deposition scene, *Richard II* had been a success on the Elizabethan stage. Historically, the deposition and death of Richard II eventually led to the death of Richard III and the assumption of the throne by Henry Tudor (Henry VII), Queen Elizabeth's grandfather. Richard II's deposition therefore triggered a course of events that eventually led to Elizabeth's ascent to the throne, but it also signalled a threat to monarchy itself, which was to culminate in the execution of a monarch and the creation of a Commonwealth. Shakespeare, in creating this play, may have courted danger but theatrically he triumphed. Many still find it one of his most compelling plays.

The English history plays 3, plus a comedy: *1 Henry IV* (1596–7); *2 Henry IV* (1597–8); *Henry V* (1599); and *The Merry Wives of Windsor* (1597–1601)

Our understanding of the *Henry IV* and *Henry V* plays is sometimes constrained by attempts to tie them down to one interpretation. While this allows us to gain valuable critical insights from reading, we are often in danger of succumbing to the realism and the directorial style of a particular performance. However, while we can choose between various critical readings, each live performance is different because every audience is different and because time moves on.

The *Henry IV* plays, for all their structural agility, have had a mixed reception. Some theatregoers love them – and Falstaff in particular. Others do not. Satisfaction with these plays depends so much on Falstaff and, indeed, the actor playing the role. For Queen Elizabeth I it is conjectured that she so enjoyed watching this fat Saturnalian rogue that she demanded that Shakespeare write another play in which Falstaff should appear 'in love'. This is the reason for including a discussion of *The Merry Wives of Windsor* in this last chapter on the English history plays, although the anecdote is one of those myths about Shakespeare that may or may not be true.

The *Henry IV* plays

The *Henry IV* plays work through a dual plot structure, with the one plot, the story of King Henry IV's reign, overlapping with the other through Prince Hal, in the parallel plot involving the Saturnalian character Falstaff, who is 'King' of the tavern world. In this we recall again William Empson's dictum of correspondence discussed earlier (see Chapter 4), whereby the two plots feed off each other. The result is a structural harmony and balance as the two narratives interact with each other, alternating until the close of *2 Henry IV*, when Prince Hal, who has cavorted with his tavern associates, becomes king and rejects Falstaff, banning him from the royal presence. The Saturnalian world has to fade away in the presence of the glorious new king – who is sometimes in performances dressed all in gold. Early in the succeeding play, *Henry V*, we hear that Falstaff is dead. War is now afoot and Prince Hal's former tavern companions go off to fight in France where one of them, Bardolph, is ordered to be hanged by the King for stealing a 'pax', which is the box in which consecrated wafers are kept for Holy Communion.

The creation of Falstaff for the *Henry IV* plays signals a different approach by the dramatist from the histories we have considered so far. In these plays Shakespeare goes well beyond creating short scenes that provide straightforward comic perspectives on serious issues raised in the plays, but rather presents two overlapping worlds: the court and politics on the one hand and the tavern and brothels on the other. The latter attempts comically to imitate the former and, in so doing, exposes issues of discontent and unease on the other.

We would be wrong to think of Falstaff merely as a comic character, a lovable rogue. He and his tavern world point in a different direction from the plays' otherwise seemingly establishment concerns. Falstaff's aim is survival within the context of his own world, which is threatened by the demands of the political establishment. Hal coldly uses the tavern world for his own purposes of personal amusement and escape from his father, although from Act 1, Scene 2 of *2 Henry IV* he appears to have a strategy to 'use' his tavern friends for a political purpose. This is expressed in Hal's direct address to the audience (1.2.190f.), which may feel a little odd, as if Shakespeare might be protecting himself by making it clear that all this bad behaviour by an heir to the throne was strategic. Falstaff plays along with the game until the end. He is an inventive opportunist since that's what his survival is all about.

When the Prince becomes king, Falstaff's heart is broken because he is denied an opportunity for advancement. Yet opportunity gave him life, allowing him the liberty even to play the king and rebuke Hal for his misdeeds, but all that is part of the Saturnalian game, of an underworld that in reality is aware of the way the world works and doesn't much like it. So there is an earthy common sense about self-preservation in the portrayal of a figure who actually questions the prevailing notions of 'honour' which lead to other men's deaths and could lead to his own in war:

> Well, 'tis no matter, honour pricks me on. Yea, but how if honour prick me off when I come on, how then? Can honour set to a leg? No. Or an arm? No. Or take away the grief of a wound? No. Honour hath no skill in surgery then? No. What is honour? A word. What is in that word honour? What is that honour? Air. A trim reckoning! Who hath it? He that died a-Wednesday. Doth he feel it? No.

Doth he hear it? No. 'Tis insensible, then? Yea, to the dead.
But will it not live with the living? No. Why? Detraction
will not suffer it. Therefore I'll none of it. Honour is a mere
scutcheon – and so ends my catechism.

(*1 Henry IV*, 5.1.129–41)

Spotlight

In contrast with this underworld is the fragile political world of King
Henry IV, a king troubled by the behaviour of his son Hal and the
security of his throne. It would be wrong, however, to consider these
two interweaving worlds as in competition with each other. The fact
that the Saturnalian is incorporated into the political world at the end of
1 Henry IV does not invalidate its purpose. Do we believe that once the
fairies have done the work expected of them in *A Midsummer Night's
Dream* they no longer exist?

We know fairies do not exist, of course, but they do in the context of the
play in performance. We know that Falstaff dies in *Henry V* after being
rejected by Hal at the end of *2 Henry IV*, but he still retains a presence
in the work of art, which is a point that Elizabeth I herself apparently
registered.

During *2 Henry IV* the King dies but the principle of kingship
remains, sustained by the strategic advice to Hal to unite the
country against a foreign foe. But by the end of *Henry V*, the
Chorus tells us that all the victories secured by the new king are
subsequently lost by Henry VI, as earlier the three *Henry VI*
plays have shown.

Perhaps those who do not appreciate the Falstaffian world,
seeing it only as a contributory factor to the development
of a great prince, risk falling into the trap of believing that
these characters on stage have an extra-theatrical existence
and are 'real' people. Falstaff is not Sir John Oldcastle, nor
is Shakespeare's Prince Hal the Prince of Wales who became
Henry V, the victor of Agincourt, and who tragically died
young. They are linguistic representations, reconstructing the
past as a means of understanding the present, and, as Kiernan
Ryan has pointed out, extending the future.

'In these works we perceive Elizabethan realities transposed into the history of Henry IV, then filtered through the lens of futurity, which twists the plays out of line with convention and into their proleptic form. Parts 1 and 2 of Henry IV afford us nothing less than a preview of the past. They project us forward to a point where we can grasp Shakespeare's version of his times as the eventual past of a still unfolding future.'

Ryan, K. (2002: 66)

THE STORY IS NOT ENOUGH

These plays all work as great examples of art though the ages, like the anticipated fulfilment of love in the expectation of a kiss depicted in the static decoration of Keats's 'Ode on a Grecian Urn', or like the characters of Michelangelo's *Prisoners* (Michelangelo died in 1564, the year that Shakespeare was born) – freeing themselves to emerge from the marble of which they were sculpted.

Spotlight

We have reached a point in our journey through Shakespeare where we perceive that the story is not enough. As a younger man in conversation with the contemporary abstract artist Bridget Riley, I asked her who was the most influential artist on her work, expecting her in my naivety perhaps to say Mondrian, but her razor-sharp reply was 'Rembrandt, of course.' I realized that she saw beyond the form of the Rembrandt self-portraits, for example, to the ways in which they were constructed and that within those constructions lay the real art. So it is with Shakespeare.

2 *Henry IV* opens with Rumour, who habitually distorts the truth when addressing the audience:

> Open your ears; for which of you will stop
> The vent of hearing when loud Rumour speaks?

(1–2)

and within that play we find Prince John of Lancaster accused of distorting his 'word' in order to gain victory without the bloodshed of his soldiers. The rebels, or traitors – and more

later about the word 'treachery' in Chapter 20 on *Macbeth* –
are immediately arrested once the army is dispersed. They had
not listened to what Prince John has said to Hastings:

> You are too shallow, Hastings, much too shallow,
> To sound the bottom of the after-times
>
> (4.2.50–51)

and so when they complain of their eventual treatment he is
able to deflect their argument:

> I promis'd you redress of these same grievances
> Whereof you did complain; which, by mine honour,
> I will perform with a most Christian care.
> But, for you rebels, look to taste the due
> Meet for rebellion and such acts as yours.
>
> (4.2.113–17)

This is no distortion of the 'word' but rather the 'word' is defined
by the powerful, those who draw up the contracts and then enact
them. In Shylock's case, in *The Merchant of Venice*, he tries, as
we have seen, to be too clever in order to have his revenge on
Antonio, but here Prince John is upholding the authority of his
father, to whom he refers as God's 'substitute' (4.2.28).

Henry V

The term 'God's substitute' is one that causes Henry IV
some anxiety since he had deposed and had murdered God's
substitute, King Richard II. Even though in Act 4 of *Richard II*
Bolingbroke says 'In God's name I'll ascend the regal throne'
(4.1.113), this anxiety remains throughout the *Henry IV* plays
and accounts for the King's political troubles. It is an issue that
surfaces again in *Henry V* where King Henry V prays before the
Battle of Agincourt:

> Not today, O lord,
> O not today, think not upon the fault
> My father made in compassing the crown!
>
> (4.1.288–90)

and goes on to say that he has had Richard reburied and paid for prayers for his soul. Even though things have moved on, the issue remains and causes Hal some difficulty on the eve of the famous battle against the French.

POLITICAL JUSTIFICATION FOR WAR

What justification is there for this war? In the opening scenes of the play, the Church, represented by the Archbishop of Canterbury, makes a long and complex case for the war, which Henry needs in order to invade France. But why does Canterbury do so? Because, as the opening scene demonstrates, the Church is likely to lose 'the better half of our possession' (1.1.8) through an act going through the Commons (Parliament). The King has the power to prevent the act, so he has been promised money by the Church for the war on which he wishes to embark. Canterbury and Ely's exaggerated admiration of the King in Act 1, Scene 1 shows the Bishops to be flatterers in the cause of their ecclesiastical self-protection, as much as the convoluted justification over the important issue of succession for going to war gives the King the authority for the invasion he wishes to undertake. This is the complex politics of yesterday, of today and of the future as time moves on at its steady pace.

THE PRICKING OF CONSCIENCE

A counterpoint to the dissembling is provided, however, when, before the great Battle of Agincourt, the King wanders in disguise among his troops. Here he encounters an ethical challenge from Michael Williams, one of his soldiers, who states:

> … if the cause [of the war] be not good, the King himself hath a heavy reckoning to make when all those legs and arms and heads chopped off in a battle shall join together at the latter day and cry all 'We died at such a place' – some swearing, some crying for a surgeon, some upon their wives left poor behind them, some upon the debts they owe, some upon their children rawly left … Now if these men do not die well it will be a black matter for the King that led them to it, who to disobey were against all proportion of subjection.

The King attempts to refute the soldier's argument with different analogies, claiming that:

> ... the King is not bound to answer the particular endings of his soldiers, the father of his son, nor the master of his servant; for they purpose not their death when they purpose their services. Besides, there is no king, be his cause never so spotless, if it come to the arbitrement of swords, can try it out with all unspotted soldiers.

(4.1.132–9, 141–4, 153–9)

Does this exchange help to support a case for this being a subversive play, swinging the pendulum away from the Tillyardian heroic image we discussed in Chapter 12? Some critics, for example James Shapiro, Michael Wood and Katherine Duncan-Jones, direct attention from that line of questioning by pointing rather to the real expectation of the Earl of Essex as he sets out at the time of the play's composition for what would prove his disastrous campaign to quell the Irish rebellion. The point, however, is that this dialogue raises some important questions about the responsibility of the monarch, and Hal's response sounds hollow. It is worth noting that while Bates' and Williams' arguments are substantive, they remain loyal to the King. Here, in *Henry V*, the subversive role of Falstaff in questioning the values of war and honour (*1 Henry IV*, 5.1.129f.) is taken up by one of those 'mortal men' who, at Agincourt, could become 'food for powder' (*1 Henry IV*, 4.2.65–6).

'For a populace increasingly weary of being ruled by a slow and cautious old woman [Elizabeth I], Henry V re-enacted the greatness England had once achieved under a young King who was full of energy and military zeal. Henry's triumph at Agincourt also figured the triumph that many hoped would soon be achieved by Elizabeth's young favourite, Essex, in crushing the rebellion of Tyrone O'Neill in Ireland.'

Duncan-Jones, K. (2010: 125), *Shakespeare: An Ungentle Life*.
London: Methuen Drama

To an extent all the critics are right: Hal is a heroic king but there is also a subversion of that myth; there is an historical context but this play, as with the other plays, gestures towards a future in performance through the centuries, as it accumulates meanings that result from the pressures of historical context. This is the art of William Shakespeare's theatre, more accomplished than any dramatist before or since, in anticipating future meanings, but at the time of composition and first production, no doubt the dramatist's mind was able to turn quickly to the resurrection of Falstaff, if that was what the Queen, or even the market, required of him.

Key idea

We should regard and evaluate Shakespeare's English history plays not as 'histories' but as works of art, which can be endlessly refashioned and reinterpreted, looking to the past, the present and the future.

The Merry Wives of Windsor

In 1893 Verdi premiered his opera *Falstaff*, with a libretto by Arrigo Boito, based on *The Merry Wives of Windsor* and elements of *Henry IV*. Boito wrote a commentary in which he states that this adaptation is true modern and Latin lyric drama (or lyric comedy), which allows for an outpouring of grace, strength and gaiety. What was happening with the musical reorientation of the Shakespearean drama was, it appears, a luxuriating in the essence of what Boito and Verdi saw as an Italian tradition behind even the Shakespearean text, to create something different, a new form of communication based on an old one, creating in the process a new artistic masterpiece.

FALSTAFF IN LOVE

However, what Shakespeare had done was exactly the same when he responded – if the story is true – to Queen Elizabeth's demand that he should write a play about the character Falstaff in love. In 14 days, the legend goes, either after completing *Henry V* or between writing *1 Henry IV* and *2 Henry IV*, Shakespeare, luxuriating in what lay within the figure of Falstaff in his *Henry IV* plays, now created something different in *The Merry Wives of Windsor*. Using a different dramatic language and creating a different experience – and one that seems to have been heavily ironical – this play has an overweening Falstaff being punished for his presumption by the honest (and 'merry') wives of Windsor.

SAME APPEARANCE, DIFFERENT FUNCTION

If you compare the character of Falstaff in *The Merry Wives of Windsor* with that in the *Henry IV* plays, you may grasp that the creation of character involves both context and genre. Falstaff in a comic play serves a different function from Falstaff in a history play. He becomes, despite his name and outward appearance, a different character. He is in a different, not a sequential play.

The structure and ambience of *The Merry Wives of Windsor*, however, appears different also from other Shakespearean comedies. This is Shakespeare's only middle-class (bourgeois) domestic comedy. It does not operate according to the formula he uses, for example, in many of the comedies or romances from *The Comedy of Errors* to *The Tempest*, where he employs particular comic templates to frame the structure. The structure of *The Merry Wives of Windsor* is different in the way it uses a number of strands that compete for our attention. Here we are not, as in the *Henry IV* plays, embroiled in debates about the ethics of political power struggles which in themselves expose either the ethical vacuity or the ethical uncertainty of a civilization. Rather, we are confronted with a tradition of stock types or dramatized figures that go back, as Boito says, to Latin lyric comedy, to Giovanni Fiorentino and to the tragic farce of *commedia dell'arte* which was later to spawn such nineteenth-century operas as *Pagliacci* and *Falstaff*.

We have in *The Merry Wives of Windsor* the man fearful of his wife's infidelity, the female trickster, the affected lovers, the duping of a husband, the joy of a romp, an escape in a buck (laundry) basket, the cross-dressing of Falstaff as a woman, the conjuration of a fairy story, the darkness of a wood, all jumbled together and hinting at the traditional Shakespearean comic structure but finding it an impossible formula to follow for the farce that is being energetically enacted.

The play provides an opportunity in this regard for hilarious acting. Falstaff's account to Ford of his plight in the 'buck' (laundry) is a great piece of comic writing for the actor playing the part (3.5.82–114). We also have the only Shakespearean scene where 'drag' definitely takes place as Falstaff, disguised as the old woman of Brentford, Mother Prat, is beaten out of doors by Ford, 'I'll prat her!' (4.2.172–3). As Wells (2012: 111) notes, it is the single example in the Shakespearean canon where we can be certain that a man rather than a boy dresses as a woman. This is because the actor, who is a man, is in character and that character dresses as Mother Prat. Although not to the liking of Puritanical authorities, it is good popular entertainment, seen in comedy to the present day. Yet the stock characters themselves force on us the Saturnalian comic power of classical comedy, mixing it with English mythology: the fairies and the comic jolly fat man who in Victorian times becomes the image of Father Christmas.

Here in *The Merry Wives of Windsor*, perhaps a drama written for the Queen, we see the versatility of Shakespeare's art as an example of the kaleidoscopic patterning prevalent throughout his writings in whatever genre. It rarely fails to please, allowing scope for some virtuoso comic acting but demonstrating also some often hilarious virtuoso scripting by an author enjoying the relief of writing something a little different.

16

Critical perspectives 4: Tragedy – some modern critical challenges; *Titus Andronicus* (1591–2)

Tragedy exposes, in one form or another, from one ideological viewpoint or another, issues relating to individual identity within or as framed by the society that produces it and participates in it – as performer, reader, student, actor or audience. This and the following chapters on tragedy are necessarily selective in the line of enquiry taken and are designed to stimulate your thoughts and reactions to Shakespearean tragedy.

Through our discussion of the history plays you will have already encountered a modern critical movement known as new historicism. Stephen Greenblatt began his book, *Shakespearean Negotiations* (Oxford, 1988) with the sentence 'I began with the desire to speak with the dead.' No sooner, however, do you express the desire to engage with the past than your present 'voice' becomes entangled with those with whom you wish to converse. This is, perhaps, one of the paradoxes of the new historicist literary critical movement of the last two decades of the twentieth century and the first of the twenty-first: the history it seeks to uncover to elucidate an understanding of Shakespeare and his contemporaries is one being explored from the perspective of 'the present', and commentators impose their present sense of pattern and values on the past. But if this is so for us, it was also the case for Shakespeare, as we have seen in his history plays and indeed also in his tragedies, where he sees the past through the lens of his (and his culture's) current concerns.

Aristotle

The title pages of the early editions of some of Shakespeare's tragedies refer to them as 'tragical histories'. To understand the nature of tragedy it is useful to keep in mind the paradox of reading history or, indeed, of reading critics reading history. Traditionally, critics, in attempting to define tragedy, have tended to go back to Aristotle's *Poetics* and his definition of tragedy and particularly his notion of catharsis.

'*Tragedy is an imitation of an action that is admirable, complete and possesses magnitude; in language made pleasurable, each of its species separated in different parts; performed by actors, not through narration; effecting through pity and fear the purification of such emotions.*'

Aristotle, *Poetics*, trans. Malcolm Heath (1996: 10). Harmondsworth: Penguin. (Note: the Greek word *katharsis* is here translated as 'purification'. In other translations the word 'purgation' is preferred.)

So let us follow tradition by looking at traditional models but then proceed to examine the way in which twentieth- and twenty-first-century critics have challenged particularly Aristotle's applicability to Shakespearean tragedy. It is for you to decide for yourself, from this understanding, how you will approach, in particular, the four major Shakespearean tragedies: *Hamlet, King Lear, Othello* and *Macbeth*.

The traditional approach to tragedy begins by viewing the drama as a 'conflict' and the plot of the play as a 'knot', which the dramatic narrative proceeds to unravel. You may recall Viola's words in the comedy *Twelfth Night*: 'O time, thou must untangle this, not I,/It is too hard a knot for me t'untie' (2.3.40–41).

Key idea

The 'time' it takes to unravel the problems of the play becomes the play's process, in comedy and especially tragedy. The structure of tragedy, however, has also traditionally been seen as a pyramid, and is sometimes referred to as 'Freytag's pyramid' after the scholar Gustav Freytag (1816–95). This involves the following progression: Exposition, Rising Action, Climax, Falling Action, Catastrophe.

Early in his career, Shakespeare was influenced in writing tragedy by the Latin author Seneca (d. CE 65). *Titus Andronicus* (1591–2) is often referred to as 'Senecan' because of its excessive violence, but Seneca's plays were written not to be acted but to be read, usually out loud. Shakespeare may not have been quite as familiar with the Greek tragic dramatists Aeschylus, Sophocles or Euripides. Nevertheless, the main plot of *Hamlet*, to take a case in point, can be related to the classical structure that is described by Freytag's pyramid. In such a reading, the climax of the play is at the turning point, Act 3, Scene 3, when Hamlet fails to kill Claudius at prayer. The plot rises to this point and then falls back towards multiple deaths that occur in Act 5. The problem with such a definition, coming from an understanding of classical drama, however, is that it can come under strain tied to another Aristotelian feature, the notion of the three Unities, which we considered in our discussion of comedy. The Unities are of time (the action should take place in a single day); of place (the action should be in a single location); and of plot (there should be just a single plot or 'action').

Clearly, *Hamlet* does not conform to the Unities, and neither do Shakespeare's other tragedies. Shakespeare is not alone in this since, although they differ from each other in all sorts of ways, other Elizabethan and Jacobean tragedies also violate the Unities, as well as incorporating comic elements into their structures. This mixture of styles, characteristic of Elizabethan popular theatre, was something to which Sir Philip Sidney (1554–86) objected in his famous essay *The Apologie for Poetrie* (or *Defence of Poesie*), written *c.*1580 and published under the two different titles in 1595.

Spotlight

Traditionally, Elizabethan and Jacobean tragedy has been defined as consisting of three types:

* The first is *de casibus* tragedy, which shows the rise and fall of a great individual (as seen, for example, in the figure of Mortimer in Christopher Marlowe's play *Edward II* (1592) and, as we have earlier considered, Richard in Shakespeare's *Richard III)*.
* The second is revenge tragedy, sometimes also called the 'tragedy of blood'. This places an individual within a corrupt society failing to find justice through legal or religious institutions. See, for example, Thomas Kyd's *The Spanish Tragedy* (1589–92) or John Marston's *Antonio's Revenge* (1599–1601).
* The third is domestic tragedy, as exemplified in plays such as the anonymous *Arden of Faversham* (*c.*1592), which deals with issues that are implicitly rather than explicitly political but nevertheless have some links with the development and progress of the tragic plays we are to discuss.

Othello is often regarded as a 'domestic' tragedy and *King Lear* demonstrates a domesticity that has far-reaching public and hence political implications. *Othello* and *King Lear*, however, would be reduced by the categorization 'domestic tragedy', as would *Hamlet* by being termed merely a 'revenge tragedy' or *Macbeth* as a '*de casibus* tragedy'. Each is much more complex than such pigeonholing allows, and each is greater in reputation than any such reductive definition can adequately contain.

The influence of A. C. Bradley

Aristotle's definition of tragedy, written before the birth of Christ, was based on his experience of Greek tragedy and its affinity with ancient Greek religion. Whereas Aristotle saw comedy as being an 'imitation of inferior people', he saw tragedy as being an 'imitation of persons better than the average man'. He believed, nevertheless, that 'character' was subordinate to 'action'. The Romantic critics of the late eighteenth and early nineteenth century, however, privileged the personality of the tragic protagonist – Coleridge, for example, declared he 'had a smack of Hamlet' within his own personality.

In doing so, they helped spawn a hybrid Aristotelian view influencing the way in which the nineteenth and early twentieth centuries perceived Shakespearean tragedy. One of the most influential of the early twentieth-century critics was A. C. Bradley (1851–1935), whose book *Shakespearean Tragedy* first appeared in 1904 and continues to influence our contemporary understanding of tragedy, although from the 1930s onwards it has sparked controversy.

Bradley's theory of tragedy owed much to the nineteenth-century philosopher G. W. F. Hegel (1770–1831), whose model of conflict and resolution bore certain similarities to the Aristotelian theory of tragic catharsis, variously understood as 'purgation' or 'purification'. This concept refers to the emotional state in which the audience finds itself at the completion of the tragic action. Through the play, feelings of pity and terror are created in the spectators and at the end these emotions and feelings are released, purged, purified and brought back into balance. This is tragic catharsis. C. L. Barber (1959), as we saw earlier, detected something similar happening in comedy when, in the conclusions of the plays, he holds that there is a 'release through clarification'. Tragic catharsis can allow the audience to feel elated at what they have witnessed while at the same time relieved that they experienced the tragedy vicariously through the agency of the fate of the protagonist.

The tragic protagonist

The protagonist, the main character in the play, is usually someone of high rank who suffers a reversal of fortune, sometimes brought about by his own pride, hubris, and his refusal to compromise. He is blind to the consequences of his pride and his actions lead to his downfall, but towards the end of the play there is the moment of recognition, anagnorisis, in which the blindness is lifted and he achieves a modicum of self-knowledge. That, however, comes too late for him to avoid the consequences of his actions. Thus, in the face of defeat, the protagonist reveals admirable human qualities. This led Bradley to lament the inconsolable 'waste' that we are left with at the end of the tragic action.

THE REACTION TO BRADLEY

In 1933 L. C. Knights published an essay, 'How Many Children Had Lady Macbeth?', which challenged some of Bradley's assumptions. Knights exposed in the very title of the essay the absurdity of thinking that Shakespeare's characters have an independent and individual life outside the confines of the play. He insisted on a close examination and appreciation of the language of the plays. Later, in *Drama and Society in the Age of Jonson* (1937), influenced by the social historian R. H. Tawney, Knights widened this critical emphasis to take into account historical, social and political issues. This began a shift away from critical attitudes founded on 'character', which had owed much to the influence of the nineteenth-century novel, to an appreciation of much wider issues that need to be considered.

Text and performance

If we return to Aristotle, he tells us that it is 'the events, i.e. the elements of plots, that are most important in tragedy' and that plot or 'action is the most important thing of all'. As early as 1933, E. E. Stoll, in *Art and Artifice in Shakespeare*, identified 'stock characters' in Elizabethan drama, an observation taken further by Bernard Spivack in his *Shakespeare and the Allegory of Evil* (1958). (See Chapters 13 and 18.) Spivak established a link between the figure of Richard III and Iago in *Othello*, suggesting that they had their origins within the tradition of the Vice figure of the medieval morality plays. From various viewpoints, other critics such as David Bevington and Robert Weimann explored the ways in which aspects of a popular tradition in medieval drama influenced Shakespeare's plays, while O. B. Hardison Jnr focused on the influence of Christian liturgy on medieval drama itself and thereby offered an alternative historical foundation for the development of Elizabethan drama.

Critical debate towards the end of the twentieth century was to intensify. A group of critics led by J. L. Styan, Stanley Wells and John Russell Brown, who owed much to the influence of the theatre director Harley Granville-Barker earlier in the century, began to look at the plays not as literary artefacts but as blueprints for performance; indeed, they were highly influential on critics such as myself in the development of my Text and Performance series of Shakespeare and his contemporaries. The Text and Performance critics tried to reconcile literary critical studies with the insistence that the plays only really come fully to life in the theatre where they are performed.

Meaning by Shakespeare

If tragedy is concerned with action rather than character, that action may be informed and, indeed, determined by social and political contexts beyond the text of the play, and these traces of the contexts maybe recovered either through critical evaluation or recognized in performance. In 1992 Terence Hawkes, in *Meaning by Shakespeare*, argued that modern scholars impose their own meanings on Shakespeare without fully realizing what they are doing. Thus critics imposed their ideologies upon the texts without a full understanding, or indeed acknowledgement, of how they were being influenced.

The landscape of critical opinion was further informed by fundamental issues relating to the notion of tragedy itself. While new historicism saw the need to locate dramatic texts in the culture of their historical moment as a means of locating historical pressures, the cultural materialists, drawing on a long dissident tradition of Marxist and socialist thought, questioned the fundamental emphasis on character in tragedy, preferring the post-structuralist category of 'subjectivity' and the complex social pressures within which it was produced. Following on from the Marxist rejection of the notion of the bourgeois 'individual' which had informed much of the characterization of the tragic protagonist since the end of the eighteenth century, emphasis now came to be placed upon how the protagonist was 'produced'.

In this regard, the writings of theatre dramatists and theoreticians such as Bertolt Brecht, who, as we saw in Chapter 9, challenged the Aristotelian methods implicit in theatre production, became highly influential on critical attitudes in the last decades of the twentieth century. His distinction between Aristotelian 'Dramatic Theatre' and his own 'Epic Theatre' took the emphasis away from the individual at the centre of the play, placing the drama directly within a social and political dimension, preferring, thereby, to expose the ways in which the tragic protagonists were produced by the political situation in which they find themselves. Brecht was an enthusiastic aficionado of Elizabethan drama, emphasizing in particular the ways in which these plays demonstrated a theatrical self-consciousness that 'realism' and 'naturalism' in the theatres sought to disguise.

The individual and society

The concept of the 'individual', however, had evolved not so much from Aristotle as from differing Christian concepts of the self, which some critics strongly challenged. Jonathan Dollimore, in *Radical Tragedy* [1984/1989: 153], insisted on a Marxist materialist interpretation of the individual: 'It is not the consciousness of men that determines their being, but, on the contrary, their social being that determines their consciousness.' In the late 1940s and 1950s Brecht had challenged what he took to be Aristotelian theatre and its alleged capacity to draw the spectator into identifying with the tragic protagonist at the expense of forsaking her/his critical distance from the action. In the 1930s Antonin Artaud augmented this challenge to accepted modes of appreciation, developing the concept of the Theatre of Cruelty:

> '[The Theatre of Cruelty is] theatre's need to steep itself in the wellsprings of infinitely stirring and sensitive poetry, to reach the furthest removed, the most backward and inattentive part of the audience, achieved by a return to ancient primal Myths, not through the script but the production, will not be solely required to incarnate and particularly to bring these ancient conflicts up to date. That is to say, the themes will be transferred straight on to the stage but incarnated in moves, expressions and gestures, before gushing out in words. In this way we can repudiate theatre's superstition concerning the script and the author's autocracy.'
>
> Artaud, A., 'The Theatre of Cruelty: Second Manifesto' (1938), *The Theatre and Its Double* (1970: 82–3), trans. Victor Corti. London: Calder & Boyars

Artaud's desire to distance the autocracy of the author and 'repudiate theatre's superstition concerning the script' in the late 1930s was the complete opposite of the bardolatory of the nineteenth-century Romantic Movement. His desire to bring the ancient myths of classical plays, for example, 'up to date' presaged a movement in Shakespearean study and performance in the 1960s and 1970s, with the writings, for example, of Jan Kott in *Shakespeare Our Contemporary* (1967) and the practice of eminent and influential British theatre directors, most notably Peter Brook (see below).

Tragedy and catharsis

The Aristotelian concept of tragedy was subsequently attacked by the South American dramatic theorist Augusto Boal (*Theater of the Oppressed*, 1974, trans. 1979), who saw in it a coercive mechanism that was specifically designed historically to ensure political harmony in a culture sustained by slavery. Boal's analysis could also be applied to any form of drama that demanded a return to social and emotional 'balance'. The concept of hamartia, or the protagonist's tragic flaw, and the retribution it provokes, is cited by Boal as a method of reinforcement of social control. In his view, tragedy creates a means of sacrificing the protagonist in order to guarantee conformity to the prevailing ethos. Thus the whole notion of catharsis as an emotional rebalancing of purgation and purification is critically questioned as being both coercive and a reaffirmation of the legitimacy of a dominant political force.

Aristotle's concept of tragedy in the *Poetics* nevertheless remains an important document from which interpretations concerning tragedy and Shakespeare's tragedies derive, but since the latter years of the twentieth century the challenges made to it have opened up debate and led to various kinds of theatrical experimentation. Much modern critical opinion respects the fact that, when we look for meanings in Shakespeare, we may actually be consciously or unconsciously imposing our own meanings upon him from our various ideologically informed viewpoints. Shakespeare's tragedies not only survive such debates but they gain from them, in the effectiveness of contemporary criticism and production.

A cruel play for cruel ages: *Titus Andronicus*

In 1955 the renowned British director Peter Brook revived Shakespeare's early tragedy *Titus Andronicus*, with Laurence Olivier and Vivien Leigh, in an uncompromising, violent production at Stratford-upon-Avon, which had some of the audience fainting at the barbarity displayed. It is important for you to recall that Elizabethan England was a violent place. In the time of Shakespeare, for example, criminals and religious dissenters, labelled as traitors, were executed as a public spectacle in the cruellest of ways – first hung, then taken down and, while still alive, castrated, their bowels drawn from them and lastly their heart removed still beating and shown to them as they died. They were then beheaded and quartered, with their limbs being sent to various parts of the country, not only as a warning to others but also to ensure that, on the day of Christian resurrection, they would find it hard to rise from the dead.

These Tyburn executions were public spectacles, in which enterprising local home owners rented out seats and viewing positions, while others sold refreshments. (See MacGregor, N. [2012] and Crawforth, H., Dustager, S., Young, J. [2015].) John Foxe's (1516–87) *Acts and Monuments* (1563), published frequently during Shakespeare's lifetime and known as 'Book of Martyrs', records the earlier horrific Protestant martyrdoms during the reign (1553–8) of the Catholic Queen Mary Tudor.

The 'revenge tragedy' *Titus Andronicus* depicts the horrific rape and mutilation of Lavinia by Demetrius and Chiron, sons of the Goth queen Tamora, who becomes the wife of the Roman Emperor Saturninus. The action of the play culminates in Titus killing his violently abused and desecrated daughter 'and thy shame (die) with thee'. His final act of revenge is to serve Tamora's dead sons, who defiled Lavinia, in a pie to be eaten by Tamora and the Emperor before he then slays the Empress. He in turn is killed by the Emperor Saturninus. This violent play written in a violent age was adapted by Brook for audiences only too aware of the Nazi barbarities in the Second World War, and also of the contemporary threats of the Cold War.

The violent atrocities of the play itself were popular with its first Elizabethan audiences, some of whom, no doubt, would have watched public executions. In one sense it was an easier play with which to challenge traditional notions of tragedy in the theatre, but Brook's famous production signalled a brave attempt to defy convention. Aristotelian catharsis was never a part of the ending of this play but Brook was later to produce a *King Lear* (1962–4) where the focus, too, was on cruelty, bleakness and contemporary relevance. His assistant director, Charles Marowitz, was subsequently to 'deconstruct' Shakespeare's plays, shattering them like a 'precious vase' in order to rebuild them for modern audiences because he thought that they had become too familiar with them (and therefore too complacent about them).

Whether, however, this bloody revenge play by Shakespeare was merely gratuitous and audience pleasing or a part of a process of learning his craft by imitating Seneca is still a matter for debate. Further modern productions have continued to expose the underlying brutality and violence of 'civilized' society itself. Perhaps in that, however, they were beginning to realize Shakespeare's vision, even at this early stage in his career, of the terrors present within historical, political regimes and within the society ruled over by the Tudor dynasty.

18

Othello (1604)

While *The Merchant of Venice* raises issues of anti-Semitism and *The Taming of the Shrew* misogyny, *Othello, the Moor of Venice* inevitably raises issues of racism when it is performed in the twenty-first century. But racism takes many forms: racism exists within what we think of as the black community and also within the white community, in addition to the racism that pits white against black or black against white. In a modern civilized society we need to talk about, analyse carefully, and thereby expose, individual and institutionalized racism as much as we need to talk about violence, or sexual gender, or religious discrimination.

In June 2015 a new RSC production of *Othello* opened in Stratford-upon-Avon, directed by Iqbal Khan with black actors playing both Othello and Iago. This production, with Hugh Quarshie playing Othello and Lucian Msamati Iago, re-energized the confrontational nature of a play in which Shakespeare may have deliberately frustrated expectations and through which he displays an unusually clear understanding of the outsider in society. This production was designed as a fresh artistic realization and dynamic interpretation of a performance script written more than 400 hundred years ago.

Louise Wise, in an interview with both actors, noted:

> 'This is an *Othello* in which race relations are turned on their head. With Iago's skin now much darker than his commander's, the reasons for the one's crime and the other's credulity become so much more intriguing. It's a definite resetting of the so-called "Othello Music".'
>
> *The Sunday Times*, 'Culture' section, 24 May 2015, pp. 8–9

In 1998 Hugh Quarshie gave a lecture at the University of Alabama, on which a subsequent paper for the International Shakespeare Association was based, in which he raised an important issue that both the paper, and, more recently, the 2015 production, tackled. He states that black actors should continue to play the role of Othello but asks:

> 'Without such casting, is it still possible to stage *Othello* without endorsing racist conventions? I think we have to accept that *Othello* is a seriously flawed play. But with some judicious cutting and textual emendation ... I think it would be possible to produce a version of the play which shifts the focus away from race and on to character. It might still be impossible to avoid the conclusion that Othello behaves as he does because he's black; but it might be possible to suggest that he does so ... because he is a black man responding to racism, not giving a pretext for it.'
>
> Hugh Quarshie (1999: 21), 'Second Thoughts about *Othello*'. Chipping Camden: International Shakespeare Association Occasional Paper, No. 7

Approaching the play in this way was what prompted in 2015 a multicultural production which was at times horrific in its representation of contemporary state-authorized tortures that were well beyond the play's own images of Islamic and Christian cultures, while at the same time offering an interesting portrayal of Emilia, influenced, it would appear, by Indian mysticism. Racism was present within the tensions of the multicultural society that the production depicted. Iago's motive was made perfectly clear from the opening scene: he had been overlooked and humiliated by Cassio's promotion and hated both him and the Moor with a deep desire for vengeance. This was no comic Vice figure from medieval drama – as some Iagos in the past have been – but a seriously disturbed man who hated to be touched physically and was obsessive, fastidiously cleansing his hands, rubbing his head, arranging furniture precisely on the stage set and wiping spots from the stage floor. This obsessive conduct grew through the performance. It was a frightening depiction of a man who, in the contemporary world of 2015, might have been at home within the brutally limited so-called Islamic State.

Othello, by contrast, was portrayed by Quarshie as a calm character, too calm perhaps compared to the traditional evaluations of the role, and, predictably, to which his critics clearly objected. Consequently, the 'madness' or 'epilepsy' scene (Act 4, Scene 1) and the 'It is the cause' soliloquy (5.2.1–22) were downplayed, with emphasis placed on the psychological fragility of a figure entrusted with the defence of Venice but who exists within a manipulative society of which Iago is a representative figure. The multicultural dimension on which this production depended insisted on the global nature of conflict manifested within the context of contemporary international anxieties. In other words, Quarshie, with his director and fellow actors, demonstrated that *Othello* could be relevant in a world where racism remains prevalent in language, culture and attitude and where those who wield power find it impossible to combat evil without practising violence themselves.

The work of the left-wing dramatist Edward Bond at the end of the twentieth century was violent because, as he states, 'Violence shapes and obsesses our society, and if we do not stop being violent we have no future.' (Bond, E. [1972: v], Author's Preface, *Lear*. London: Methuen). So it is with racism in the multicultural world that is the global village.

Shakespeare's *Othello* is about racism and modern productions of the play cannot avoid depicting issues that we confront in our own society. The 2015 production did not succeed entirely in resolving difficulties, but its direction of travel was logical and, rightly, confrontational in its exposure of controversial issues that it was able to develop from Shakespeare's text.

We can gauge the extent and the complexity of the problem from the following quotation by the feminist critic Catherine Belsey:

> *'In written works it matters who addresses whom, in what situation and with what authority. When the works in question are fictional, it matters that we differentiate between the fictional speaker and the text. The views of the villain are probably contrary to what the audience is invited to believe: Iago's racism and misogyny, for example, should not necessarily be taken for the play's.'*
>
> Belsey, C. (1999: 14–15), *Shakespeare and the Loss of Eden: The Construction of Family Values in Early Modern Culture.* Basingstoke: Macmillan

Othello's credulity

Othello has tantalized critics and audiences with questions through the centuries. How could Othello be so credulous as to be duped through insinuation, and over a handkerchief? What is the motive for Iago's villainy? What are the politics behind the play? Dramatically, the black general and the white ensign make a powerful visual statement on stage. It is not necessarily the main statement of the play, but it is one indicative of its level of tension, whether it involves black and black or white and white. Racists and bigots exist, and the list of oppositions they produce is lengthy: for example, Christian and Jew, Protestant and Catholic, Capulet and Montague. Shakespeare exposes in drama how individuals become victims of discriminatory attitudes, of social mores, and we have to judge whether, in the context of our society rather than his, we can interpret and perform them with their tensions as challenging artefacts for contemporary audiences, in what is our own violent, racist world.

Certainly, in Shakespeare's play, Iago uses the colour of Othello's skin, particularly in the opening scenes, to promote a prejudicial opinion of the military leader. Shakespeare parodies Iago by placing in his mouth a series of coarse animalistic descriptions of which the following is perhaps the most striking: 'Even now, now, very now, an old black ram/Is tupping your white ewe!' (1.1.87–8). This is the language of extreme right-wing fascism and, as we know, such ultra far-right-wing prejudices are still, sadly, to be found within established political opinion in the West. Shakespeare could not have known this but this tension still comes through in the play in modern interpretation and performance. Iago's gruff, insulting language is in marked contrast to the measured dignified language employed by Othello when, for example, Brabantio comes with others to arrest him. The dignified General politely assumes control:

> Keep up your bright swords, for the dew will rust them.
>
> Good signior, you shall more command with years
>
> Than with your weapons.

$$(1.2.59–61)$$

Spotlight

What emerges from the play's dramatic structure is an awareness of a whole series of developing oppositions and a process of manipulation into which the audience is drawn by being invited to form judgements that the dramatic characters themselves have prompted. Of course, it is the playwright who is manipulating the dramatic characters and audience alike, making available to each different levels of knowledge. This mechanism, which critics have called 'discrepant awareness', is a familiar strategy in the comedies where the audience is given information denied to the characters themselves. But in the tragedies, and in *Othello* in particular, it is a major source of tragic irony in that it allows us to see clearly the errors of judgement that the protagonist is forced into making.

Stereotypes

In *Macbeth*, as we will see in Chapter 20, there is equivocation. What may have been popularly considered to be 'foul' is made to look 'fair' and vice versa. Something similar occurs in this play in the interaction of black and white. We also find it in Shakespeare's Sonnet 147, where the dramatist draws a relationship between darkness, evil, night and hell:

> For I have sworn thee fair, and thought thee bright,
>
> Who art as black as hell, as dark as night.

> (13–14)

Some of this, at first sight at least, might offend modern sensibilities, but putting aside the fact for the moment that Shakespeare was writing 400 years ago, we might ask what he is making of such stereotypical images and contradictions in *Othello*? What we find is that Shakespeare turns the stereotype, Iago, who in some measure does have a relationship with the Vice figure in medieval drama, into a white exemplar of an evil, manipulative and dishonest individual. The reason for his success for most of the play is that he preys upon fears and anxieties with which his victims identify: Brabantio is anxious about his daughter, as any patriarch would be, and that anxiety spreads fears of miscegenation, a prejudice that lurks underneath the surface of Venice and that Iago mobilizes as he pursues his evil scheme. Similarly, Othello is represented both as a black 'outsider' or 'stranger' and a 'Noble Moor', both of which are stereotypes. Thus the play expresses clear racial attitudes and in that reflection, no doubt, racist tendencies within Elizabethan society, indicated in some of the laws that were passed excluding 'Moors' from England.

Scholarship has found, for example, that in 1596 the Queen had 'ten blackmoors (of which kind of people there are already here too many)' deported and urged her subjects to give up Moors as servants in favour of their 'own countrymen than with those kind of people'. Julia Briggs observes that 'the intolerance of the Queen and her officials is even more distressing in view of the fact that most, if not all, of the Africans in England had been brought over by force rather than choice' (Briggs, J. [1997: 95–6], *This Stage-play World: Text and Contexts, 1580–1625*. Oxford: Oxford University Press).

Key idea

Shakespeare dares to expose these prejudices on stage, reversing the norm of his society's expectation. He places virtue with black, evil with white. In doing so he places naivety and goodness with the outsider and exploitation and offence with the Christian European community, foregrounding the foul-mouthed insults and malign actions of the manipulator, Iago, who is both jealous and vengeful. He is, thereby, questioning the moral norms of his own society and its hypocrisy.

Othello the outsider

Shakespeare would probably have known that the Republic of Venice depended for its defence on mercenary soldiers. Outsiders were appointed because Venice was a trading republic and not a military state. One of the play's literary sources, a novella, Cinthio's *Gli Hecatommithi*, first published in 1565, stimulated Shakespeare's imagination, although some elements of *Othello* are found in embryo in the earlier play *The Merchant of Venice*. What if a prominent outsider fell in love with a daughter of a member of the Venetian ruling class and eloped with her? If, at the same time, Venice were to be in danger from the Turks, how would the politicians react? Would they support the father of the woman who had eloped or try to appease him?

The hypocrisy of government was as much a subject for theatrical exploitation in Shakespeare's day as it is now. If necessary, the outsider would be tolerated whatever he had done – and in this play we are never quite sure what he has done since the dramatist implies that the father at first encouraged Othello's relationship with his daughter (1.3.129f.). Make the outsider 'black' and the dramatic potential is even greater.

Othello intensifies the theme of the outsider, which Shakespeare had developed before in some of the comedies, most notably *The Merchant of Venice*, but in that comedy his treatment of that outsider (Morocco) reflects rather badly on Portia. In the later play, Brabantio's curious treatment of Othello, guided by Iago's and Roderigo's insinuation, points towards a deep-seated fear of miscegeny that lies beneath the surface of the claim that Venice was known to be hospitable to strangers.

Craftsmanship

In its craftsmanship, *Othello* confirms what we have already seen as the underlying structure of problems, journeys, arrivals, complications and silence.

The problem is threefold:

▸ First, Othello, the outsider, has secretly married Brabantio's daughter, Desdemona.

▸ Secondly, the Turks are attacking the Venetian island of Cyprus.

▸ Thirdly, there is the malevolence of Iago towards the General, allegedly as a result of being passed over for promotion.

The journey takes the protagonist to Cyprus, and to a location on the border between Venice and the Ottoman Empire where the Turkish fleet is destroyed. One problem has been solved but others remain. It is on the Cyprus frontier that Iago develops his plot to destroy Othello with jealousy, and he succeeds to the point where Desdemona is publicly abused and finally murdered. The scene of her death begins with an erroneous self-justification on Othello's part that involves an appeal for justice but in a nameless cause.

But herein lies the complication. The actual self-knowledge or anagnorisis occurs only after Desdemona has been killed, and it is followed by the protagonist's own characterization of the problem in terms of a confrontation between a 'Venetian' and a 'turbaned Turk'. The result is the death of the protagonist by suicide, although the act itself is expressed in terms of the conflict between a 'Venetian' and an 'outsider'. The 'Hellish' agent of the destruction, Iago, meanwhile, remains steadfastly silent but it is expected that torture will loosen his tongue: 'The time, the place, the torture: O, enforce it!' (5.2.369). Of course, when Iago next speaks, the play will begin again, rather like the tale that Horatio promises to tell at the end of Hamlet: the play advertises its future performances.

Iago's motivation

There has been much debate, particularly since the early nineteenth century, about Iago's motive for what he does. Coleridge coined the term 'motiveless malignity' to explain his behaviour. But that debate leads us into the Bradleyan fallacy, which endows a fictional character with a human reality. Of course, in rehearsal, actors such as Lucian Msamati try to find a motive for Iago's scheme. The works of E. A. J. Honigmann may also be useful to actors in the distinction he makes between the 'motiveless malignity' and the character's 'contemptuousness'. He refers to the passage at 1.3.384f.:

> ... I hate the Moor
> And it is thought abroad that 'twixt my sheets
> He's done my office. I know not if't be true,
> But I for mere suspicion in that kind
> Will do as if for surety.

The speech concludes with:

> The Moor is of a free and open nature
> That thinks men honest that but seem to be so,
> And will as tenderly be led by th'nose
> As asses are.
> I have't, it is engendered! Hell and night
> Must bring this monstrous birth to the world's light.

In an unpublished conversation with me, Terry Hands, the director of the 1985 RSC production with Ben Kingsley as

Othello and David Suchet as Iago, was quite explicit about his advice. Iago is jealous because he has been passed over for promotion and also because Othello, whom he loves, has fallen in love with Desdemona. In such a theatre-based interpretation, Iago transposes his own jealousy on to the one he loves, driving Othello to distraction and murder. This is a useful example of how a 'theatre director' motivates an interpretation from actors.

What may interest us further is that it is the white man, Iago, who is summoning hell and night. The conflict between fair and foul is not initially, or indeed ultimately, between Othello and Desdemona but between Othello and Iago. Shakespeare in this respect may have manipulated Elizabethan racial assumptions and expectations by reversing that which was thought to be evil with that which was assumed to be good on the part of his contemporary audience. The complication arises because Othello initially disregards his skin colour, as does Desdemona, but the action and society force him to become consistent with his appearance as they, or at least one of their number, force him to move from 'noble Moor' to 'black devil'. Both alternatives are kept before us throughout the play, and this division within the figure of the protagonist remains at the end as Shakespeare wrote it. There is racism in this play, just as there is violence in the plays of Edward Bond, which raises tough questions of the audience in exposing and not reinforcing prejudices.

Truth and falsehood

Whether portrayed by a black or a white actor, Iago is created as a manipulative character inviting the spectators on the stage and in the theatre into his confidence, thus setting up a bridge between the fictional world of the play and the extra-theatrical reality of the audience. In this, he certainly resembles the medieval figure of Vice, attracting and amusing spectators, inviting their complicity and diverting them with comedy. Shakespeare has created a confidence trickster that the audience may well find attractive.

There may be critical debate over Iago's motives, but those he does reveal are always plausible even if they are, sometimes, by his own admission, fanciful. In being taken into his humour, the audiences gradually realize that they too are victims of liking and trusting him. His appeals to them are part of the complex web of suggestion and persuasion that involves questions of proof and the manipulation of evidence; indeed, it is no accident that the play raises issues of 'truth' and 'falsehood' that the audience cannot fully resolve. For example, what has led up to Desdemona's elopement? What has her father done to encourage the relationship between her and Othello? Who is Bianca? What is her relationship with Cassio?

In short, the audience is asked to go through the same process of evaluating evidence that Roderigo, Brabantio, Cassio and, finally, Othello are confronted with on stage. There, only the Duke of Venice relies on established fact, withholding judgement about the destination of the Turkish fleet until he has received all the evidence about its strategic movements, and this exemplary behaviour is preceded by two examples (Roderigo and, especially, Brabantio) where the evidence has already been distorted by Iago to have the desired effect on his victims. What happens to them (and later to Cassio) are dry runs for the much more devastating assault on Othello.

Even when audiences reflect on Othello's tragic error in accepting Iago's story about the whereabouts and destiny of Desdemona's handkerchief as proof of her infidelity, they remain divided both within and outside the frame of the illusion that Shakespeare has created. William Empson, in his essay 'Honest in Othello', noted over 50 uses of the words 'honesty' or 'honest' in the play. (Peter Davison's count in *The Critics Debate* is 56 [1988: 50].) This repetition, as Empson suggests, allows the words to accumulate irony, similar to the way in which Mark Antony's subtle manipulation of his onstage audience in *Julius Caesar* (1599) in the 'Friends, Romans, countrymen' speech (3.2.74f.) gradually undermines the case that Brutus has already made for the murder of Caesar. *Othello* contains a further twist to this rhetorical subtlety since the audience, unlike the characters, having been taken in by Iago, come to realize just how hollow the epithet 'honest' is when applied to the character. Of course, all the manipulation is Shakespeare's, as he creates an engagement with but eventual withdrawal from Iago's character.

Who is the protagonist?

One issue that has interested critics, commentators and theatre practitioners alike is the question of who the protagonist is in *Othello*. Is it Iago or Othello, or both? Martin Wine discusses the relationship between the two characters in twentieth-century productions:

'We cannot be sure how Iago was played in Shakespeare's day. Possibly he ... was hissed and booed as a Machiavellian villain. But there seems no doubt that Richard Burbage's Othello, remembered and praised long after his death, was not too small for the Globe stage. We do not know who his Iago was.'

Wine, M. L. (1984: 66), *Othello: Text and Performance*. London: Macmillan

A balance has to be found to sustain the relationship between the two characters across the entire play. Some Iagos have tried to dominate the play through their humour and their studied intimacy with the audience. Some have been kept down by 'star' performers in the role of Othello. When balance is lost, so are integrity and coherence. This balance permits us to think of *Othello* as a play involving a fall, through manipulation. Shakespeare exposes a love being led to destruction, with the protagonist-turned-murderer asking pitifully, 'Where should Othello go?' (5.2.271). There is nowhere for him to go. It is Iago, ironically, who takes a vow of silence: 'From this time forth I never will speak word' (5.2.303). He is, as Greenblatt says, 'cut off from original motive and final disclosure. The only termination possible in his case is not revelation but silence' (1980: 236–7). Silence is silence but the causes of silence vary. As Wine succinctly puts it, Iago's retreat into silence places him 'once and for all outside the pale of humanity' (1984: 35).

Spotlight

In contrast to his treatment of Iago, Shakespeare almost parodies his tragic creation of the Moor, who calls for quiet before embarking on a rhetorical tour de force: 'Soft you, a word or two before you go' (5.2.338). The 'Soft you' calls for the audience's attention as much as it does for that of the characters on stage:

Speak of me as I am. Nothing extenuate,

Nor set down aught in malice. Then must you speak

Of one that loved not wisely, but too well;

Of one not easily jealous, but, being wrought,

Perplexed in the extreme; of one whose hand,

Like the base Indian, threw a pearl away

Richer than all his tribe;

(5.2.342–8)

The protagonist here gives an epilogue before killing himself. Shakespeare is still tempting us to question, to judge. Do we agree or disagree? Is this what we have witnessed? Is this a perverse judgement that Othello turns upon himself as a means of rectifying the murder he has committed? Is this justice? Of course, in dramatic terms the active protagonist cannot be allowed to sink into inactivity. Othello's ending is a dramatization of the main conflict in the play, and it is one that is geographically located on a frontier between the ideal republic (Venice), which, as in *The Merchant of Venice*, falls a little short of the 'ideal', and her hostile adversary (the Turks):

And say besides that in Aleppo once,

Where a malignant and a turbanned Turk

Beat a Venetian and traduced the state,

I took by th'throat the circumcised dog

And smote him – thus!

(5.2.352–6)

Shakespeare portrays Othello, the outsider, as acting for Venice to the last, executing himself as he had done her traditional 'malignant' enemy. We may wonder if, through the machinations of the Iago character, Shakespeare may have been prompting us to consider still whether this fictional man was himself a victim of the Venetian state or whether, as he claims, a figure who 'loved not wisely but too well'. In a world still riven by racial and religious conflict, it is for us to decide and for us to reconsider, as it will be for the generations that follow.

19

King Lear (1605–6)

In our journey through Shakespeare's plays, we have now come to the play that many consider to be his finest achievement, *King Lear*. It is a play widely regarded today as one of the most significant works of art in Western culture. It emphasizes a more extreme version of Hamlet's 'slings and arrows of outrageous fortune' (*Hamlet*, 3.1.58), boldly placing them on stage as an expression of the precarious realities of experience.

If we begin to interpret the play, however, through, for example, Aristotelian theories of audience reaction (catharsis), we have to take care that we do not obscure the difficulties that are not fully or satisfactorily resolved at the end. Are we offered anything to offset the bleakness of the play's vision, and is all restored in the conclusion to some sort of 'balance'?

Modern materialist criticism, as exemplified by Terry Eagleton, Malcolm Evans or Terence Hawkes, provides different radical perceptions of the play. John Drakakis notes that Eagleton's materialist approach, for example, is one where '*King Lear* generates a rhetoric which devalues language'. It thereby 'introduces a contradiction into the process of sign production whereby language is urged to surpass material reality at the same time as it is contained by it' (Drakakis, J. [1996: 388–9]).

Similarly, if we look within the play for a universal value statement, we will be deluding ourselves about the nature of the work. Modern audiences or readers, for example, question the misogyny present in the work, just as they ask questions about the anti-Semitism of *The Merchant of Venice* or the racism in *Othello*.

Key idea

King Lear portrays the absurdity, vacuity and chaos upon which humanity seeks to impose order. It does so within the confines of an established dramatic structure that Shakespeare deliberately frustrates and strains to the very limit, affirming thereby his faith in the communicative function of art itself.

'Feminist doubts about King Lear ... come up in the discussion of the apparently excessive nature of the play's misogyny. They [are] also raised in relation to the play's ending and Lear's appropriation of Cordelia. No one who discusses the play with women or girls today can be very confident in asserting that its values are "timeless" or "universal"; teachers find themselves apologizing for Shakespeare's enthusiastic endorsement of what is at last being widely seen as the unfair and unjustifiable ideology of patriarchy ... We can still find King Lear an excellent play in its own terms, but we must be aware that those terms are no longer our terms.'

Thompson, A. (1988: 76), *King Lear, The Critics Debate*. Basingstoke: Macmillan

This is a play that, however excellent in itself, needs to be handled with great care and for the twenty-first century it presents a very real challenge. Ann Thompson, earlier in her *The Critics Debate* volume, makes the point that there is a distinction between a critical approach to, and a critical judgement of, a play – that is, between interpretation and evaluation. So let us begin our discussion by looking at the mechanics of the play.

Structure and emblem

King Lear employs the fivefold structure of Shakespearean tragedy – problems, journeys, arrivals, complications and silence – and makes use of parallel plots and characters – the King, Gloucester and the Fool; Regan and Goneril; Edmund and Edgar. You will need to explore all of these in your consideration of the text. Many of the greatest productions of *King Lear* have circled around the problem implicit in its raw dialectic concerning nature, natural justice and the function of politics.

Whether in its quarto or First Folio versions, Shakespeare's original 'scripts' contain a pattern or series of stark visual emblems: the King dividing his kingdom; Kent in the stocks; Edmund inflicting an injury on himself; Lear stripping himself naked on the barren heath; Gloucester's eyes being put out; Gloucester throwing himself from the top of a non-existent cliff; the old King entering with the body of his dead daughter.

These visual signs are linked to the language the characters deploy as they bewail, manipulate, prevaricate or court each other in a world of power, violence and lust. These epic moments bring to the fore a number of contradictions at the centre of the play, and are presented in the two parallel plots: one concerning King Lear and his daughters, the other Gloucester and his sons.

The test

As the action progresses, the issues of the play seem to reflect Cordelia's stringently sparse response to Lear's demand that she speak of her love for him. She says she has 'nothing' to say.

This is the first of a number of set pieces in the play which have real substance, but which at face value appear to be 'nothing'. What is this challenge that Lear has set for Cordelia and his other daughters? Lear demands of them:

> Which of you shall we say doth love us most,
>
> That we our largest bounty may extend
>
> Where nature doth with merit challenge.

(1.1.51–3)

However, this episode is not a competition, since as soon as Goneril has spoken the King gives her a portion of land and as soon as Regan has spoken he gives her hers. This exchange is telling, in that Lear is asking his daughters to measure something that is immeasurable. You cannot quantify love, and in this staged exchange we are to be invited to support Cordelia against her garrulous and, it turns out, deceitful sisters.

If this is a staged exchange and not a competition, then what is this test about? It may be suggested that Shakespeare sees it as an indication of the way this fictional king imposes his authority on his children: how does he perceive and construct reality here? Cordelia is going to get the best share because he believes that she will say that she loves him most and, as his youngest daughter, it is implied, he expects her to look after him in his old age. Regan and Goneril will get their just share because they are his daughters. But behind this is a division of Lear's power base, his land.

Spotlight

Shakespeare depicts Lear as having the power to construct his own reality, but, because he is a king, he can impose it on his subjects. Because he has authority, everyone has to conform to the order, the ceremony, the games, the tests that he creates. But Cordelia will not conform; she is a woman who resists, her resistance attracting sympathy since Lear is clearly wrong in what he is doing. Like Hamlet, she 'knows not seems'.
Her love simply 'is' and so does not have to be proved: to do so would be to demean it. This is what Lear is unable to understand.

In this respect, Lear is in somewhat similar to another of Shakespeare's dramatic artefacts, Richard II, who, as we have seen (Chapter 14), at the beginning of *Richard II* relies on the great ceremonial order of the court that is later undermined by the politically pragmatic Bolingbroke. In *Richard II* the game is overtly political and the King may have an ulterior motive for hiding behind ceremony, but we also see the emotional toll it takes on the protagonist, when he comes to realize his dilemma as he gradually loses his power. This is explored further in *King Lear*, in which the King's 'family' extends to embrace the entire community for which he has responsibility. Everything the King does, especially and including the treatment of his daughters, is necessarily political.

Telling the truth

Modern sensibilities may well approve of Cordelia's behaviour in that she refuses to be sycophantic. She tells the truth: that she will love her husband as a husband and her father as a father. Audiences old and new will recognize this as part of a familiar collective perception of reality, and an important issue of identity for women in the early seventeenth century. But there is, however, something disturbing in Cordelia's response. Just as in *Richard II* the King refuses to recognize that his questionable use of authority will lead to revolt, so in his plan for retirement Lear refuses to countenance any opposition to his patriarchal power. In fact, Lear wants to separate the position of king from the responsibilities of kingship.

Shakespeare has Lear warn Cordelia, '… nothing will come of nothing' and there is a certain truth in that. But in refusing to conform to a ritual, Cordelia has placed herself outside the existing order of things. It's not that nothing *will* come of nothing but that nothing *can* come of nothing because Cordelia refuses to be part of the material world that Lear constructs, in which everything is susceptible to measurement. Although there is biblical support for the simple use of language here, her candour is set against 'the precious square of sense' that allows Goneril and Regan to speak in garrulous but, as we shall soon see, duplicitous terms.

Goneril and Regan

The further irony is that Cordelia's revolt, together with Lear's decision to abdicate, allows Goneril and Regan to pursue the logic of Lear's strategy to a horrifying conclusion:

GONERIL   Pray you let us hit together. If our father carry authority with such disposition as he bears, this last surrender of his will but offend us.

REGAN   We shall further think of it.

GONERIL   We must do something, and i'the heat.

(1.1.304f.)

What they determine to create is a new domestic and political order into which the King, deprived of the symbols of his regal power, will have to fit. So it is that the play's patterns begin to take shape. The argument about the hundred knights, for example, is a direct extension of Lear's own flawed quasi-mathematical logic. Within a very short time, Lear's hundred knights have been significantly reduced and Kent, in the stocks, asks why Lear has so few followers about him. The Fool replies:

All that follow their noses are led by their eyes but blind men, and there's not a nose among twenty but can smell him that's stinking. Let go thy hold when a great wheel runs down a hill lest it break thy neck with following it; but the great one that goes upward, let him draw thee after. When a wise man gives thee better counsel, give me mine again.

(2.4.61–8)

Thus the argument that follows between Lear and Regan and Goneril turns Lear's argument against him, and serves to reduce him to 'nothing'.

Parallel plots

When we turn to the parallel plots, similar issues confront us. Here, Edgar and Gloucester are tricked into believing a story that is fictitious, and that is fabricated by the deceitful and illegitimate Edmund. The result is that Edgar is forced to flee and in order to survive in a hostile environment he retreats to the inhospitable heath and takes on the persona of 'Poor Tom'. Many productions of the play, and many criticisms of the play, seem to view Poor Tom as some kind of Elizabethan John the Baptist, sent out in a loincloth to eat insects and wild honey in the wilderness. He in fact becomes the emblem of the 'unaccommodated man' of whom Lear has, up to this point in the play, taken no account, and he retains this persona until he encounters his father, Gloucester, who agrees with his evaluation of human purpose that 'Ripeness is all' (5.2.11). It is Edgar who leads his father to recognize his past errors, and in a way not too dissimilar from that in which Cordelia's return forces the chastened Lear to admit his.

> '[Shakespeare uses] "nothing" to suture together the Lear and Gloucester plots. Even as Cordelia's initial response to her father is the words "Nothing, my lord", so too, in his first exchange with his father, Edmund, when asked by Gloucester about the contents of the letter he has hastily hidden, replies, chillingly, with the very same words: "Nothing, my lord".'
>
> Shapiro, J. (2015: 61)

The heath

The heath is the place where the two plots come together. It is a barren waste of nothing, except for the elemental forces of nature that bear down on the characters that have resorted to its confines. As such, its function is similar to, though much darker than, the forests of the comedies, although even there the harsh consequences of elemental experience are alluded to in *As You Like It*. In that play, for example, Old Adam's weariness and hunger lead him to the verge of death. But Lear's heath is a place without trees, open to the storms and the reality of endless rain, which was described in Feste's pessimistic closing song of *Twelfth Night* (5.1.381–400). Here the Fool echoes the same song as he coaxes Lear (3.2.73–6) into the shelter which they find to be Poor Tom's hovel (3.4.37).

Key idea

A fine line can exist between comedy and tragedy. In the twentieth century G. Wilson Knight wrote of '*King Lear* and the Comedy of the Grotesque', while Jan Kott discussed the bleakness of Shakespeare's play in the context of Samuel Beckett's *Endgame*, which has been seen as a play within what is called 'the theatre of the absurd'. Such mid-twentieth-century bleakness informed the tenor of Peter Brook's famous production of *King Lear* at Stratford-upon-Avon in 1962 with Paul Scofield as Lear.

The portrayal of Poor Tom

The portrayal of Poor Tom can be a challenge to the actor playing Edgar. How does he develop the role once Edmund's deceit has taken place and the character has fled to the heath, where he is flimsily clothed, crying out 'Tom's a cold'? Shakespeare gives the clue through what he is saying. Tom calls out that he is cold because exposure to the cold is the only reality that Tom knows. All other measures of reality, including his name, have been usurped by lies masquerading as truths. Edgar's own perception of social order has disappeared: it has been stolen by his illegitimate brother, who is aware that the currency of power is land. But the heath to which those who have been displaced resort is a wasteland, barren, worthless, open to the ravages of the elements.

Edgar isn't on the heath just to lead Gloucester. He is there as an emblematic figure, reconstructing an identity that has been taken from him. He has had to begin again and with a new name in order to rediscover himself. You may recall the plight of the usurped Richard II: 'I have no name, no title;/ No, not that name was given me at the font,/ But 'tis usurp'd' (*Richard II*, 4.1.255–7).

As with his earlier kings – Henry VI and Richard II – Shakespeare exposes Lear's self-centred sanctimony as he wants to enter the hovel, kneeling in the rain to meditate on those over whose plight he has 'ta'en/Too little care' (3.4.32–3). He never enters Poor Tom's shelter but rather, in encountering cold reality in the figure of the semi-naked Tom, Lear exposes himself to the elements (3.4.100f.).

Interactive narrative

It seems that Shakespeare, in a complex pattern of interactive narratives, is examining aspects of identity, experience and perception in order to pose questions about the nature of reality. The very opening of the play offers us some indication; the puns Gloucester makes about Edmund's conception are not just for comic effect. Gloucester's narrative of Edmund's birth exposes an issue that informs the whole play: that at the heart of 'order' there lies disorder. Indeed, Gloucester may laugh and joke about Edmund's bastardy, but Edmund shows in his Act 1 soliloquy that he can turn his illegitimacy to his political advantage, and he does so by appealing to the unmediated biological truths of 'Nature'. (1.2.1–22). Edmund transforms Gloucester's jokes into a new alternative reality by engineering a shift of emphasis in the very foundations of domestic society, so that his brother Edgar becomes the victim rather than the legitimate heir. He can do this because Shakespeare depicts him as realizing that society's rules are not hard and fast, that there is a gap between the values and attitudes prescribed by law and actual human behaviour, and that this gap can be exploited.

It is not so much that Tom is 'poor' but that he is victimized and Shakespeare depicts him as having to suppress his bitterness in order to combat the turning of the ideological tide. On the heath he becomes the victim of the 'cruelty' of nature, subject to the wind, rain and tempest, with only a hovel to accommodate or protect him. But he recovers a strong enough identity for himself at the end of the narrative to be able to defeat Edmund and regain his birthright.

Questions of identity

The play asks: Who are you when you have been rejected, stripped of your power and social status or sent out on to the heath blinded or robbed of your birthright? What is the devil that Edgar describes (4.6.69–72), who he claims to see at the top of the cliff, a devil that has led Gloucester to contemplate suicide? Some might argue that it is something that Shakespeare has Edgar use to help educate Gloucester, although we should bear in mind that Edgar is employing an allegorical cloak to protect himself in what is a hostile environment. Gloucester himself is also a victim of that hostility but, after he throws himself from the imaginary cliff, he does not know whether he is alive or dead, whether he has fallen or not. The disguised Edgar claims to provide a particular experience for his disillusioned and blind father, and he does so from a position in which he is himself marginalized from society.

Moreover, the play seems to offer a perverted view of Christianity, in that the secularized Lear, realizing his own potentially tragic situation and fearing for his sanity, calls not on a god or a religious figure in his anguish but on his self-determination, tempered by his fear of insanity:

> No, I'll not weep.
> I have full cause of weeping, but this heart
> Shall break into a hundred thousand flaws
> Or e'er I will weep. O fool, I shall go mad.

(2.2.475–8)

Belief offers no consolation for the pain and anguish that Lear suffers and which will eventually result in his death. In an incisive exchange towards the end of the first act, when the Fool had told him 'Thou shouldst not have been old till thou hadst been wise', Lear had similarly prayed, this time to heaven:

> O let me not be mad, not mad, sweet heaven! I would not be mad.
> Keep me in temper, I would not be mad.

(1.5.41–5)

But there is no heaven to be found here, just as in *Richard II* there are no angels to come to the king's service, however much he protests that they could. These are earthly kings suffering rejection and loss of identity.

In an early Jonathan Miller production, the director had an old Lear and an old Fool come face to face, mirrored in their expression of such anxiety. All of this may have had what is traditionally seen as a tragic effect but there is something mingled with it that is more challenging than the Aristotelian notion of anagnorisis, or self-recognition, will allow.

'Unaccommodated man'

Clothes are the trappings of the society Lear is responsible for having ruled, and yet, as he comes to realize, in his encounter with Poor Tom, 'unaccommodated man' is something that he has failed to consider. On the heath he has to become as Poor Tom. He has to find out who he is now that language, ceremony and order have been stripped from him. He has to stand naked, exposed to the elements. Shakespeare takes King Lear beyond the realms of civilized communication to a point where he addresses Nature – the wind, rain and cold – rather than society:

> Blow winds and crack your cheeks! Rage, blow!
> You cataracts and hurricanoes, spout
> Till you have drenched our steeples, drowned the cocks!
> You sulphurous and thought-executing fires,
> Vaunt-couriers of oak-cleaving thunderbolts,
> Singe my white head! And thou, all-shaking thunder,
> Strike flat the thick rotundity o'the world,
> Crack nature's moulds, all germens spill at once
> That make ingrateful man!
>
> (3.2.1–9)

In the twenty-first century we sit and witness the tragic farce of this man reduced to nakedness and at the mercy of a violent storm. If he takes off everything, as did G. Wilson Knight as an 85-year-old actor in the 1970s, and Ian McKellen, somewhat younger, in 2007, there is a danger of distracting the audience. Through Lear's stripping off of his clothes, audiences are being challenged to witness the breakdown of the stability of the self and the social context that sustains it. In the end, the body is primarily natural, not social, and therefore, once rejected by society, divorced from an identity within society, all that remains as a yardstick for judgement is Nature: the body outside the institutions of society, the body that will die and decompose, the naked body that on the scaffold and gibbet of Elizabethan and Jacobean England was literally 'torn apart'. How this is achieved, without modern-day sniggering or offence, is a challenge for any director or actor, but does that matter?

In the play Shakespeare confronts social perceptions of reality. If Lear constructs a reality that ultimately collapses, so do Regan and Goneril, so do Gloucester and Edmund, and so, in a curious way, does Cordelia. This is a domestic affair but at the same time it is not a family affair. All the characters are frustrated, more or less, in their individual attempts to resolve satisfactorily the problems that they either make for themselves or that they encounter. The result is that the play offers us a raw expression of the agony of what it can mean to be human in an inward, self-harming society driven by vicious ambition and cruelty.

The recognition scenes

Shakespeare provides three recognition scenes. The first is one between 'the mad' Lear and 'the blind' Gloucester, which concludes with these lines:

> If thou wilt weep my fortunes, take my eyes.
>
> I know thee well enough, thy name is Gloucester.
>
> Thou must be patient. We came crying hither:
>
> Thou knowst the first time we smell the air
>
> We wawl and cry.

(4.6.171–6)

The second is when Lear wakes in Cordelia's arms:

> LEAR   Pray do not mock me.
>
>   I am a very foolish, fond old man,

> Fourscore and upward, not an hour more or less;
>
> And to deal plainly,
>
> I fear I am not in my perfect mind.
>
> ...
>
>   Do not laugh at me,
>
> For, as I am a man, I think this lady
>
> To be my child Cordelia.
>
> CORDELIA And so I am, I am.

>   (4.7.59–63, 68–70)

In these two he deliberately frustrates our expectation of closure, since neither of them is allowed to close the play satisfactorily. The strained frustration of the dramatic structure is thus an indication of the dark chaos of human experience that remains once the social and political context of what were formerly Lear's identity, mind, sanity and kingdom have been taken from him. There can be no neat solutions to the dilemma for which he has himself been responsible, and we can say the same is true, in a less extreme form, of Gloucester.

A third recognition scene is to follow at the end of the fight between Edmund and the disguised Edgar, when Edmund asks who it is that has 'slain' him. But even this recognition, which concludes the subplot, does not arrive in time to prevent the deaths of Cordelia and Lear. The play, therefore, concludes with a curt statement that acknowledges the prevailing sadness that demands attention, while at the same time recognizing the difference between the link between 'feeling' and truth and the superficial demands on an imposed utterance:

> The weight of this sad time we must obey,
>
> Speak what we feel, not what we ought to say.

>   (5.3.322–3)

It is precisely this conflict between what is felt and what ought to be done that cannot be resolved, largely because there is a gulf between signification (the capacity of language to express a stable reality) and reality itself. Gloucester, too, is dead and so are Cornwall, Regan and Goneril and all for nothing, for the impotence of office. Even the Fool, the touchstone of reality, has been hanged.

Spotlight

In *King Lear*, despite anagnorisis, the triple recognition scenes can provide no catharsis. Indeed, in allowing the action to lead to an inevitable and unavoidable conclusion, Shakespeare departed significantly from an anonymous earlier play, *King Leir*, which was one of his principal sources. Perhaps he had even acted in that earlier play with the Queen's Men. In it, Cordelia and Lear survive and live happily together, but this is not a conclusion possible for Shakespeare's play, in which he takes his audience to the abyss both structurally and thematically and forces us to contemplate its darkness, where possibly there remains a glimmer of light to be detected in the context of the artistry of the play that has just been performed.

If this is still regarded as a great play – which has not always been the case – I would venture to suggest that it is precisely because of the way Shakespeare pushes the action well beyond his own established rules of dramatic art. In deliberately frustrating and straining his structural template, testing it to its limit, he demonstrates his confident belief in his artistic abilities, as the greatest artists in music, literature, painting, sculpture and, today, the electronic media invariably do.

20

Macbeth (1606)

Equivocation is at the core of *Macbeth*, posing questions and challenges for the audience on a level that goes beyond character and informs the historical context of the play.

The playwrights of the period were craftsmen who, like Shakespeare, understood how truth could be transformed into falsehood by insinuation, as in *Othello*, or by equivocation, the exploitation of the instability of language itself, as in *Macbeth*. Social control could be exercised and maintained through language – through, that is, the political control of language – as has been the case through the ages. The Roman historian Tacitus' realization that, if you wished to bring down a political regime or country, you should first undermine its language, was as true in Elizabethan/Jacobean times as it was for the Romans and as it is for the present day.

What is a traitor?

In John Marston's play *The Malcontent* (1603/4), the disguised and usurped Duke Altofronto asks Bilioso, a courtier, 'What religion are you of now?' The courtier replies, 'Of the Duke's religion, when I know what it is. What religion else?' The incident brings into sharp focus religious uncertainties, the need for self-preservation, the professional hypocrisy of courtiers and their lack of integrity, all of which are indicative of the social anxieties prevalent in early Jacobean England.

Let us take, for example, the word 'traitor'. By his control of the Church, Henry VIII allowed for a change of language to take place in which the words 'heretic' and 'traitor' became almost synonymous. The punishment, of course, might remain the same but traitor has a more secular, political force to it and is dependent on the government in power. It individualized the notion of treachery as an act directed against the monarch, but when the King was, as Henry VIII became, the head of the Church of England, the terms 'heresy' and 'treachery' were synonymous: to oppose the monarch was also to oppose the religious institution of which the monarch was the supreme head, and vice versa. It all depended, of course, on the religion of the reigning monarch. So while prominent Protestants were executed as 'traitorous heretics' under the Catholic Queen Mary, so under Elizabeth, who was excommunicated by the Pope, Catholics were regarded as traitors to the realm. Some of them then paid the price by being publicly 'unseam'd … from the nave to th' chops' (*Macbeth*, 1.2.22) on the scaffold, just as the traitor Macdonwald is reported to have been killed by Macbeth on the battlefield.

Such hangings and evisceration continued with James, especially after the Gunpowder Plot (November 1605) was uncovered, in which Catholics had engaged in planning high treason in the attempt to kill the King and the whole of his government. As Catholics, the conspirators were 'heretics' but in their design to assassinate the King and his parliament they were also guilty of 'treason'. But one of the linguistic devices that captured

Catholics used to claim their innocence was to 'equivocate', and so another term, 'equivocation', acquired popular currency. Equivocation was a means of exploiting the instabilities of language in order to obscure the truth as defined by the State, and it was a favoured strategy of Jesuit dissidents.

The Old Testament commandment 'Thou shalt not bear false witness against thy neighbour' is only 'false witness' if it distorts or flatly contradicts the 'truth'. Equivocation suggests that the 'truth' is unstable, allowing for more than one interpretation. *Macbeth* takes this problem a stage further to ask the following question: Can those in power create a situation in which language itself is abused in order to reverse the normal meanings of 'good' and 'bad'? To do so would be to invert the normal order of things.

'What is a traitor?' Lady Macduff's son asks. 'Why, one that swears and lies' is the reply:

SON	And must they all be hang'd that swear and lie?
LADY MACDUFF	Every one.
SON	Who must hang them?
LADY MACDUFF	Why, the honest men.
SON	Then the liars and swearers are fools; for there are liars and swearers enow to beat the honest men, and hang up them.

(4.2.46–7, 51–7)

The audience knows, of course, that in this case it is not Macduff who is the 'traitor', although he opposes the new king, Macbeth. At the end of the scene, the 'Poor prattler', as his mother calls him, is stabbed to death because he denies his father's treachery; nonetheless, the First Murderer calls him 'Young fry of treachery!' (4.2.85). By this point in the play we are convinced that 'fair' has become 'foul' and 'foul' has become 'fair', thereby inverting normal moral categories.

Macbeth and interpretation

Macbeth was written in 1606 in the aftermath of the
Gunpowder Plot and the executions of Catholic 'traitors' and
priests and at a time when the concepts of 'truth' and 'justice'
were being undermined.

'Shakespeare's Macbeth – *likely in repertory with (Jonson's)*
Volpone *at the Globe shortly after the resumption of playing
after Easter (1606) – managed to do something ... profound,
registering deeper tectonic shifts taking place in Jacobean
England ... By early 1606, the fear was all too real that once
equivocation took root, "in short time there will be no faith, no
troth, no trust". One of Shakespeare's most powerful insights in*
Macbeth *is that in so infected a climate... the good, along with
the evil, embrace equivocation.'*

Shapiro, J. (2015: 228–9)

As we have seen throughout our journey, there is a relationship
created in drama between the writer, the performers and
the spectators, who are part of a conversation through the
agency of the text in performance or in reading. The historical
circumstances of the text's inception need, therefore, to be
considered if that conversation is to be meaningful, even
though a modern interpretation will impose modern meanings
upon it, from current cultural perspectives. Religion cannot be
far away from the discussion of Macbeth, nor can the fact that
a Scottish king had recently ascended the throne of England,
and that a significant political change had taken place with the
movement from the Tudor to the Stuart dynasty. At this period
monarchical power, whether Tudor or Stuart, was absolute and
thus invited flattery. It may be that *Macbeth* was intended to
flatter the new king, although Shakespeare's method, as we will
see, seems to have been much more subtle than mere 'flattery'
would suggest.

'Reading' *Macbeth*

How do we today read or interpret *Macbeth*? The play appears to question the reduction of 'history' to single organic narratives such as 'the Elizabethan world picture'. Some contemporary criticism has set out to challenge the readings of liberal humanist critics who start from the position of a singular established universal 'truth' that prevails through history. Thus Alan Sinfield, writing in 1992 on *Macbeth* (in Brown, R. D. and Johnson, D. (eds) [2000: 130, 136]), challenged prevailing orthodox interpretations. For example, he points to the fact that Macbeth, in killing the rebel Macdonwald, is hailed as a great warrior by King Duncan, who calls him a 'valiant cousin' and a 'worthy gentleman', but when Macbeth kills King Duncan he is subsequently seen as a murderer.

Sinfield writes, 'Violence is good ... when it is in the service of the prevailing dispositions of power; when it disrupts them, it is evil', and he argues that '*Macbeth* focuses on major strategies by which the state asserted its claim at one conjuncture.' Sinfield argues further that, although certainly portrayed as 'a murderer and an oppressive ruler', Macbeth is, in effect, 'one version of the absolutist ruler, not the polar opposite'.

Readings such as Sinfield's, in the context of changing ideologies, notions of historical accuracy or universal truth, prompt the modern critic to challenge and review what has been hitherto regarded as critical orthodoxy.

Macbeth in the past may sometimes have been seen as an easier play to study than the other three great tragedies, but today it foregrounds the complexities of interpretation by asking questions about the definitions of 'good' and 'evil' as determined by society, by politicians or by anyone who tries to limit meaning. The play itself shifts its perspectives, working through a series of equivocations. In 1986 the Marxist critic Terry Eagleton was providing a very different interpretation of the Weird Sisters than conventional readings allow:

> *'The witches are the heroines of the piece, however little the play itself recognizes the fact, and however much the critics may have set out to defame them. It is they who, by releasing ambitious thoughts in Macbeth, expose a reverence for hierarchical social order for what it is, as the pious self-deception of a society based on routine oppression and incessant warfare.'*
>
> Eagleton, T. (1986, 1987 p/b: 2), *William Shakespeare*. Oxford: Basil Blackwell

Later, Eagleton revised his view, arguing that the witches, in their negativity, display an abhorrence of the positivity of existence (Eagleton, T. [2010], *On Evil*. New Haven: Yale University Press), but his subsequent reconsideration illustrates the divergence of views within critical perception, even at times with a single scholar's reading of the plays.

The murder of a Scottish king as a central concern of the play can also be read in two ways. The first is in accordance with a traditional literary orthodoxy, which would see the regicide as a potentially subversive, dramatic event and a challenge to the philosophy of the 'divine right of kings' that James I was known to support. This was the philosophy to which Claudius had appealed in *Hamlet* when confronted by the rebellious Laertes: 'There's such divinity doth hedge a king / That treason can but peep to what it would, / Acts little of his will' (*Hamlet*, 4.5.123–5). A second reading is more subversive, in itself questioning the methods of King Duncan, and would seek to determine whether within the claim to 'divine right' there lurked a force that the King's own militaristic regime actually encourages. It would also question the focus of 'evil' in the play in female characters such as the Weird Sisters or Lady Macbeth.

Spotlight

The play here exposes equivocation. James I was a voyeur who used his power over his courtiers for his own vicarious sexual pleasure. Duncan is portrayed often as a holy man (as, for example, by Griffith Jones in the renowned 1976 RSC production), but another reading might suggest that he is the man who sends his thanes off to war while he looks on. Duncan says, 'There's no art/To find the mind's construction in the face' (1.4.11–12) but this, too, is an equivocal statement: from one perspective it asserts that you can never know what another person is thinking from looking at their face, thus reaffirming the existence of the hypocrisy and deception which permeates the play. From another perspective it also suggests that there is no need of an 'art' to find out what a person is thinking because it will show in the speaker's face.

Hell's gate

In the spring of 1606 the Jesuit priest Henry Garnet was executed for his supposed complicity in the Gunpowder Plot. One of the 'main crimes' levelled at the Jesuits (members of the Society of Jesus, a Roman Catholic order of priests) was that of equivocation, of saying one thing to disguise something potentially more incriminating. Indeed, at his trial, Garnet had attempted to justify the practice. Shakespeare alludes to Garnet as one of those entering the hell's gate of Macbeth's castle in the Porter's scene:

> Faith, here's an equivocator, that could swear in both the scales against either scale; who committed treason enough for God's sake, yet could not equivocate to heaven: O! come in, equivocator.

> (2.3.8–12)

But, as James Shapiro points out, the person knocking at the gate is Macduff, who in the eyes of the audience is far from being represented as a traitor and even in the Porter's quipping the equivocator has done so 'for God's sake', which makes his fate ambiguous.

At the end of the play Macbeth himself comes 'To doubt th'equivocation of the fiend,/ That lies like truth' (5.5.43–4). Indeed, with the Weird Sisters' chant 'Fair is foul, and foul is fair' the normal referential properties of language are inverted so that meanings are the opposite of what we might expect. In this way, Macbeth encounters a Birnam Wood that is not Birnam Wood, and he finally dies at the hand of an adversary who was not, albeit only in a technical sense, 'of woman born'.

Temptation and conscience

The myth of Adam and Eve's sin is also not far away in this play. Macbeth is encouraged to undertake his treacherous murder by Lady Macbeth, who is charged with sexual power. What she says about ripping the suckling child from her breast and dashing its brains out (1.7.54–9), in her determination that her husband should secure power through murder, is a powerful image of the destruction of innocence. The crime of the mother killing her child is presented as being as 'unnatural' as the subject killing the monarch. Yet it goes beyond it, since monarchs lose their innocence but babies cannot. So maybe we have here a further reading of Lady Macbeth's image in the overall narrative context of the play. This is the power of the Shakespearean text: the rich ambiguity of possibility (which is not to be confused with 'equivocation') at its heart, which invites a variety of responses.

Macbeth and the Weird Sisters

Macbeth is given a conscience, which emerges in the illusions he sees – the dagger before him (2.1.33f.) and the ghost of Banquo (3.4.44–73). Throughout the play there is a dark inevitability suggested about his curiosity in an underworld where he cannot tell whether the phantoms before him, the Weird Sisters, are male or female, and whether they speak the truth or not. Is what they say true or false? Ironically it is both, as they prove their credibility in pointing to the future to the very end. Because of their grotesque appearance, the strange rituals in which they engage and their gruesome pot of broth, the audience is exposed to a palpable form of evil but we should remember that Shakespeare creates them as symptoms and not the cause of the evil into which Macbeth descends.

All that the Weird Sisters predict actually happens but does what they say make it happen? To ask that question is to demonstrate that Shakespeare has drawn us into the play. We are uncertain in our response because of the ways in which the play unsettles the stability of language. It is the dramatist who makes the play happen; his dramatic characters are vehicles that carry the action forward to its conclusion. But we, the audience, ask such questions and respond accordingly. In the soliloquy at 1.3.127f. Macbeth balances probabilities against realities, imaginings against conclusions, with the equivocal tautology, 'And nothing is, but what is not' (142). In this way Macbeth draws attention to the process of equivocation as well as to the temptation that it seems to offer him. The Christian man is being drawn to heinous sin, to what in the world he desires, but along with the desire comes a consideration of its consequences – a 'conscience', in other words – that recognizes the sinfulness of the temptation even as Macbeth succumbs to its attractions. His is a more intense version of Claudius's more perfunctory stirrings of conscience in *Hamlet* (3.4.36f.). Here Macbeth says:

> ... Present fears
>
> Are less than horrible imaginings.
>
> My thought, whose murther yet is but fantastical,
>
> Shakes so my single state of man,
>
> That function is smother'd in surmise,

> (*Macbeth*, 1.3.137–41)

Shakespeare has Macbeth say in the same speech that the 'horrid image' of the deed he imagines 'doth unfix my hair'. The portrayal is of energy and an excitement for what, at this stage, is nothing more than a fantasy encapsulating a desire to do the almost unthinkable, by living what is imagined. It is a strange voyeurism of one's own thoughts, a submission to what Christianity terms 'temptation'. Dramatically, these temptations are spurred on by the embodiment of the Weird Sisters' evil. Yet the consequences that occur are not postponed to the afterlife but follow immediately on from the deed itself, as surely as did the arrest and death, mostly by executions, of the Gunpowder plotters upon the 'stage' of the scaffold.

The soliloquy 'Is this a dagger, which I see before me, ... A dagger of the mind, a false creation, / Proceeding from the heat-oppressed brain?' (2.1.33, 38–9) appears similarly to be the product of temptation, a pre-vision of the deed and its danger but also a luxuriating in it, an enjoyment of its process. These reflections are not specifically about right or wrong but about the process of a deed that in the context of the play is clearly being portrayed as wrong. Even Macbeth's statement to his wife that 'We will proceed no further in this business' (1.7.31) can be interpreted as a request for further confirmation of the resolution to realize in action a dangerous fantasy.

'Unsex me here'

Lady Macbeth's invitation to the 'Spirits/That tend on mortal thoughts, unsex me here' (1.5.37–8), comes in the second part of her great soliloquy (1.5.14f.), which must rank as an example of Shakespeare's darkest, most intense writing. In her determination to be 'unsexed', Lady Macbeth deploys a stringent sexual imagery that aligns, but in a sadomasochistic manner, sexual union with personal gratification. The negative wish invokes the positive enjoyment of the self-cursing: 'make thick my blood,/Stop up th'access and passage to remorse'(42–3); 'Come to my woman's breasts,/And take my milk for gall' (46–7), 'Come, thick Night,/And pall thee in the dunnest smoke of Hell'(49–50). This is a sexual union that comes close to an association with the darkness of death itself. At the end of the soliloquy Shakespeare depicts Lady Macbeth as changing sex, in crying that her phallic 'keen knife see not the wound it makes,/Nor Heaven peep through the blanket of the dark,/To cry, "Hold, Hold!"' (51–3). Here, under the 'blanket' of the night, as in a bed, is the sexual climax of the deed: the spirits that she invokes at the start of the passage all point to her enjoyment of the act. It is a speech of impressive sexual power exposing a disturbed imagination. Lady Macbeth has become one with the darkness that accompanies her desire, and it is a path that Macbeth himself will shortly follow.

Consequences

With the deed done, and with the hands of both Macbeth and Lady Macbeth physically covered in blood (2.2.58f.), Shakespeare starts to move us from the world of temptation and diseased imagination into the world of consequences. Macbeth deludes himself, as Lady Macbeth has done, that he has the power to see 'the future in the instant' and that he can, therefore, control events. However, even though in the stages leading up to the regicide he is fully aware of the moral implications of the act, in the wake of the deed itself he becomes paranoid as the future begins to slip away from him. Believing in the accuracy of the Weird Sisters' prediction that it is Banquo's lineage that will succeed to the throne of Scotland,

Macbeth muses that 'To be thus is nothing, but to be safely thus' (3.1.47). To secure his own future he must kill Banquo but, no matter what he does, there is always something – in this case, Banquo's son Fleance – that escapes his grasp.

'In Macbeth, Shakespeare brings an audience to recognize the power of language and performance to create their own versions of reality, to manipulate and shape the ways we understand and respond to events. Outside the play, either as a private citizen or a head of state, Macbeth would be what Malcolm judges him: a butcher. But in it, for all the ways his evil is made clear and his poetry is undercut, he can still retain the sympathy of an audience even after his death. In the end, the play leaves audiences (and critics) trying to reconcile two contradictory impulses: the impulse to condemn Macbeth as evil and the impulse to mourn and celebrate his courage and perverse magnificence.'

Collins, M. J. (1989: 94–5), 'Macbeth and Its Audience' in Dotterer, R. (ed.) (1989), Shakespeare, Text, Subtext, and Content. London and Toronto: Associated University Presses

The fantastical imaginings of the aspiring protagonist and his ambitious spouse, once converted into actions, return to torment the perpetrators. The rich and vivid imagery of the play invites us to experience vicariously the act of murder: Macbeth hears a voice crying, '"Sleep no more!/Macbeth does murther Sleep,"' (2.2.34–5), and later Lady Macbeth is seen sleepwalking, which is described by the Doctor as 'A great perturbation in nature, to receive at once the benefit of sleep, and do the effects of watching!' (5.1.9–11). In washing her hands in her sleep, 'Out, damned spot! out, I say!' (5.1.36), she contradicts her statement following the murder, when she claimed 'A little water clears us of this deed' (2.2.66). On the whole, the horrifying consequences of their deeds far exceed even the imaginations of the protagonist and his wife, to the point where, as Lady Macbeth laments, they have fulfilled their desire but unwittingly sacrificed their 'content': 'Nought's had, all's spent,/Where our desire is got without content' (3.2.4–5).

Macbeth's earlier question, 'Will all great Neptune's ocean wash this blood/Clean from my hand?' (2.2.59–60), is answered through the process of the play in the negative. Textually, it might remind us of an opposing statement in *Richard II*, 'Not all the water in the rough rude sea/Can wash the balm off from an anointed King;' (3.2.54–5). In the same speech Richard draws a comparison between darkness and light, when the sun rises, 'And darts his light through every guilty hole', exposing 'murthers, treasons, and detested sins' (43–4), making his treacherous cousin Bolingbroke 'tremble at his sin' (3.2.53). To secure the crown, Macbeth has spilt the 'sacred' blood of an anointed king and will, like Claudius in *Hamlet*, assume the role of a 'player king' himself, when 'invested' at Scone.

Whether balm or blood, the realities appear to depend on political pragmatism. The guilt-ridden Macbeth is destroyed by political strategy – a union between Scotland and England, with Malcolm appealing to the English King for support (4.3.43–4) – and the nature of kingship in this union is articulated by means of the vocabulary of saintliness. Macduff refers to Malcolm's father as 'a most sainted King' and the Queen as one who 'Died every day she liv'd' (4.3.109, 111). The King of England, Edward the Confessor, is endowed with divine power and he can solicit heaven to cure people of sickness: 'sundry blessings hang about his throne,/That speak him full of grace' (4.3.158–9). This utilizes the language of the traditional Catholic prayer to the Virgin Mary ('Hail Mary, full of grace, the Lord is with thee'), but is here associated with the King who may have been watching the play, full of the hypocrisy of his own 'holiness'.

Shakespeare may appear to be flattering King James, but at the same time he may also be teasing out some of the moral issues surrounding the power of monarchy that inform the play. We might wonder, for example, in Act 4, Scene 1, whether Macbeth's words 'Horrible sight' elicited by the witches' vision of one of Banquo's successors carrying the 'twin balls' and 'triple sceptres' of the monarch of a united Scotland and England under James, elicited the same response in the King watching the play at a royal performance as it might have done in a possible 'closet' dissenter in the audience? The whole issue of the Union of England and Scotland was, historically, one in which James was being frustrated. Of course, images are received in different ways and words can be understood in different contexts by different people.

Signifying nothing

Equivocation, as we have seen, is established as a language for the play from its opening, when the Weird Sisters comment that 'Fair is foul, and foul is fair' (1.1.11). It sets the scene and paves the way for further prophecies, for Macbeth's journey and arrival. It leads ultimately to that final recognition of the futility of his actions when he hears of the death of Lady Macbeth:

> ... Out, out, brief candle!
> Life's but a walking shadow; a poor player,
> That struts and frets his hour upon the stage,
> And then is heard no more: it is a tale
> Told by an idiot, full of sound and fury,
> Signifying nothing.

> (5.5.23–8)

Lady Macbeth has left the stage, the light of life has gone out like a burnt candle, and all is darkness. Without the natural rhythms of life and the institutions that are designed to support them, all life, including royalty, is without substance and devoid of meaning. Macbeth's 'nothing', however, may go deeper, reflecting the variety of discourses that feed into the play's demonstration of the consequences of equivocation. As Malcolm Evans points out, 'The "nothing" signified is not merely an absence but a delirious plentitude of selves and meanings, always prior to, and in excess of, the self-naturalizing signs and subjects of the discourses it calls perpetually to account' (1986: 117).

Key idea

In that 'nothing' we may find not only, therefore, the fate of the protagonist but also the enigma of the play's progress. It both flatters and questions divine kingship and authority by placing a focus on events such as war, murder, executions, treachery and loyalty, and exposes in the process royal succession, the emerging instability of language and the equivocation that lies at the heart of both power and dissent.

21

Critical perspectives 5: Searching for and interpreting the text

It is difficult to find an absolutely original text of a Shakespearean play, since play texts even after first and subsequent publication change according to the dynamics of performance. Early texts may be versions designed for particular performances, and those texts that emerged to be published in the first collected edition of his works may have been altered for performances over time. Textual critics have to make choices to publish a modern text and directors and performance companies have to decide which text to use and how they may wish to change it to suit their interpretations.

'Good' and 'bad' quartos and the First Folio

Where do we find the original text of a Shakespearean play? It is not as easy as some imagine. Let us begin with *Hamlet* as an example. *Hamlet* first appeared in print in 1603 in a quarto-sized edition known now as Q1 and often referred to as the 'bad Quarto'. It was published again in a 1604 quarto edition, known as Q2 or sometimes as the 'good Quarto'. It was later published after Shakespeare's death by two of his fellow actors, John Heminges and Henry Condell, in the first collected edition of his plays, the First Folio, in 1623.

Why is there a 'bad' Quarto and a 'good' Quarto? There were no copyright laws in Shakespeare's time, and consequently his company, the Lord Chamberlain's Men, which later became the King's Men, did not rush to publish plays in performance since they may not have wanted rival companies to steal them and make money from them. Actors might move from one company to another, having memorized major parts of a popular play. Members of the audience or rival company actors may have tried to memorize, albeit sometimes inaccurately, particular parts of the play. The result would not only be a rival production but also the publication of an unauthorized and sometimes garbled version of the play. This is what may have happened with the 1603 version of *Hamlet*.

In 1592 Shakespeare himself, as noted earlier, was accused by a fellow writer of 'stealing' plays and ideas. As a dramatist he used many sources for his plays, including *Hamlet*. An earlier play of the same title had probably been performed in 1594 by the Lord Chamberlain's Men and the Lord Admiral's Men in a joint production. The text of this early *Hamlet*, which is sometimes referred to as the ur-*Hamlet*, is now lost. It is likely that it was never printed and it may not have been a particularly good play. As G. R. Hibbard notes in his introduction to *The Oxford Shakespeare: Hamlet* (1987: 13), 'one aspect of Shakespeare's genius was his ability to take an old-fashioned drama and utterly transform it'. The following example gives an indication of Q1 in relation to the Folio. In Q1, the 'bad Quarto', Hamlet's most famous soliloquy begins:

To be, or not to be, I there's the point,

To Die, to sleepe, is that all? I all:

No, to sleepe, to dreame, I mary there it goes ...

> (*The Tragicall Historie of Hamlet Prince of Denmarke*
> [1603], Edinburgh: Edinburgh University Press [1966: 28])

Compare this Q1 version with the more familiar version taken from the 'good' 1605 Quarto and the First Folio:

To be, or not to be, that is the question:

Whether 'tis nobler in the mind to suffer

The slings and arrows of outrageous fortune,

Or to take arms against a sea of troubles

And by opposing end them. To die – to sleep,

No more;

...

To die, to sleep;

To sleep, perchance to dream – ay, there's the rub:

> (3.1.56–61, 64–5)

The texts of Shakespeare's plays, including *Hamlet*, that we read or produce today are interpretative texts, compiled by modern editors who make choices between readings from the quarto editions and the First Folio, although sometimes they produce an edition based on the Folio text or what they consider to be the most authoritative of the quartos.

As we saw in Chapter 1, the terms 'quarto' and 'folio' refer to the book size. While single editions were published in quarto, the first *Complete Works* was published in folio. There appears to be an 'authorized' text of *Hamlet*, the Quarto of 1605 that purports to be 'Newly imprinted and enlarged to almost as much again as it was, according to the true and perfect Coppie' but there are certain differences between it and the Folio edition. Each of the three early texts we have give a number of interesting clues about early performances as well as providing stimulus for modern interpretations. The 'bad' Quarto of 1603 may reflect aspects of the first performance of Shakespeare's play or it may be influenced by one or more earlier lost plays. The 1605 Quarto is probably a response by the Lord Chamberlain's Men designed to reassert ownership of a popular play in their repertoire. The First Folio edition, published 18 years later, may reflect changes made to the play during its many performances over the years since 1605. The modern editor has to make decisions. Take, for example, Hamlet's first soliloquy, that is, the first speech he makes when alone on the stage. In the *RSC Complete Works*, based on the Folio edition, the speech that appears in Act 1, Scene 2 (129f.) begins:

> O, that this too too solid flesh would melt,
>
> Thaw, and resolve itself into a dew!

In the Arden and Penguin editions, the word 'sullied' is used rather than 'solid'. Both Q1 and Q2, however, actually use the word 'sallied'. The use of 'sullied' in these modern editions appears to follow an amendment made in an edition by John Dover Wilson for the New Cambridge Shakespeare (1934), although the Hudson Shakespeare (1909) also refers to an 'anonymous conjecture' of 'sullied' rather than 'sallied'. A critical judgement, nevertheless, was made by a respected twentieth-century textual critic concerning a word not found in the original texts, but which has subsequently become embedded in certain established editions.

Much of this may be dismissed as academic pedantry, but actually the words 'solid', 'sallied', 'sullied' indicate important differences for an actor who is to deliver this speech or, indeed, for anyone reading this famous soliloquy. The example helps to demonstrate that the texts we buy or pull up on our laptop are the results of editorial choices. This leads us into another important issue. Shakespeare's *Hamlet* was originally written not as a literary text but as a performance script. As it became a 'literary text' over the centuries, its ambiguities surfaced, confirming the view that, despite the 1605 'authorized' version by the company, there can be no authoritative single original text. The history of *Hamlet* criticism, however, is one that consists of numerous attempts to 'fix' the play's meanings, or indeed to reduce them to one organic meaning.

Attempts to fix meanings

Some dramatists who have harboured literary aspirations over the years – for example George Bernard Shaw – have attempted, unsuccessfully, to fix the meaning of their plays by legislating how a play should be performed and what its meaning should be. As noted earlier, Chekhov famously complained that the Russian director Constantin Stanislavsky actually misinterpreted his plays, turning his 'comedies' into 'naturalistic tragedies'. Stanislavsky, committed as he was to a naturalistic style of performance, nevertheless, gives us a clue: Shakespeare's texts, including *Hamlet*, have the capacity to generate multiple interpretations, dependent on the influence of the historical conditions and cultural assumptions of the performances and their audiences, which change over time.

Different kinds of Hamlet

It is because of these historical and cultural shifts that we talk about different kinds of Hamlet – Romantic Hamlet, Political Hamlet, Tragic Hamlet, Violent Hamlet, Alienating Hamlet, all of which depend on the interpretations of particular actors and, in modern theatre, different directors. We also talk about Hamlets in terms of an actor's name: Asta Neilsen's Hamlet, Gielgud's Hamlet, Olivier's Hamlet, Nicol Williamson's Hamlet, Jacobi's Hamlet, McKellen's Hamlet, Frances de la Tour's Hamlet, Angela Winkler's Hamlet, David Tennant's Hamlet, Jonathan Slinger's Hamlet, Benedict Cumberbatch's Hamlet, and so forth.

The actor Jonathan Slinger, for example, in the 2012 RSC production proved to be an uncomfortable Hamlet, deliberately preventing the audience from empathizing with him, in particular by his violence towards Ophelia. During the Vietnam War, Nicol Williamson's Hamlet was a man in the shadows, fearful of big politics. In 1975 Ben Kingsley's Hamlet concentrated on weighing the balance between life and death, a performance that coincided with an extra-theatrical tragedy of the untimely death of the first female director at the RSC, Buzz Goodbody. In 1979 Frances de la Tour played the title role in an all-female cast at the Half Moon Theatre in London, following a tradition of female Hamlets. The nineteenth-century actress Sarah Bernhardt, for example, played Hamlet in 1899.

In 1980 Jonathan Pryce created another of the great Hamlets of the twentieth century in a production at the Royal Court Theatre in which the Ghost was portrayed as coming from within the depths of the protagonist's own being. In 1988/9 Mark Rylance interpreted Hamlet as insane and he appeared for much of the play wearing pyjamas in a performance that became known as the 'pyjama *Hamlet*'. At the turn of the century and into the new millennium, David Tennant (RSC) and Rory Kinnear (National Theatre) have portrayed Hamlets that reflected the growing isolationism of the individual in society and the fragmentation of Western values. This aspect was present also in Slinger's performance, which was set in a school hall reminiscent of a 1950s English grammar school that had fallen into disrepair. The production programme included an image of gallery visitors milling round Damian Hirst's challenging work *The Physical Impossibility of Death in the Mind of Someone Living* (1991).

Original performance

Shakespeare's original theatres, their architecture, location and ambience, the nature of their audiences and the competitive business of the theatrical environment, naturally influenced the nature of the plays' composition. Some pioneering work on the nature of the audience and also on what is often called 'the War of the Theatres' or 'the Stage Quarrel' – but which at the time was termed by the dramatist Thomas Dekker (*c.*1570–1632) Poetomachia, the Poet's War – was undertaken by Alfred Harbage in the mid-twentieth century. As we have seen, like other critics and directors of that period, Harbage was influenced by the dominant ideologies of the time, but his work firmly established an area of importance for further study.

Andrew Gurr, in *Playgoing in Shakespeare's London*, warns about the complexities involved with trying to understand the composition and interaction of the first players and playgoers with the text:

'Shakespearean receivers were far from passive objects. They are likely nowadays to be invoked all too often in a vicious circle of internal evidence, as arbiters of this or that otherwise inexplicable or undesired feature of the plays. Understandably, because they are the most inconstant, elusive, unfixed element of the Shakespearean performance text, their contribution is presented as an easy means of explaining away features of the dramaturgy which seem incongruous to modern audiences.'

Gurr, A. (1987: 3), *Playgoing in Shakespeare's London*. Cambridge: Cambridge University Press

Gurr asks, for example, how a soliloquy may have been delivered before an audience of 3,000 people at the Globe, some of whose heads were at the actors' feet. We may have some indication of this today since the opening of the replica of the Globe in 1997, but the modern audience is not the same as that of the early seventeenth century. Gurr also provides a corrective to any stereotypical formulations that make out that audiences were mainly 'artisan' or 'privileged'. As we journey through the plays, we are noticing possible interactions between actor and audience being signalled in the text. We're also noting changes of dramatic style, including music and song reflecting the years going by and the changes of audience market demand, particularly from Elizabeth I to James I.

Further, the type of playhouse in which the original performances was to take place must have had an influence on the writing of the play even if it was going to be performed at both the private and the public theatre. Gurr prefers to call the public theatres, which as we saw in Chapter 1 probably first started in the 1567 with the Red Lion in Whitechapel, amphitheatres. The 'private' smaller indoor theatres or 'Halls' began in 1575 at St Paul's Cathedral Choir School and also included The Blackfriars. They became venues for plays, often satiric, performed by boy actors.

It was the competition of the boys' players, 'an eyrie of children, little eyases, that cry out on the top of question, and are most tyrannically clapped for't' (*Hamlet*, 2.2.340–42), that is the reason, Rosencrantz tells Hamlet, for the 'tragedians of the city' to be on tour. Hamlet asks if the writers of the private theatres 'do' the boy actors 'wrong to make them exclaim against their own succession?' (351–2), since they might well wish one day to be members of the adult companies. The boy players had come into particular prominence at the turn of the century, promoting the works of the satiric dramatists of which John Marston was one.

The relationship of his *Antonio's Revenge* with Shakespeare's *Hamlet* is a vexed question. Which play was written first? Were they both dependent on the 'ur-*Hamlet*'; or were the two dramatists knowingly writing plays on a similar story but from different angles as if they were shadowing each other? Certainly, the two plays reflect each other at times. David Farley-Hills believes, for example, that 'Shakespeare does everything he can to encourage us to identify with the revenge hero', while 'Marston uses dramatic techniques ... to exclude audience feeling ... not unlike that of Brecht's *Verfremdungseffekt*, to keep the intellectual sightlines clear of emotional clutter' (Farley-Hills, D. (1990: 17), *Shakespeare and the Rival Playwrights, 1600–1616*. London and New York: Routledge). So much depends, as we've seen throughout our journey, on how we read, produce, perform and 'receive' the plays today. This is an ephemeral undertaking that allows for a plethora of interpretation.

Modern adaptations

We saw in Chapter 13 how Peter Hall and John Barton adapted the *Henry VI* plays and *Richard III* into a sequential work, *The Wars of the Roses*, in which John Barton even wrote some of the scenes. In Shakespearean production the freedom to adapt the Shakespearean text or sequences of plays subsequently became less controversial. Directors and theatre companies realized that Shakespeare's plays were blueprints for performance that could include the kind of dynamism and creativity that could be released by adaptation and modernization.

At the far end of the spectrum, Shakespeare's plays were deconstructed by Charles Marowitz or entirely new plays written, such as Arnold Wesker's *The Merchant* or Edward Bond's *Lear* within the political context of the later twentieth century. Radical productions by, for example, the Half Moon Theatre and Cheek by Jowl created compelling interpretations of Shakespeare's plays, while productions at the Donmar Warehouse in London appeared to have greater freedom than the larger mainstream theatres, especially under the direction of Sam Mendes but not only during his tenure. In the mainstream 'establishment' companies, however, experimentation and interpretation also took place, and continue to do so. For productions of Shakespeare's plays, an appropriate Shakespearean text still has first to be found, which, as we've seen, isn't as easy as it may at first appear. In this, *King Lear*, for example, presents a number of challenges, not only for directors but also for editors.

Editorial decisions

There are two versions of *King Lear*, one published as a quarto in 1608 and the other in the First Folio of 1623. When editing the play for The Oxford Shakespeare in 1988, Stanley Wells and Gary Taylor made a decision to include both versions of the play rather than, as was usual, conflating the two into a single text:

'King Lear *first appeared in print in a quarto of 1608. A substantially different text appeared in the 1623 Folio. Until now, editors, assuming that each of these texts imperfectly represented a single play, have conflated them. But research conducted mainly during the 1970s and 1980s confirms an earlier view that the 1608 quarto represents the play as Shakespeare originally wrote it, and the 1623 Folio as he substantially revised it. He revised other plays, too, but usually making small changes in dialogue and adding or omitting passages, as in* Hamlet, Troilus and Cressida *and* Othello ... *But in* King Lear *revisions are not simply local but structural, too; conflation, as Harley Granville-Barker wrote, "may make for redundancy or confusion", so we print an edited version of each text.'*

Wells, S. and Taylor, G. (1988: 909), 'Introduction to *The History of King Lear*', *William Shakespeare: The Complete Works*. Oxford: The Clarendon Press

Jonathan Bate and Eric Rasmussen, in producing their complete edition in 2007, *The RSC Shakespeare Complete Works*, based it on the First Folio, ordered the texts of the plays as printed in 1623 but included the texts of *Pericles* and *The Two Noble Kinsmen* that were originally missing from the Folio. With *King Lear* they published, therefore, only the Folio text: *The Tragedy of King Lear*, with Quarto *The History of King Lear*, variations appended. *The Arden Shakespeare Complete Works* (2011), which is being used as the text for this book, brings together individual texts edited by a variety of scholars, published as single editions of the plays from the Arden Shakespeare 2 series. The general editors Richard Proudfoot, Ann Thompson and David Scott Kastan order the plays alphabetically, but as we have seen in our discussion of *The Merchant of Venice*, there are differences between John Russell Brown's edited Arden 2 version of the play included in Arden's *Complete Works* and the more recent single revised Arden Shakespeare 3 version, 2010–13, edited by John Drakakis.

Aligning plays with events

In recent years, as we will see in Chapter 24, a popular critical vogue for historical biography has developed that has been fused with new historicism. Stephen Greenblatt's *Will in the World: How Shakespeare Became Shakespeare* (2004) perceives *Hamlet* as 'a highly political play' of its time 'about betrayal and assassination' written immediately before the Essex Rebellion, and he notes the 'remarkable scene' in which Laertes, leading an insurrection, breaks into the royal palace to confront the King and Queen. He also notes that the play was written shortly after the death of Shakespeare's own son Hamnet, in August 1596, suggesting that the names Hamnet and Hamlet 'in the loose orthography of the time … were virtually interchangeable'. He comments: 'Even if the decision to redo the old tragedy were a strictly commercial one, the coincidence of the names – the act of writing his own son's name again and again – may well have reopened

a deep wound, a wound that had never properly healed.'
(Greenblatt, S. [2004: 310, 311], *Will in the World: How Shakespeare Became Shakespeare*).

Greenblatt proceeds to the very edge of critical speculation by seeking to align the play with the death of Shakespeare's father in September 1601, and asks a provocative but unanswerable question, 'How did the father's death become bound so closely in Shakespeare's imagination with the son's?'

Nostalgia

In *Performing Nostalgia* (1996), Susan Bennett offers a different perspective. She suggests that there is nostalgia for the past which comes from the present, and that in our materialistic, consumerist age historical artefacts are transformed into commodities.

> 'Re-enactments of history are perhaps the most literal, if not always the most spectacular, examples of what Patrick Wright refers to as a trafficking in history. Whilst (Michel) Foucault has persuasively accounted for history as "inertia and weight, as a slow accumulation of the past, a silent sedimentation of things said" ... it is also true that what has been accumulated has also been appraised for is currency (both cultural and economic) ... The past, in the present, has become a powerful (element of a) trading economy on a global scale.'
>
> Bennett, S. (1996: 15), *Performing Nostalgia*. London: Routledge

There is, of course, a significant difference between a theme-park 'Globe Theatre', as in Busch Gardens in the USA, and the meticulously researched and reconstructed Shakespeare's Globe in London, which since its opening in 1997 – the year after Bennett's book was published – has demonstrated in its productions an intellectual grasp of some of what it means to perform the plays in a reconstructed playhouse that is in many ways similar to Shakespeare's own. But, even so, Bennett's remarks rightly reflect issues of our own society that influence our interpretations and expectations.

Interpretation and performance

These examples serve to indicate the range of critical and performance interpretations not only of *Hamlet* but Shakespeare's plays in general. It is easy for someone to say, 'Go back to the original' but we have to ask 'What or which original?' Plays are subject to what is sometimes called 'cultural transformations', allowing the often-changing contemporary relevance of the plays to become a significant issue to discuss. Integrated with that we, of course, have to ask questions concerning the original context and any dangers of drift into cultural nostalgia. Historicize and we sometimes fall into mere speculation. Dismantle or deconstruct the plays, and we have to ask ourselves in what order, and how do we reconstruct.

However we attempt to locate a text and an interpretation, Shakespeare appears to keep asking questions. As Shakespeare's contemporary John Marston said, 'Remember the life of these things consists in action.' These tragedies are dynamic. They live in performance and develop through interpretation. Each age, each production, and each interpretative or imaginative reading has to find its *Hamlet* or its *King Lear*, *Macbeth* or *Othello*.

Greeks and Romans 1: *Timon of Athens* (1605) and *Troilus and Cressida* (1601–2)

Shakespeare's first venture into the era of the Greeks and Romans was, as we saw in Chapter 16, *Titus Andronicus*, a play from early in his career containing horrific and gruesome violence which clearly appealed to his audiences. *A Midsummer Night's Dream*, discussed in Chapter 4, is set in Athens. *Pericles*, which we will consider in Chapter 27, involves the protagonist journeying to several Mediterranean port cities all round the Roman Empire. In this chapter, however, I want to consider two satiric plays related to Greece, *Timon of Athens* and the slightly earlier *Troilus and Cressida*, which challenge audience expectations with their bitter cynicism.

Timon of Athens

Timon of Athens is not a particularly popular play in production and it is only periodically performed by the major companies. At the RSC, the performances by Paul Scofield (1965), Richard Pasco (1980) and Michael Pennington (1999) stand out, as does Jonathan Pryce's Timon for Jonathan Miller's BBC TV Complete Shakespeare series. Simon Russell Beale (2012) at the National Theatre, London, played the role as amiable and pleasant with a heart of gold in the first half and a heart truly broken in the second. But when you can see the play on stage or on TV or in the cinema, you'll note not only some rather laboured speeches and the episodic nature of the play but the sheer bitterness of the work.

A BITTER PLAY

Is this bitterness deliberate on Shakespeare's part? Anthony Holden, in his sympathetic biography of the dramatist, searches for a reason for the bitterness in Shakespeare's life at this time but can find nothing in the evidence of the period. That doesn't mean to say that there wasn't anything. Critics also note that the script we have is 'rough', as if it were an early draft in which Thomas Middleton most likely had a hand as a collaborator. Not published in quarto, it appears only in the First Folio of 1623.

Why, therefore, spend time on an incomplete, unreliable text that was apparently only partly written by Shakespeare and not published in his lifetime? The reason is because of its differences in tone, structure and approach from the majority of Shakespeare's plays. There are, for example, no major female roles in the play at all. This bitterness is of a male world where the only females that appear, and then just briefly, are prostitutes. Love is nowhere to be found, but money, or the lack of it, is everywhere, even more so than in *The Merchant of Venice*. As for the gods, their presence is acknowledged in the curses that Timon rains down on an ungrateful and inhospitable Athens, but there is no regenerative energy to be found in a recognition scene or in the reconciliation of the protagonist with his fate:

The gods confound – hear me, you good gods all –
Th'Athenians both within and out that wall;
And grant, as Timon grows, his hate may grow
To the whole race of mankind, high and low!
Amen.

(4.1.37–41)

It is a bitter 'Amen' to his prayer that is directed towards a
society that has shown him no love, no mercy, no kindness.

Spotlight

This is a secular condemnation of a secular society, at the centre
of which is money and its uses. Perhaps that is why Karl Marx was
attracted to the play, in that it exposes the obsession with goods,
whether they are being generously given away or withheld. It is almost
a manifestation of the emerging, secular, monetarily obsessed society of
early capitalism, which was being ruthlessly satirized on the Elizabethan/
Jacobean stage of the time by Ben Jonson, in plays such as *Volpone*
(1605–6) and *The Alchemist* (1610).

THE STRUCTURE OF THE PLAY

Jonson in his satiric comedies is sometimes seen as severe
but his plays are quite different from those of Shakespeare in
this respect. So what has Shakespeare done? He has divided
his play into two parts. In the first we see the generosity
of Timon, who takes delight in giving, to the point of
recklessness – which his servant Flavius tries to point out. In
the second part his appeal for loans is turned down by those
to whom he had formerly been generous. Consequently, he
loses faith in his fellow man and retreats to the woods, railing
against the city and humankind.

MISANTHROPOS

In Act 1, the malcontent cynic Apemantus, a grimmer figure
than Jaques in *As You Like It*, will have none of Timon's
munificence. As the 'opposite to humanity' (1.1.292), he intones
a grace at Timon's feast:

> Immortal gods, I crave no pelf;
>
> I pray for no man but myself.
>
> Grant I may never prove so fond,
>
> To trust man on his oath or bond;
>
> …
>
> Or my friends if I should need 'em.
>
> Amen. So fall to't:
>
> Rich men sin, and I eat root.

(1.2.63–6, 70–72)

The prayer presages what Timon is to become, devoid of
friends and wealth and searching for roots in a barren ground
that will ironically yield gold but only rarely the roots that will
keep him alive.

Spotlight

As it progresses, *Timon of Athens* appears to be a secular morality play. In the medieval morality plays such as *Everyman*, death is the enemy. With death approaching, all man's friends, senses and intimates gradually leave him. You might recall Jaques' Seven Ages of Man speech, which concludes in the seventh age with ageing man, 'Sans teeth, sans eyes, sans taste, sans everything' (*As You Like It*, 2.7.166). You will recall that in *King Lear*, Edgar, when rejected, flees out to the barren heath – as Timon does to the Athenian woods – and there, dishevelled, finds a means, through helping his blind father, to provide some redemption for himself and eventually, re-establish his identity. But Timon resolves that 'I am *Misanthropos*, and hate mankind' (4.3.54), railing earlier in this particularly grim scene against gold, which makes:

> Black, white; foul, fair; wrong, right;
>
> Base, noble; old, young; coward, valiant.

(4.3.29–30)

Timon's friend Alcibiades, in a subplot, turns against Athens, which has also rejected him, and with the help of Timon's money discovered in the woods defeats Athens, but then shows mercy. But for Timon there is ignominious death and, for the audience, no relief from the character's situation or pain, no catharsis, no anagnorisis – just the report that he has gone. It is as bleak a play as anything that was to come hundreds of years later from the Russian writer Maxim Gorky or the Irish dramatist Samuel Beckett. Perhaps Shakespeare left the play rough and unfinished because the bleakness was too extreme, the experiment too emotionally draining or, perhaps, the market was not ready for such a work. But that would be to speculate, which, as we have already seen, Shakespeare so often tempts us to do. You realize you have become a connoisseur of Shakespeare when you begin to be fascinated by this play, *Timon of Athens*.

THE DYSTOPIAN VISION

In his recent paper 'Shakespeare and Greece: Hospitality, Friendship and Republicanism in *Timon of Athens*', John Drakakis provides an insight into the play by referring to Ulysses' often-quoted speech from *Troilus and Cressida*. In this speech, Ulysses, frustrated at the lack of progress of the war and similar lack of commitment from Achilles, articulates the dangers to the structure of a model society, which can unravel through a failure to recognize and respect the principles of order and degree:

> Take but degree away, untune that string,
>
> And hark what discord follows. Each thing meets
>
> In mere oppugnancy.
>
> ...
>
> Then everything includes itself in power,
>
> Power into will, will into appetite;
>
> And appetite, an universal wolf,
>
> So doubly seconded with will and power,
>
> Must make perforce an universal prey
>
> And last eat up himself.

(1.3.109–11, 119–24)

> *'To service his own munificence, Timon, a bankrupt "Lord",*
> *is forced to mortgage his own lands in order to finance the*
> *"hospitality" that he dispenses to artists, poets, merchants and*
> *senators. As his substance diminishes, so he becomes more*
> *conscious of the devaluation of language, the medium through*
> *which he articulates his friendship and his hospitality. What*
> *was primarily and constitutively a means of sustaining and*
> *reinforcing the bonds that hold society together now becomes*
> *hopelessly entangled in quicksands of Athenian power. The*
> *consequence of this diminution is the emergence of a vision*
> *of Athenian chaos that echoes the dystopian vision outlined by*
> *Ulysses in* Troilus and Cressida.*'*
>
> Drakakis, J. (2016: 29), manuscript

Drakakis's insight neatly links these two bitter plays written within just a few years of each other. The devaluation of language, the reference to sexual disease, the railing against 'women as purveyors of that disease', the distasteful images of the body and flesh, all permeate *Troilus and Cressida* as much as they do *Timon of Athens*. What holds them together in *Troilus and Cressida* in describing such a similar dystopian society is the Trojan War.

Troilus and Cressida

This discussion of *Troilus and Cressida* will concentrate on Shakespeare's narrative, since it is precisely through the story – from the relationship that is interwoven between what occurs within and immediately outside the walls of Troy – that we find the social and political environment of a dystopian world emerging.

THE NARRATIVE

The play focuses not on the story of Paris and Helen, but of Paris' younger brother Troilus, and Cressida, the daughter of Calchas who defects to the Grecian camp. These two lovers are brought together by Pandarus, Cressida's uncle – hence the term 'pander' meaning a procurer. But after a wooing and one night only together, Cressida is exchanged by the Trojans for one of their generals, Antenor, who has been captured by the Greeks. Troilus and Cressida swear undying love to each other but when Cressida arrives at the Grecian camp, she finds that her only safety is to enter a relationship with Diomedes, which will protect her against the advances of other soldiers.

Love itself is reduced to a commodity to be transferred apparently from Troilus to Diomedes. Despite Cressida's protestations, when Troilus has secretly entered the Grecian camp and finds out the truth, any explanation of her conduct is rejected. Cressida's 'unfaithfulness' is a symptom of the breakdown of society, and of a piece with the unheroic death of Troilus' brother Hector at the hands of Achilles' Myrmidons, and of Troilus' own resolve to continue fighting, even though there remain no ideals for which to fight.

Within the framework of the war, Achilles, the famed warrior of the Greeks, is in a dalliance with Patroclus and is spurned by the Trojan generals for his refusal to fight. The great warrior of the Trojans is Hector. Eventually, when Achilles, taunted by the foul-mouthed Thersites, is shamed into fighting Hector by the Greek generals – who pretend to favour the bullish Ajax – he has Hector butchered by his followers, the Myrmidons. Hector's death is indicative of the fall of both civilizations, but in the narrative is a crushing blow for Troy and King Priam. The distraught Troilus, who has lost both Cressida and his brother Hector, vows revenge:

> Hector is gone.
> Who shall tell Priam so, or Hecuba?
> Let him that will a screech-owl be called
> Go into Troy, and say their Hector's dead.
>
> ...

And, thou great-sized coward,

No space of earth shall sunder our two hates.

I'll haunt thee like a wicked conscience still,

...

Hope of revenge shall hide our inward woe.

(5.11.14–17, 26–8, 31)

Spotlight

Cressida unfaithful and lost, Hector dead, Troilus enraged with grief: the play concludes pessimistically with Pandarus promising to bequeath his sexual diseases to the audience.

CYNICISM

Throughout the play the character of Thersities, in the role of the Fool, who in Shakespeare's plays provides a commentary on the follies of others, does so here in obscene terms fitting for the degeneration of the world that the war has created (see, for example, 5.4.1–17). Meanwhile, in Troy, Cassandra, King Priam's daughter, prophesies the death of Hector, and, although this worries Priam, the Trojans do not heed her warning (5.3.80–94). Of course, the root cause of the war is the abduction of the Greek Menelaus' wife, Helen, by the Trojan Paris, so that the origin of the war lies not in a chivalric ideal but, as Thersites indicates, unrestrained sexual desire or 'lechery'.

So this play is no *Romeo and Juliet*, with its romanticizing of the lovers and its move from comedy to tragedy, but a hard-hitting, cynical account of human conduct, accompanied by betrayal and the degradation of language as indicative of sexual decadence and social disintegration.

> 'Troilus and Cressida *is distinguished by its image clusters of diseases, animals and food ... the imagery of disease and animals ... serve to caricature and degrade the activities of the dramatis personae ... Eating and tasting ... construct a profound metaphor for human activity, and its exploitation in* Troilus and Cressida *goes far to establish an intellectual critique of the actions recorded there ... The vehicle is food, but the tenor is Time: Time viewed as an inexorable determined process in which the end is contained in the beginning, the conclusion in the premise.'*
>
> Berry, R. (1978: 75–6, 80), *The Shakespearean Metaphor: Studies in Language and Form.* London and Basingstoke: Macmillan

Some critics have been tempted to suggest that the images of sexual disease in the play indicate that Shakespeare may have contracted syphilis around this period. The later sonnets take up the theme, as do *Timon of Athens* and the later *Pericles*, but this is conjecture and speculation and it cannot be validated. It is also an inadequate explanation for what this complex play is imagining and how it works as a play, the process of which draws a landscape of malign humanity. The Trojan Hector remarks to the Greek Ulysses:

> ... The end crowns all,
> And that old common arbitrator, Time,
> Will one day end it.
>
> (4.5.224–6).

For the present, the deadly war continues. The images of flesh, animals, food and disease work through the play, creating an overall image of a foul unsavoury society, one that is no longer dependent on itself to bring an end to the misery but rather on that 'old common arbitrator, Time'. It is a refrain we meet in various manifestations throughout Shakespeare in his comedies, tragedies and histories, but rarely as bleakly and terrifyingly as in this savage conflict.

THE LANDSCAPE OF WAR

In *Troilus and Cressida* Shakespeare paints the landscape of war. He introduces a revolting, foul-mouthed commentator, Thersites, to rail at and taunt the Greeks from within. There is decadence in the war itself, exposed by Thersites in his railing at Ajax or Achilles and, however foul-mouthed he is, the picture of war as a metaphor of human conduct seems brutally realistic.

Although the story of Troy and the manner of the war's end was and is well known, the story of the Trojan Horse is ignored by the dramatist. He chooses rather to focus on a story within war, creating a pattern of images on which we may impose our own understanding and knowledge of war. The arbitrator 'Time' places the issues beyond the age of Classical Greece or Elizabethan England. For the twentieth or twenty-first century, this might mean the First World War, the Second World War, the Falklands War, the invasion of Iraq or, on the very day I am writing this chapter – 2 December 2015 – the debate in the UK Parliament leading to a vote to bomb Syria in order to help eradicate the barbarity of the so-called Islamic State.

I recall that Terry Hands produced this play in 2004/5 at Clwyd Theatre Cymru, in North Wales, following the 2003 invasion of Iraq. It was performed as the text dictated. There was no overt reference to the war in Iraq, no gimmicks but just the reality of war itself. The production spoke volumes. Hands' sensitivity to the text was all that was needed for the audience to realize that what was being said 400 years ago was being re-enacted yet again in the real politics of the contemporary world. In conversation with me on 21 January 2016, Hands told me that he never discussed the Iraqi War in rehearsals. He didn't have to. He did, however, point to the relationship between the two sets of lovers Paris and Helen and Troilus and Cressida in the play and their correspondence, a statement which takes us back to Empson's concept of the double plot.

'The political theorising in Troilus (chiefly about loyalty, whether to a mistress or a state) becomes more interesting if you take it as a conscious development by Shakespeare of the ideas inherent in the double-plot convention... Troilus compares the sexual with the political standards, and shows both in disruption. The breaking of Cressida's vow is symbolic of, the breaking of Helen's vow is cause of, what the play shows (chiefly by the combat between Hector and his first cousin Ajax) to be civil war; Shakespeare's horror of this theme... may in part explain the grimness of his treatment.'

Empson, W. (1935, repr. 1950: 34–5), *Some Versions of Pastoral.* London: Chatto & Windus

As noted from the start of this book, Shakespeare doesn't mean what we mean by Shakespeare. Anthony Holden wryly notes that 'we do not read Shakespeare, he reads us' (Holden, A. [1999: 2]). Like *Timon of Athens, Troilus and Cressida* is a confrontational play, and its structure allows its narrative consistently to provide glimpses of the 'present' in the experience of war. In one sense the play has no ending, since its subject can provide no revelation or relief. It is the process of the play that engages us, without tempting us with any expectation of closure. To use a Shakespearean tautology, it is the play that is. His focus is on the insistence on the process of the narrative, rather than on a structure that will conveniently produce a satisfactory ending. In this, *Troilus and Cressida* presages some of the issues and structural incongruities we have already found in our discussion of *King Lear*. It is a play designed to disturb.

Greeks and Romans 2: *Julius Caesar* (1599); *Antony and Cleopatra* (1606–7); *Coriolanus* (1608)

These three plays on Roman themes provide a further variant or dimension of 'tragic history' from the ones we have discussed earlier in our consideration of the English history plays or the four great tragedies. These are histories taken from a variety of sources but principally Plutarch's *Lives*, published as *Lives of the Noble Grecians and Romans* in a translation by Thomas North in 1595. In being dependent on a particular source, the structure of each play follows the historical narrative.

The structure of the plays

These three Roman plays exploit a dimension of tragedy by foregrounding a dialogue between the private and the public sphere and the effect each has on the other. To do so, Shakespeare follows his source and creates his own discipline for their structure, which often challenges expectations.

In *Julius Caesar*, Brutus justifies the murder of his friend Caesar to himself thus:

> It must be by his death: and for my part
> I know no personal cause to spurn him
> But for the general. He would be crowned:
> How that might change his nature, there's the question.
> It is the bright day that brings forth the adder,
> And that craves wary walking.

(2.1.10–15)

In *Antony and Cleopatra*, Antony's friend Enobarbus justifies his betrayal of Antony because of what he terms 'A diminution in our captain's brain', which has made Antony 'outstare the lightning', concluding:

> When valour preys on reason,
> It eats the sword it fights with. I will seek
> Some way to leave him.

(3.13.204–6)

In *Coriolanus*, the protagonist's mother Volumnia does not desert him in the same way but, in persuading the banished warrior not to wreak his revenge on Rome by sacking the city, she condemns him to his death at the hands of the Volscian general Aufidius. At the conclusion of Volumnia's great appeal for her son's mercy on the city (5.3.94–124, 133–84), Coriolanus replies:

O mother, mother!

What have you done?

...

You have won a happy victory to Rome;

But for your son, believe it, O, believe it,

Most dangerously you have with him prevail'd,

If not most mortal to him.

(5.3.185–6, 189–92)

Antony and Cleopatra moves across the years and across the ancient world with astonishing rapidity because the dramatist seeks to represent a history in which the characters did move from Rome to another part of the Roman Empire, but he has to represent these movements within the timespan of a performance. Shakespeare is pragmatic. He tells a vast story within the restricted limits of a theatrical production on a particular stage. He does not focus on a single aspect but opens up the narrative to produce an episodic structure which not only allows him to violate the unities of time, place and action but also to provide an opening or debate among the play's political adversaries. These necessarily involve plebeians and common soldiers, faced with the attitudes and decisions made by their generals. So, for example, in Act 3, Scene 7 of *Antony and Cleopatra*, he introduces a character that Antony respectfully terms a 'worthy soldier'. The soldier then pleads with Antony not to fight at sea (as Cleopatra plans to do) but on land:

O noble Emperor, do not fight by sea.

Trust not to rotten planks. Do you misdoubt

This sword and these my wounds? Let th'Egyptians

And the Phoenicians go a-ducking; we

Have used to conquer standing on the earth

And fighting foot to foot.

(3.7.60–66)

Antony ignores his advice but, in creating the scene, Shakespeare introduces a number of issues: the scepticism and unhappiness of the common soldier with regard to the general that he has followed for years, and the determination of Antony not to listen to any advice but that of Cleopatra, however incorrect others deem it to be.

Similarly, in *Julius Caesar* the people have to make up their minds about why Caesar has been assassinated, and *Coriolanus* opens with the people nearing revolt because of famine and identifying Caius Martius (Coriolanus) as their chief enemy. It is no surprise, perhaps, that Bertolt Brecht, the twentieth-century advocate of Epic Theatre and political drama, was stimulated to make a translation and adaptation of *Coriolanus*, commenting on the plebeians in the first scene, 'Think how reluctantly men decide to revolt! It's an adventure for them: new paths have to be marked out and followed; moreover the rule of the rulers is always accompanied by that of their ideas' (Willett, J. [1964: 252], *Brecht on Theatre*, ed. and trans. by John Willett. London: Eyre Methuen).

Exploring social conduct through the drama

By the time of writing *Coriolanus*, Shakespeare appears to have moved on from the dialogue that we saw in *Henry V* – written at approximately the same time as *Julius Caesar* – between the soldier Michael Williams and the King on the eve of the Battle of Agincourt (see Chapters 13 and 15). In this Roman play he provides a greater exploration of the significant social tensions, not just among ruling hierarchies and with soldiers but among the people themselves.

Each of these three Roman plays is termed a 'tragedy' but none of them lends itself to being regarded as 'cathartic' in quite the same way that critics have traditionally considered the four 'great tragedies'. Some critics, of course, will argue about whether they are 'tragedies' or 'histories' and try to pigeonhole them, while others might politicize them in a different way, as does Brecht. But on our journey through these Shakespearean plays we are considering how plays open up debates, asking questions by illuminating social conduct as reflected through dramatic narrative.

What we find with *Julius Caesar* and *Coriolanus* in particular is a merging between stage and audience, insofar as an affinity is established between the people within the audience and the plebeians being depicted. Even so, there is a different emphasis with regard to the depiction of the Roman populace between *Julius Caesar* and *Coriolanus*, where in the latter the people are treated more sympathetically.

'*Coriolanus* exploits the conditions within the playhouse which produces such close contact between audience members; the play contains many scenes involving Roman citizenry, which, when we consider the atmosphere within a crowded playhouse, draws in the spectators, transforming them momentarily into the very people whom *Coriolanus*, reluctantly, has had to work so hard to win over. The protagonist needs the people's voices as much as the actor playing him needs the approval of the audience. Thus it is hard to miss the irony when *Coriolanus* remarks that he doesn't like to speak to the people – "It is a part/That I shall blush in acting, and might well/Be taken from the people" (2.2.144-6).'

Karim-Cooper, F. and Stern, L. (eds) (2014: 221), 'Touch and Taste in Shakespeare's Theatres', in *Shakespeare's Theatres and the Effects of Performance*. London: Bloomsbury (Arden Shakespeare Library)

But this understanding comes from the fact that the plays themselves are telling a good story, which other, later, writers such as Bertolt Brecht and Günter Grass (1927–2015) readily recognized.

'Even with popular ballads or the peepshows at fairs the simple people (who are so far from simple) love stories of the rise and fall of great men, of eternal change, of the ingenuity of the oppressed, of the potentialities of mankind. And they hunt for the truth that is "behind it all".'

Willett, J. (ed. and trans.) (1964: 265), Brecht, B., 1957, *Brecht on Theatre*. London: Eyre Methuen

Merging stage and audience

Julius Caesar may have been the first play to be staged at Shakespeare's new theatre, the Globe, in 1599. As we have seen, this theatre was constructed in 'the stews' of London. The play opens with the rabble, with people out on the streets. The Tribune Flavius commands them:

> Hence! home, you idle creatures, get you home!
>
> Is this a holiday? What, know you not,
>
> (Being mechanical) you ought not walk
>
> Upon a labouring day, without the sign
>
> Of your profession? Speak, what trade art thou?
>
> (1.1.1–5)

A new theatre, a new play, the early afternoon, and who are the audience? Shouldn't some of them at least be at work? Shakespeare, with these opening words, draws attention to the very notion of the play as a representation, not just of the fictional history, but as entertainment itself involving the audience in a relationship with the characters on stage, the first of whom answers Flavius' question with, 'Why, sir, a carpenter.' It's not impossible that someone watching that afternoon – perhaps more than one – was a carpenter, since this, after all, was possibly the first production in the wooden theatre – the wooden O – that had been recreated from the timbers of the old playhouse in Shoreditch, 'The Theatre'.

As with the later *Coriolanus*, in *Julius Caesar* a connection is being made from the start between the governed and those who govern, the audience and the action on stage, whether they are playing nobility or commoners. We have from this dramatic opening a communal event being enacted, suggesting a shared understanding which involves everyone in the theatre. The 'well-heeled' audience in the sixpenny seats might even have wondered why those standing around the stage were not at work. But that is, of course, speculation. What is of further interest is the emphasis, within the representation of the Roman context, of the interaction of the plebeian with the governing classes, and the fact that the celebration is stimulated by a series of political events.

Spotlight

Rome, the greatest empire of which Shakespeare's time had knowledge, is used by the dramatist to develop dramatic entertainments around the lives and fates of noble men depicted as individuals, within the context of a society that was in some ways not unlike the one engaged in the dramatic experience of the performance itself.

In an ingeniously meta-dramatic moment in *Antony and Cleopatra*, Shakespeare makes the defeated Queen of Egypt refer to the very action of the drama itself. She recoils from the fact that she could be 'staged':

> ... Saucy lictors
> Will catch at us like strumpets, and scald rhymers
> Ballad us out o' tune. The quick comedians
> Extemporally will stage us and present
> Our Alexandrian revels; Antony
> Shall be brought drunken forth; and I shall see
> Some squeaking Cleopatra boy my greatness
> I'th' posture of a whore.

> (5.2.213–20)

Remember that this is the boy actor, the subject of Cleopatra's prophecy or denial, who is speaking these lines. *Antony and Cleopatra* was written nine years after *Julius Caesar* and the meta-theatrical reference had become within that time ever more assured than at the opening of *Julius Caesar*. But even that play, like *Antony and Cleopatra* and *Coriolanus*, defies categorization. Once termed a 'tragedy', however, debates occur as to whose tragedy it is, or who is the tragic protagonist. Is it Julius Caesar, who dies in Act 3, Scene 1 (the apex of Freytag's pyramid) or is it Brutus, whose death comes at the conclusion of the play? We began our journey through Shakespeare's plays by defining structures and their underpinning of the dramatic plot and action, but we've now arrived at a point in our discussion where we can see that Shakespeare is so much in command of his material that he can open the structure expansively without it collapsing.

Elizabethan contemporary issues

Although eighteenth-century critics complained about the lack of structural decorum, *Julius Caesar*, like *Henry V*, involves itself in contemporary issues such as the reign of the ageing Queen, the famines that afflicted the rural communities of early Jacobean England, and the continued outbreaks of plague in London. The nature and make-up of the original audience in the new London theatre had knowledge of contemporary events of the day, and they were mirrored in the stories of the past that Shakespeare exploited.

Even in our contemporary theatre, the great orations to the people by Brutus and Antony following Caesar's assassination are sometimes made directly to the audience. But to the Elizabethans watching the spectacle, the bloody nature of Caesar's body which Antony displays, the tears in Caesar's robes, the wounds still oozing blood, all emphasized by Antony's rhetoric and also, to an extent, indicative in 'theatrical terms' of the actual executions that they could watch across London at Tyburn, were immediate experiences for which there were plenty of extra-theatrical analogues. There is in Shakespeare's theatre a realization of the theatrical potential of earlier morality plays. In the old medieval *The Play of the Sacrament*, the defiled consecrated host of the Catholic Mass bleeds in the hands of those desecrating it, just as Caesar bleeds again on stage or the traitors bleed at their execution. Within that context, the plays refer not only to the larger context of Elizabethan/Jacobean society itself but also to the public discourses that sustain them.

Manipulation of perception

It is the language, the manipulation of perception, the stage management of the oratory, which works within the play, and as in a play, it sways an audience this way and that.

Spotlight

Antony and Cleopatra opens with a statement that the great general has been compromised, with his own soldiers complaining:

> Nay, but this dotage of our general's
>
> O'erflows the measure. Those his goodly eyes,
>
> That o'er the files and musters of the war
>
> Have glowed like plated Mars, now bend, now turn
>
> The office and devotion of their view
>
> Upon a tawny front.

(1.1.1–6)

He has been entrapped, as far as his soldiers are concerned, by the 'tawny front' that is Cleopatra. The image of Mars, the god of war, is introduced, which is to be counterbalanced in the play by that of Venus, the goddess of love. The images do not make characters into gods but put them in the

On the other hand, in *Julius Caesar* the audience does not witness the offer of the crown three times to Caesar – although some film directors cannot resist the temptation to visualize it. Shakespeare knew his business of writing in a disciplined way, omitting distractions, but also, as in the later *Othello*, forcing the audience to make up its mind from conflicting narratives. The audience hears the off-stage noise but the conspirators use the noise to persuade Brutus to join them. This is part of the continuing unfolding drama of the play, one episode leading to the next and that to the following, rendering the narrative complex and ambiguous until it is drawn to a conclusion. Indeed, although Caesar dies in Act 3 of the play, his presence prevails until the end when Brutus 'runs on his sword'.

The domestic and the public

You will recall that, except for the prostitutes, there are no female roles in *Timon of Athens*, which allows for the restrictive dominance of the masculine world of Athens. In the earlier *Julius Caesar*, however, aspects of the play work by the exposure of the feminine attempt to ward off the determination of the masculine. Calphurnia, Caesar's wife, begs him not to go to the Capitol because of the dream she has had. She attempts to impose domestic discipline upon him:

> What mean you, Caesar? Think you walk forth?
> You shall not stir out of your house today.

(2.2.8–9)

Caesar is momentarily shown to be vulnerable and is tempted by her:

> Mark Antony shall say I am not well,
>
> And for thy humour I will stay at home.

(2.2.55–6).

The domestic, however, gives way to the public through Decius' explanation of the dream as a means to exalt Caesar with the promise that 'the Senate have concluded/To give this day a crown to mighty Caesar' (2.2.93–4). Caesar's domestic subservience is shown to give way to politics and pride and male hubris overcomes Calphurnia's female intuition.

Brutus's wife, Portia, similarly shows a wife's concern about her husband's mental and physical state:

> What, is Brutus sick?
>
> And will he steal out of his wholesome bed
>
> To dare the vile contagion of the night?
>
> And tempt the rheumy and unpurged air
>
> To add unto his sickness? No, my Brutus,
>
> You have some sick offence within your mind ...

(2.1.262–7)

As a proof to her husband of her loyalty, love and strength, she has voluntarily wounded herself in the thigh (2.2.298–300), and later she dies, as Brutus reports to Cassius, by swallowing fire (4.3.154). In these plays the feminine adds a dimension of humane opposition to the political, an element of humanity to a world of masculine competitive power.

The argument between Brutus and Cassius in *Julius Caesar* (Act 4, Scene 3) is in itself, however, a tense prelude to a coming public display of masculinity – the final war that will send them both to their deaths. 'O my dear brother,' Cassius says to him about their argument, 'This was an ill beginning of the night./Never come such division 'tween our souls./Let it not, Brutus' (4.3.231–3).

The personal and the political

In *Antony and Cleopatra*, Enobarbus in making his decision to leave Antony and join Caesar discovers that Antony has sent his treasure after him and that Caesar does not look kindly on such deserters, placing them in the van of battle, ensuring they face their former comrades. But there is more to it than this. Enobarbus realizes that he has deserted his friend, which causes him greater anxiety than anything the political struggle can elicit:

> I am alone the villain of the earth,
> And feel I am so most
> ...
> I fight against thee [Antony]? No, I will go seek
> Some ditch wherein to die; the foul'st best fits
> My latter part of life.
>
> (4.6.31–2, 38–40)

Within all of this, although ideologies and/or pragmatism in both *Julius Caesar* and *Antony and Cleopatra* lie behind the choices being made, human behaviour is still questioned in detail within the framework of these plays.

'In Antony and Cleopatra *those with power make history yet only in accord with the contingencies of the existing historical moment – in Antony's words: "the strong necessity of time"* (1.3.43).'

Dollimore, J. (3rd edn. 2004: 207), *Radical Tragedy: Religion, Ideology and Power in the Drama of Shakespeare and His Contemporaries.* Basingstoke: Palgrave Macmillan

Political decisions are made by Shakespeare's Roman generals in public and it is within the same arena that their private fragilities are exposed. Coriolanus has to fight his pride first to gain the 'voices' of the people to become consul (*Coriolanus*, Act 2, Scene 3), but eventually he cannot hide his disdain. The people's Tribune, Junius Brutus, reveals his knowledge of the man's weakness as a sure way to bring him down:

> Put him to choler straight; he hath been us'd
> Ever to conquer
> …
> Be rein'd again to temperance; then he speaks
> What's in his heart, and that is there which looks
> With us to break his neck.

(3.3.25–6, 28–30)

Spotlight

Coriolanus cannot reconcile the political with the personal. He despises the people, although he fights on their behalf against external enemies, and he cannot see why he needs their approval, 'their voices', to become a Consul. He cannot fully play the role of the professional political hypocrite because he is conscious of his own achievement of authority, bravery and experience. To have to stand as on a stage and gain the approval of a citizenry for whom he has absolute contempt is anathema:

> Most sweet voices!
>
> Better it is to die, better to starve,
>
> Than crave the hire which first we do deserve.
>
> Why in this wolvish toge should I stand here,
>
> To beg of Hob and Dick that does appear
>
> Their needless vouches?

(2.3.111–16)

At first he does what is required of him:

> For your voices I have fought,
>
> Watch'd for your voices; for your voices, bear
>
> Of wounds two dozen odd; battles thrice six
>
> I have seen and heard of; for your voices have
>
> Done many things, some less, some more: Your voices!
>
> Indeed I would be consul.

(2.3.125–30)

Thus far he sways the populace, who remain suspicious, until Junius
Brutus turns them with the revelation that his request was shot through
with hypocrisy:

> Did you perceive
>
> He did solicit you in free contempt
>
> When he did need your loves; and do you think
>
> That his contempt shall not be bruising to you
>
> When he hath power to crush?

(2.3.197–201)

Coriolanus is subsequently banished and turns against Rome,
but towards the end of the play when he does have the power
to 'crush', which is to lead the Volscians against the city, the
feminine, in the person of his mother, dissuades him by her own
appeal to him to save Rome. It is a maternal appeal but one
directed to his pride. What will be his legacy if he should lay
waste his own lands?

> ... but this is certain,
>
> That if thou conquer Rome, the benefit
>
> Which thou shalt thereby reap in such a name
>
> Whose repetition will be dogg'd with curses,
>
> Whose chronicle thus writ: 'The man was noble,
>
> But with his last attempt he wip'd it out,
>
> Destroy'd his country, and his name remains
>
> To th'insuing age abhorr'd.

(5.3.143–50)

She possesses a theatrical rhetoric which he could not master
as she instructs his wife Virgilia, his son young Martius, Valeria
and their attendants to 'shame him with our knees' (5.3.171).
For him to show mercy, which he proceeds to do, will result in
his own death.

Challenging the audience

What *Coriolanus* does show is the impossibility of the choices that the tragic protagonist is forced into making by his contradictory commitments. Shakespeare doesn't end the play, however, with the Volscian conspirators and Aufidius, Coriolanus' great competitor in arms, sadistically repeating the word 'Kill, kill, kill, kill, kill him!' while they butcher him and then stand over his corpse in triumph. Rather, Shakespeare has the Lords around them cry out 'Hold, hold, hold, hold!' counterbalancing the repetition of the word 'kill'. They chide Aufidius for his lack of valour, for which he first makes excuses and then, perhaps in keeping with the political hypocrisy of the play as a whole, states:

> My rage is gone,
> And I am struck with sorrow.
>
> (5.6.146–7)

How the actor playing Aufidius delivers the lines is for him and his director to decide. There is even in the ending of this play a certain fluidity. Coriolanus is dead. Is what Aufidius says to be truly believed by the audience? Or is it a further testament to the hypocrisy of politics that the play has systematically exposed? Or is it merely a reflection of Aufidius' own sense of deflation after an event that he had longed to experience? If these and other such questions are left in our minds as we leave the theatre, then the only certainty lies in the mastery of the writing that has left us conflicted, perhaps horrified, and still ruminating on what has been portrayed. In other words, the conclusion throws the challenge of the play's dilemmas back to the audience – the real people, not the fictional characters of drama.

It would be a mistake, however, to think the Roman plays are without emotion. Mark Antony grieves, Coriolanus despairs and Cleopatra loves. Her great argument in Act 1, Scene 3, with Antony, who will 'desert' her to return to the politics of Rome, concludes with a moment of intensity. Antony begins to storm out of her presence, 'I'll leave you, lady', but is halted as she calls him back with an expression of love of which the audience can be in no doubt:

> Courteous lord, one word:
> Sir, you and I must part, but that's not it;
> Sir, you and I have loved, but there's not it;
> That you know well. Something it is I would –
> Oh, my oblivion is a very Antony,
> And I am all forgotten!

> (1.3.88–93)

It is through that break at the end of line 91, 'I would – ' leading to the great statement of her incapacity to be anything but her love, that Shakespeare shows his artistic control of that extraordinary play. Indeed, it is with Cleopatra that the 'poetry' and the imagination reside in this play: Egypt is the place of sensuousness, fecund femininity and poetry, whereas Rome is the place of a rational politics that is no match for the feminine wiles of Egypt.

Key idea

In the Roman dramas the public and the private play off each other, highlighting aspects of both. In this, they can both conjure up and modulate emotion while engaging the intellect of the audience in debate.

Critical perspectives 6: Some 'isms'; a glossary; and selected biographies

At this point let us take a brief pause in our journey so that you can refresh yourself with some definitions of the critical movements we have been coming across in getting to know Shakespeare. This chapter also includes a glossary of technical terms used in the book. In addition, you might find it useful to have a guide that will help you find out more about Shakespeare's life. In recent years a number of interesting biographies of the poet/ dramatist have been published, based on some incisive historical research, and these are listed here.

Some definitions of 'isms'

CATHOLICISM

Christianity provided a central authority, located in Rome under the figure of the Pope, and a unifying intellectual and spiritual influence in Western Europe after the fall of the Roman Empire. By the fourteenth century, however, the Church's increasing worldliness and its venal abuses led to growing dissatisfaction. The Renaissance, or Early Modern period, heralded a re-examination of Christianity by humanists (such as Erasmus and More) who nevertheless rejected wholescale reform when radical clerics such as Martin Luther and his Protestant supporters sought to diverge from traditional teaching. The Roman Catholic Church, which places an emphasis on sacramental liturgy and 'historic' episcopal papal authority, initiated a movement (1545–63) to counter the Reformation that had been initiated by Luther in 1517. After Henry VIII's break with Rome (1533), papal authority was briefly reinstated in England in the reign of Mary I (1553–8), but when Elizabeth I became queen a Protestant settlement was engineered and her role as head of state and supreme governor of the Church of England was affirmed.

HUMANISM

This is the general term for the renewed interest in classical ideas and literature that developed in Italian city-states during the fourteenth century, and particularly after the fall of Constantinople in 1492, spread throughout Europe in the fifteenth and sixteenth centuries, helped by the invention of the printing press (c.1450). Inspired by a desire to access knowledge of the ancient world, it emphasized the use of primary sources, encouraging intellectual curiosity and self-improvement. Renaissance humanists believed that 'the new learning' created good Christians, good citizens and a deep appreciation of humankind and the created world. It transformed European thought, leading to an expansion in the curriculae of schools and universities. Italian writers like Pico della Mirandola (1463–94), Marsilio Ficino (1433–99), the poet Petrarch (1304–74) and others were influential in emphasizing the centrality of man in the universe. These beliefs have been subsequently modified in modern times by other linked ideologies such as Christian humanism and liberal humanism.

PROTESTANTISM

Protestantism originated in the protest by a German theologian from Wittenberg, Martin Luther (1483–1546), who in 1517 attacked church practices he felt needed to be reformed and who (it is generally believed) nailed his 95 theses to the church door in that town. Luther's protest was inspired by the ideals of humanism. Protestantism based its authority not on tradition or on the primacy of papal interpretation of the Scriptures but on the Bible as the only source of truth, and placed much greater emphasis on the individual conscience. Protestantism soon divided into a number of denominations that championed differing theological emphases. In England, Henry VIII did not embrace Protestantism but seceded from papal authority to create an anglicized Catholic Church of which he was the supreme head. A more Protestant theology was introduced under Edward VI, who produced the influential *Book of Common Prayer*, and was consolidated by Elizabeth I, but elements of Catholic theology remained enshrined in Church of England doctrine, causing conflict with some forms of extreme Protestantism, particularly Puritanism, in the reigns of Elizabeth I and the early Stuart monarchs.

NEOCLASSICISM

This movement emanated mainly from the 1660s and became prominent throughout the eighteenth century. It promoted the concepts of order and decorum necessary within a work of art, deriving its inspiration from the classical age for definition and interpretation. There was an understanding that literature concerned itself with form, with 'What oft was thought but ne'er so well expressed' (Alexander Pope (1688–1744): *An Essay on Criticism* [1711]). The neoclassical rules for that expression worked with established generic principles rather than allowing the writer the freedom of the imagination or the individualism fostered in Renaissance humanism, although Elizabethan writers such as Sir Philip Sidney (1554–86) were drawn towards such formal rules.

ROMANTICISM

Romanticism developed in the late eighteenth and early nineteenth centuries. It regarded art and literature in the context of its 'organic nature', developing from laws within itself. It looked towards the ideal, found in myths and also in the innocence of ordinary people expressed in simplicity of language. It thereby rejected the neoclassicism of the eighteenth century. It also privileged a free autonomous individualism. For the Romantics, Shakespeare's art came from his 'natural genius', a view advocated particularly by the poet Samuel Taylor Coleridge (1772–1834).

REALISM

Realism was a reaction against the Romantic notion of the ideal, and was evident in the realist novelists of the nineteenth century, for example Charles Dickens (1812–70) and George Eliot (1819–80), who depicted as clearly as possible what they considered to be the realities and experiences of life in all strata of society. It is a mimetic form that could easily be transferred to the stage, with the plays of Henrik Ibsen (1828–1906) in particular. Realism influenced dramatic criticism in its concentration on characters that behave as they would do in real life.

ARCHETYPAL CRITICISM

This movement grew out of Jungian psychology in the early twentieth century, taking realistic and psychological aspects of Shakespearean criticism into a new dimension. Primordial myths and patterns within the collective unconsciousness could be detected in, and aroused by, a variety of different texts: for example, *Hamlet* displays a similar pattern of myths that can be found in the plays of Aeschylus (525–456 BCE) or Sophocles (496–406 BCE), and the play could reveal similar archetypal modes of behaviour, as represented in figures such as Orestes and Oedipus in mother–son relationships or in the concentration on the taboo of incest, and on the subsequent retribution of the gods.

MODERNISM

Modernism rejected the nineteenth-century concept of the 'organic nature' of art, and in the early twentieth century also rejected realism. Modernist writers such as James Joyce (1882–1941) and Virginia Woolf (1882–1941) made the reader aware that they were 'reading' something that had been 'written', thereby forcing the reader into a self-conscious acknowledgement of the role that language played in the shaping of literary response. In the theatre, modernist-influenced movements such as constructivism arose around the same time as communism and the Russian Revolution. In Germany they were followed by the politically oriented theatre of Bertolt Brecht (1898–1956), although modernism was not politically partisan since it also had exponents on the right such as Ezra Pound (1885–1972) and T. S. Eliot (1888–1965).

POSTMODERNISM

Postmodernism arose out of modernism and the experience of a war-torn Europe, which led to the rejection of authority by some. Like modernism, this movement rejected the linearity of an artistic product and worked through presenting patterns of experience that did not have to express a 'sense of meaning'. It conveyed a vacuity of existence and an absence of purpose, exemplified in drama such as *Waiting for Godot* by Samuel Beckett (1906–89).

NEW HISTORICISM

This approach questions contemporary interpretations that look for the 'relevance' of drama, insisting that Shakespeare can be understood only by being located within the period of the plays' inception and composition. It draws on historical evidence from outside the text, including sources not necessarily connected with the text, such as medical cases, historical tracts, tax records and gravestones, and aims to locate common structural patterns in all forms of narrative. It sought to combine elements of materialism with the poststructuralist writings of Michel Foucault (1926–84), and emphasized the various ways in which power operated to contain resistance.

FEMINIST CRITICISM

Shakespearean studies as well as literary studies were influenced the feminist movement of the mid- to late twentieth century and its antecedents. There are broad definitions and differing expressions of feminism in literary criticism generally. Nevertheless, significant areas can be discerned: the first relates to politics, feminist philosophy and gender as seen in the work, for example, of Marilyn French, who exposes in cultural terms how gender determines the identity of the 'female' who is subordinate to the 'male'. A second approach is related to the location of women within Shakespeare's society, as found in the work, for example, of Lisa Jardine, Juliet Dusinbere, Catherine Belsey and Germaine Greer. A third is concerned with Shakespeare in performance in theatre and film. In this, the growing voice of many female directors and actors in both experimental and mainstream theatre became prominent from the 1970s onwards.

CULTURAL MATERIALISM

Cultural materialism attempts to understand the 'materiality' of a work of art within the context of its historical production and location. It denies the universality of truths contained in the text and emphasizes areas of resistance that the text privileges or disguises. It argues that texts do not mean something in themselves but have meanings conferred upon them and those meanings have a political charge. Cultural materialism anchors meaning in an overtly stated political understanding of material reality. It draws heavily on the philosophies of writers such as Raymond Williams (1921–88) and Louis Althusser (1918–90), but also makes some reference (like new historicism) to the writings of Jacques Derrida (1930–2004) and Michel Foucault.

STRUCTURALISM

This is a complex idea that takes the structure of language as a model for the structure of all forms of human endeavour. It is concerned to establish patterns that can be replicated across the human sciences in order to establish hitherto obscure connections. In literary discourse it distinguishes between the 'word', or 'signifier', that is comprised of arbitrary elements, and 'the signified', which is the concept that lies behind it. In literary criticism structuralism divides texts according to the tension between binary elements that derive meaning from their relation to each other. Meaning is generated by selecting elements from language (*la langue*) and combining them into meaningful units (*la parole*). So, 'put crudely, structuralism is (at least in its early or "pure" form) interested rather in that which makes meaning possible than in meaning itself: even more crudely in form rather than content' (Hawthorn, J. [1992: 174]).

POST-STRUCTURALISM

As Hawthorn says, this is a term 'that is sometimes used almost interchangeably with Deconstruction' (Hawthorn J. [1992: 137–8]). In literary criticism it follows on from structuralism's attempt to discover mechanics of meaning but it questions the overt distinction between 'the signifier' and 'the signified'. For structuralists, the 'death of the author' represents a challenge to the principle of a single controlling authority of meaning. For post-structuralists, the relative stability of any 'structure' is undermined by what is perceived to be a constant deferral of meaning. Any structure, according to post-structuralism, can be undermined or reduced to the conditions under which its structure is formulated.

Unlike modernism, which is content to reflect the fragmentary nature of reality, post-structuralism challenges all attempts to anchor knowledge, and asserts that there are only 'knowledges' whose authorities are always capable of being undermined. Consequently, post-structuralism rejects attempts to interpret texts which claim to have a finality of meaning or any authority that cannot be deconstructed (see Hawthorn, J. [1992: 137–8]). Post-structuralists consider texts as asking questions rather than giving answers, and as revealing the conditions under which meanings are produced. They look for 'the differences between what the text says and what it thinks it says' (Selden, R. [1985: 102]). Thus post-structuralism opens the way for other forms of criticism such as new historicism and cultural materialism. The title of Malcolm Evans's *Signifying Nothing: Truth's True Contents in Shakespeare's Text* (1986) not only references Macbeth's soliloquy following the news of the Queen's death (5.4.28), but points also to Evans's own post-structuralist approach to be found in his book that you, maybe, are about to read, whether as a whole or in parts.

For definitions of the Renaissance and the Reformation, see Chapter 4.

Glossary

Anagnorisis: The moment of discovery or recognition.

Aporia: When characters ruminate on issues that are irresolvable. An example is Hamlet in the opening lines of the soliloquy 'To be, or not to be' (3.1.56–88), but it isn't just a simple weighing up of alternatives. It points also to those moments in a text where gaps appear and meaning risks falling into a void. In that respect, it is an area of interest in post-structuralism whereby deconstructivist critics are 'centrally concerned with looking for the aporias, blind spots or moments of self-contradiction where the text begins to undermine its own presuppositions' (Peck, J. and Coyle, M. [1993, 2nd edn: 135]).

Catharsis: A purging or release of emotions of pity and fear in the audience.

Hamartia: The fatal or tragic flaw within the protagonist, arising usually from an error of judgement but often interpreted wrongly as weakness of character.

Hubris: Excessive or outlandish pride, which in Greek tragedy tries the patience of the gods too far and leads to nemesis.

Nemesis: The retribution of the gods and the cause of the resulting downfall.

Onomatopoeia: A term denoting words that imitate what is being expressed, e.g. 'fizz' or 'sizzle' or 'shiver'; so Bottom's humorous 'The raging rocks,/And shivering shocks' (*A Midsummer Night's Dream*, 1.2.28–9).

Pathos: Stimulating pity or sorrow in the audience for the 'casualties' of an event; distinct from the downfall of the protagonist.

Peripeteia: A reversal of fortune leading to the downfall of the protagonist.

Pentameter: The poetic line of five feet, each foot characterized by two stresses – that is, iambus (soft/strong) or trochee (strong/soft). Shakespeare predominantly employed the iambic pentameter but he often varied both line length and the position of the stresses for effect.

Soliloquy: A substantial speech in which a character voices his or her innermost thoughts to the audience or provides them with important information. As these are 'private' thoughts being exposed, the character is 'alone', so Hamlet's 'O what a rogue and peasant slave am I!' is prefixed by the words 'Now I am alone' (2.2.549). But it is not always the case that no one else is on the stage. Directors and actors in contemporary productions tend, for example, to decide whether they wish Ophelia to be on stage in the 'background' for Hamlet's 'To be, or not to be' (3.1.56) soliloquy. Desdemona, asleep, is on the stage for Othello's 'It is the cause, it is the cause, my soul!' (5.2.1f.). Lady Macbeth's soliloquy 'Glamis thou art, and Cawdor; and shalt be/What thou art promis'd' (1.5.14f.) is preceded by her reading a letter from Macbeth.

Stichomythia: Short, sharp, quick-fired repartee or banter between characters. For example:

QUEEN	Hamlet, thou hast thy father much offended.
HAMLET	Mother, you have my father much offended.
QUEEN	Come, come, you answer with an idle tongue.
HAMLET	Go to, you question with a wicked tongue.

(*Hamlet*, 3.4.8–11)

Selected recent biographies

This introduction to Shakespeare has taken its structure from a desire to look at how the dramatist's plays work. Another way to introduce Shakespeare is to look at his life and what we know about the man himself.

To a great extent the work of Samuel Schoenbaum, in his *Shakespeare's Lives* (1970) and *William Shakespeare: A Documentary Life* (1975), has provided the basis for a number of lively and interesting biographies over recent years. Bill Bryson's *Shakespeare: The World as a Stage* (2007) is an entertaining introduction to the dramatist's life. Michael Wood's *In Search of Shakespeare* (2005) is a tremendously enjoyable read, written with the enthusiasm of an accomplished historian who has the skill to engage his readers and television viewers in the historical stories he tells. Here he draws out the influence of Mary Arden, Shakespeare's mother. Jonathan Bate's *The Life, Mind and World of William Shakespeare* (2008) and Stephen Greenblatt's *Will in the World: How Shakespeare Became Shakespeare* (2004) come from literary critics whose lives have been steeped in Shakespearean scholarship and research but who in their wide-ranging forms of biography make the dramatist highly accessible.

Katherine Duncan-Jones, in her *Shakespeare: An Ungentle Life* (2010), thinks that Bate and Greenblatt stray into the realms of the historical novel in their approach. She attempts to be more objective, though she often still has to qualify her views with admissions of speculation. In her determined objectivity, Duncan-Jones work is a useful warning and corrective to any sentimentalism.

Peter Ackroyd is an accomplished biographer–author, writing, for example, a weighty biography of London. His *Shakespeare: The Biography* (2005) demonstrates the professionalism that you would expect to find, locating Shakespeare particularly within the city and town environments where he lived. Anthony Holden's *William Shakespeare* (1999) is a sympathetic and at times forgiving biography. His journalistic background allows his enthusiasm to be unfettered and yet sound, providing a good read.

Germaine Greer's *Shakespeare's Wife* (2007) takes a different line of enquiry, writing an informative book on Anne Hathaway, but it is a book also seen by Duncan-Jones as an example of a tendency towards novel writing. In order to shape a biography of Hathaway, Greer has to comb records of how women made their way in Elizabethan and Jacobean society. She is one of the few biographers, however, who has recourse to the anthropological and demographic research of writers such as Peter Laslett, in *The World We Have Lost* (1983). In the same year as Greer's book appeared, Charles Nicholl's *The Lodger: Shakespeare on Silver Street*, and René Weis's *Shakespeare Revealed* were published. The first looks at

Shakespeare particularly in London with the Mountjoys, with whom he lodged, and the second considers the context and influence of his family and friends. Clare Asquith's *Shadowplay: The Hidden Beliefs and Coded Politics of William Shakespeare* (2005) challenges established critical opinion. She provocatively considers many of the plays as political allegories influenced by the formidable Magdalen Browne, Viscountess Montague, and her Catholic aristocratic circle which appears to have supported Shakespeare in the 1590s.

Work on detailed aspects of events or years in Shakespeare's life have provided some excellent studies by James Shapiro: *1599: A Year in the Life of William Shakespeare* (2005) and *1606: William Shakespeare and the Year of Lear* (2015), while Chris Laoutaris's *Shakespeare and the Countess* (2014) approaches an aspect of Shakespeare's life from the perspective of a particular event, the opposition of Elizabeth Russell to the Blackfriar's Theatre, which had a knock-on effect in the building of the Globe and the subsequent development of Shakespeare's plays. Shapiro's work, and that of Laoutaris, provide a fresh approach but in an area which over recent years has produced an excellent array of biographies.

Another biography that might be of interest is by Ian Donaldson about one of Shakespeare's contemporary playwrights: *Ben Jonson: A Life* (2011). Finally, Stanley Wells's *Shakespeare for All Time* (2002) is not a biography as such but is a good introduction to Shakespeare's life and subsequently his reception across the centuries and, in the final chapter, worldwide.

The next chapter considers two plays that in the past have had the label 'problem' linked to them.

25

All's Well That Ends Well (1605) and *Measure for Measure* (1604)

You may recall how, following *The Comedy of Errors* – and even in plays before it – Shakespeare broke neoclassical rules, developing his own structure to underpin his romantic comedies. Once we realize, as critics and admirers of his work, what he has done, we tend to pigeonhole his work again, perceiving an aesthetic harmony that we accept as being part of the genre as Shakespeare conceived it. But great artists rarely stay within the structures that they create or that we define. They continue to experiment, pushing the frontiers of their art, testing its limits as we have seen, for example, in *King Lear, Timon of Athens* and *Troilus and Cressida*. So it is also with two further comedies, *All's Well That Ends Well* and *Measure for Measure*, where Shakespeare deliberately strains the relationship between structure, narrative and content, disturbing some critics who have tried to create another term, 'problem plays', to describe these texts and the puzzlement that they have produced.

Key idea

The term 'problem play' to describe these plays by Shakespeare was taken over from the description of some early twentieth-century dramas that dealt with social problems. In Shakespeare's case the 'problem' is much to do with an acknowledgement of the gap between form and content, between the expectations that the drama arouses in readers and audiences, and its refusal (or failure) to satisfy those expectations.

All's Well That Ends Well

In our earlier discussions of the romantic comedies, and the hybrid romantic tragedy *Romeo and Juliet*, I invited you to consider the relationship between the plays and fairy tales. In the case of the tragedy of *Romeo and Juliet*, the romantic narrative, 'children of an idle brain' (1.4.97), ridiculed by Mercutio, goes wrong, first with the deaths of Mercutio and Tybalt, and subsequently with the deaths of the lovers. In a fairy tale, Romeo should kiss the sleeping Juliet for her to awake, but in Shakespeare's play, thinking that she is dead, he kills himself, and she follows suit when she wakes from her drug-induced sleep. Here, as we have seen, is an echo of the classical tale of 'Pyramus and Thisbe', an intended 'tragedy' amusingly portrayed by the artisans in *A Midsummer Night's Dream*.

Spotlight

Shakespeare toys with these tales and their genres asking questions of them and posing variants on and within comic conventions. What happens, he asks, if the expectations of the traditional narrative do not adhere to convention? He would have known traditional fairy tales and romances such as those written, for example, by Geoffrey Chaucer (c.1345–1400).

In *The Wife of Bath's Tale*, one of Chaucer's famous stories, the Wife holds that the reason why fairies no longer exist is because of 'holy friars' who 'seem to have purged the air' but that, in 'ancient days', 'This was a land brim-full of fairy folk./The Elf-Queen and her courtiers joined and broke/Their elfin dance on many a green mead …/But no one now sees fairies any more' (Chaucer, G., *The Wife of Bath's Tale*, trans. into modern English by Coghill, N. [1960, rev. edn: 299]. Harmondsworth: Penguin). In that tale a knight who has raped a young woman is condemned to death unless he can solve a riddle given to him by the Queen: 'What is the thing that women most desire?' The answer is eventually given to him by an old foul-looking woman who thereby saves his life, 'A woman wants the same sovereignty/Over her husband as over her lover,/And master him; he must not be above her' (301, 304).

The payment for the answer, however, is that he has to marry the deformed old woman. He does so but recoils from her because of her poverty, her lack of status and her ugliness. But she gives him another question to answer. He can choose for her to be old and ugly until she dies but faithful always to him, or to be young and pretty but possibly flirtatious, even, adulterous, risking making him a cuckold. He responds that the choice has to be hers. In this way, she has 'mastery' over him and transforms herself into a beautiful woman. But what if she did not? Or what if she then did become unfaithful? Those are the kind of questions Shakespeare asks in the Jacobean comedies, not necessarily of the women, but of the men.

The Chaucerian tale is not the source of *All's Well That Ends Well*; that is a story from Boccaccio's *Decameron* that Shakespeare probably encountered through William Painter's English translation, *The Palace of Pleasure* (1566). But Shakespeare would have known many fairy tales, fables and mythic narratives such as Chaucer's with their twists and turns. Like many of us, his mind would have been a cultural repository which retained specific narratives, and which contributed to a facility for storytelling on which he consistently drew. As we journey through these plays, therefore, it is not only the immediate source that can inform our understanding but also the culture of a lost age of fairy and folk tale, which appears to have interested him.

With such tales, he discovers that there are elements of human conduct which, we may find, continue to exert a certain force in the modern world or which run counter to our predilections and expectations, thereby confronting us with 'problems'. Some of these predilections over the ages, as we've been discussing throughout our journey, relate to the issues of harmony and consistency between form, plot, character and thematic development. In this, certain judgements are made and, as in the case of *All's Well That Ends Well*, they are invariably almost apologetic.

FEELINGS AND THE 'BOX OFFICE'

'Shakespeare cannot have been entirely satisfied with the way All's Well *turned out. The idea is brilliant, but the play is padded out with some dreary material. It is the ending, however, that is the real trouble. Helena at the beginning of the play is an extraordinarily interesting person; at the end she has become a kind of smothering Amazon with the feeble male cowering at her feet.'*

Edwards, P. (1986, 1987 p/b edn: 164), *Shakespeare: A Writer's Progress.* Oxford: Oxford University Press

How can we possibly know what Shakespeare felt about the play? One of his performance indicators would have been 'box office' pressure. In reading the play it does appear a little laboured and forced. It is generally talked and written about less by critics than some of the other plays but, as we have noticed, dramas, such as *King John*, for example, go in and out of fashion according to the time. In modern performance *All's Well That Ends Well* has had notable and enjoyable successes on the modern stage, although it does not appear in the modern repertory as many times as *Twelfth Night* or, indeed, *Measure for Measure*.

HISTORICAL LOCATION: DECONSTRUCTING THE FAIRIES OF EARLIER PLAYS

The critical trend for historically locating the plays at the time of their composition has, as we've already seen, been informative. Stanley Wells, for example, has noted that there could be an affinity between the conduct of Bertram in *All's Well That Ends Well* and the Earl of Southampton's personal history of a refusal of an arranged relationship and the later tempestuous love affair that led to his marriage.

> 'At the age of seventeen Shakespeare's patron the Earl of Southampton, who was ward to Lord Burleigh, faced an enormous fine and his influential guardian's serious displeasure for refusing to marry Burleigh's granddaughter, Lady Elizabeth Vere, simply, it would seem, because she did not attract him and in any case he – like Bertram – did not want to marry ... But a few years later Southampton made the Queen furious by seducing Lady Elizabeth Vernon, whom he later married ... It is not impossible that Shakespeare had these real-life events in mind as he wrote *All's Well That Ends Well.*'
>
> Wells, S. (2010: 141), *Shakespeare, Sex and Love*. Oxford: Oxford University Press

There is an affinity between this story, as Wells also notes, and that of Shakespeare's classically based poem *Venus and Adonis*. There is so much in this play, however, particularly in the context of Helena's curing of the King's illness and her subsequent choice of a husband, that has a fairy story ambience, and yet Shakespeare appears almost to be deconstructing the nonsense of the fairies of his earlier plays as the reality of the world is allowed to bear down upon the romantic plot. Helena's motivating force from the start is to win Bertram for her husband, although she is poor and not of his social class. She is also portrayed – as her early dialogue (1.1.107f.) with Parolles makes clear – as sexually and socially aware of the disparity between the genders concerning not just the loss of virginity but the power of sexuality. She – remember, originally played by a boy actor – is given an overt sexual awareness in her jibes, for example, 'Bless our poor virginity from underminers and blowers-up! Is there no military policy how virgins might blow up men?' (1.1.121–3) – bawdiness which the audience may have appreciated.

THE BED TRICK

The play contains a bed trick, a device we also find in *Measure for Measure*. Wells suggests (2010: 146) in both that it is 'a kind of rape by a woman of a man', commenting that 'rape is the ultimate consequence of lust, the very opposite of love' even though 'the physical act is identical' (147). In the case of this play, however, Helena makes it evident in her discussion with the Countess, Bertram's mother, that, despite her poverty, she is in love with Bertram.

> I love your son.
>
> My friends were poor, but honest; so's my love.

> (1.3.191–2)

Similarly, in *Measure for Measure*, Mariana, who takes Isabella's place in Angelo's bed, does so because she still loves him, despite his prior off-stage rejection of her when her fortune was lost. These are not simple issues relating merely to a dichotomy of lust or love, which, as Jacqueline Rose notes, in traditional criticism often 'traces the problem of interpretation to the woman' (Drakakis, J. (ed.) [1985: 229], *Alternative Shakespeares*). Rather, they contain a more open exploration of human conduct – male and female – in relation to audience expectations. When plays represent life, why do they have to be consistent? What happens in life is not bound by a narrative harmony or an ultimate teleology. So why do plays, even if drawing on myths and fables, have to conform to the exterior rules used in other plays? May they not each create their own discipline through which they can find expression that challenges aesthetic expectations?

Disrupting the dramatic structure

We have seen that this is the way in which Shakespeare has consistently approached his writing from the mid-1590s onwards, perhaps experimenting with a number of plays to find the right structure but then moving on, deliberately frustrating at least some of the elements of those structures to create something challenging and fresh. So it is with *All's Well* and with *Measure for Measure*. We may have become relatively comfortable with the way that structure, plot and content coalesced in the romantic comedies but in these two plays he certainly disrupts his own structure, asking questions of it through the nature of the stories he wishes to dramatize. This is not, however, necessarily a chronological issue. We have seen earlier, for example, 'life colliding with art' in *Love's Labour's Lost* and *Much Ado About Nothing*.

MODERN PRAGMATISM AND SEXUAL POWER

There is, however, another aspect to consider. *All's Well That Ends Well* and *Measure for Measure* concern love, sex, status and power. Over the last 70 years, in Western culture, we have experienced a sexual revolution, a freeing of sexual attitudes and controls, which are reflected in the contemporary production and interpretation of these plays. What we see now in Helena and the Countess in *All's Well*, and Isabella and Mariana in *Measure for Measure*, may therefore be different from what audiences first saw then, or, indeed, in subsequent performances over the last 400 years of these plays' histories.

Helena is in love. She wants her man and will do what is necessary to achieve her desire. The King's illness allows her achieve her ambition. She has, maybe for us, a modern pragmatism:

> Our remedies oft in ourselves do lie,
>
> Which we ascribe to heaven; the fated sky
>
> Gives us free scope; only doth backward pull
>
> Our slow designs when we ourselves are dull.
>
> ...
>
> The king's disease – my project may deceive me,
>
> But my intents are fix'd, and will not leave me.

> (1.1. 216–19, 228–9)

Here, of course, the medieval fairy-story element surfaces, but what is this disease of the King? We may think of archetypes and go back to myths of the sick King, representing the waste of the land, the loss of fertility. Critics have noted that there is a sexual power in the way Helena cures him of the fistula, a malignant growth usually situated in the lower region of the body, although the play's source places this tumour near his heart. The language of the interaction between Helena and the King is in rhyming couplets, reminiscent of an incantation or spell, suggesting that she is endowed with a mysterious power inherited from her father's learning. The King agrees to the application of the remedy but with a warning:

> Sweet practiser, thy physic will I try,
>
> That ministers thine own death if I die.

(2.1. 184–5)

There is risk to her, but if all goes well then there will be a reward. The King makes his solemn promise:

> Here is my hand; the premises observ'd,
>
> Thy will by my performance shall be serv'd;

(2.1.200–201)

This is a solemn bargain made in private between the two of them. It may be something sexual, sacred or satanic but it is certainly intimate as they leave the stage:

>   ... If thou proceed
>
> As high as word, my deed shall match thy deed.

(2.1.208–9)

Deeds will be matched and wonders will ensue, new life will be given to the ailing King and all seems to go ahead as planned.

CHOICES TO BE MADE

It is as if at the conclusion of Act 2, Scene 1 we have come to an end of one movement in a sequence of tales in this play. The next movement of the main narrative is reminiscent possibly of *The Merchant of Venice*'s cabinet-choices scene in Belmont. The King having recovered, Helena examines various lords for her to choose a husband. Lafew, the commentator for the audience, wishes that he was one of them, wondering why 'all they deny her' (2.3.88), but it is she who is discouraging them. This is clever writing by Shakespeare as he increases the tension of the scene right up to Bertram's actual rejection of Helena:

My wife, my liege! I shall beseech your highness,
In such a business give me leave to use
The help of mine own eyes.

(2.3.107–9)

She may not be ugly or old as in Chaucer's Tale, but in his 'eyes'
it is as if she is, since she is poor and lacking social status. She
has cured the King but his 'proxy' of her reward in marriage
is refused. The expectations from old tales are turned upside
down in order to produce an innovative alternative narrative.
In this, the second, more complex tale, Bertram is forced to wed
her but refuses to bed her, which allows for a new riddle to be
introduced with the impossible challenge given to her by letter:

> When thou canst get the ring upon my finger, which never
> shall come off, and show me a child begotten of thy body
> that I am father to, then call me husband; but in such a
> 'then' I write a 'never'.

(3.2.55–8)

There is, however, more to this inversion of the traditional
folk–tale mode. In rejecting Helena, Bertram is also challenging
the King's promise since it is he who undertakes to decide on any
adjustments to the social hierarchy. It is also unusual since here it
is not the daughter who objects to a patriarchal instruction (as in
A Midsummer Night's Dream), but the son who does so.

Key idea

We are now deep into traditional tales of trickery and deceit, but with a
difference, since this narrative reflects the tensions and the emotions as
well as machinations of characters embedded in complex social situations.

In *Shakespeare and Decorum* (1973: 17), Thomas McAlindon
writes, '… the thoroughly inept title of *All's Well That Ends
Well* underscores the tragic seriousness of the comic action and
the unsatisfactoriness of the marriage denouement for which
a decent girl has indecently schemed.' Such a view, however,
too easily moves the play into a naturalistic world and takes it
away from that of fable and fairy tale, where, if babies can be

changed in cradles, so women can certainly change places with one another in bed. Also, on the surface of it, the riddle that Bertram sets Helena as a condition of marriage seems, in view of his behaviour towards her, impossible to fulfil. But in a story such as this, Bertram can be deceived by Helena's ingenuity in his night of sexual pleasure with the person he thought was Diana: even her name, the goddess of chastity, gives us a clue. So Bertram then has to make up fantastical excuses to explain how he came to be in possession of the King's ring given to Helena, from whom it should never have been parted. This is all integral to the wider fantastical but engrossing story.

THE PLAY AS SOCIAL 'METAPHOR'

We may, nevertheless, still consider the story as a parable, or what Parolles ironically calls 'a metaphor' (5.2.11). It is a fairy tale – with classical reference – revealing love, lust, faithfulness, deceit, absurdity, status and motivation, with some psychology being applied by Shakespeare especially in his portrayal of the Countess, who plays the part of a mother to her son to whom she remains as close as she is to Helena:

> Which of them both
> Is dearest to me I have no skill in sense
> To make distinction.

> (3.4.38–40)

Spotlight

The first person questioned by the King in Act 5, Scene 3, in an attempt to get to the truth, is, fittingly, Parolles, who as his name implies is just 'words', and who the King sees as being 'too fine in thy evidence' (5.3.267). Yet he has a particular function in the play. The comic Parolles subplot deflects us from taking the Bertram story too seriously, and a correspondence is implied between him as the boastful, wordy braggart and Bertram, the Count of Rossillion, who makes up stories to protect himself. When placed in a corner both characters act similarly. It is the folly of denial. Through the play, the Clown is a perceptive witty commentator on both the action of the play and the ambiguities inherent even in the language of the society:

CLOWN	O madam, yonder's my lord your son with a patch of velvet on's face; whether there be a scar under't or no, the velvet knows; but 'tis a goodly patch of velvet. His left cheek is a cheek of two pile and a half, but his right cheek is worn bare.
LAFEW	A scar nobly got, or a noble scar, is a good liv'ry of honour; so belike is that.
CLOWN	But it is your carbonado'd face.

(4.5.93–100)

A face scarred for life with carbonadoes or incisions was common, not necessarily as a mark of military honour but as the result of syphilis, over-activity in the 'sex wars', as Shakespeare's audience would have known only too well.

All's Well That Ends Well isn't always given the credit that is due to it. Perhaps we expect something from it that runs against the context of fable that is at its heart. Possibly, however, Shakespeare does endow too much character into the parts within a setting which hasn't been distanced enough from realism and a genre that cannot adequately contain it. But in performance the play does work, implying in its fable motif the collision between life and fiction which confronts us throughout its progress. In this play, more appropriately perhaps than with *Measure for Measure*, Chaucer's comments about his own tales have a resonance: 'Consider then and hold me free of blame;/ And why be serious about a game?' (*Words between the Host and the Miller*, Coghill's translation, p. 104).

Measure for Measure

If *All's Well That Ends Well* has caused critics 'problems' of incredulity in the mixing of the narrative genres and the perceived perfunctoriness of its conclusion, then *Measure for Measure* became in the mid-twentieth century almost a battleground between two influential critics. F. R. Leavis (*The Common Pursuit*, 1952) launched what could only be seen as an intellectual assault on his 'friend' L. C. Knights ('The

Ambiguity of *Measure for Measure*', 1942*)*, accusing the latter of a departure from his early work where, as we have seen, he had professed that the better the language, the better the play. In his 1942 essay Knights was sympathetic to the ambiguities of *Measure for Measure* and this caused some consternation for a number of twentieth-century evaluations of the play. The problem for these critics resided in their frustration with both the progress and the conclusion of the play.

Criticism has moved on considerably since then and the term 'problem plays' is now rarely employed, although G. Wilson Knight's interpretation (1930) of the Duke of Vienna as a Christlike figure is one that, despite causing much critical concern, nevertheless still retains a need for attention:

> O my dread lord,
> I should be guiltier than my guiltiness
> To think I can be undiscernible,
> When I perceive your Grace, like power divine,
> Hath looked upon my passes.

(5.1.363–7)

'To G. Wilson Knight (1930), these lines made clear that their speaker, Angelo, represented Fallen Man, while their addressee, Duke Vincento, represented Almighty God. Other critics rightly took the dramatic context of the speech more seriously. They pointed out that, among other things, it is a particular character in a particular situation who sees the Duke as "like pow'r divine"; no other character in Measure for Measure praises the Duke so abjectly; while from the start of the play the Duke engages in morally dubious intrigues for the purpose of astounding his subjects and humiliating Angelo.'

Knapp, J. (2002: xi), *Shakespeare's Tribe: Church, Nation and Theater in Renaissance England*. Chicago and London: The University of Chicago Press

MEASURE FOR MEASURE IN THE TWENTY-FIRST CENTURY

In the twenty-first century the exposure of religious hypocrisy in society has been often foregrounded. We live in an age when priests, bishops and even cardinals, so critical of modern sexual culture and practices, have had to confess to 'inappropriate' criminal and sexual conduct in their own lives. The scandals that have rocked the modern Church have raised all sorts of questions about the nature of morality itself, which may make some of the issues in *Measure for Measure* look tame by comparison. Nevertheless, the play appears to ask a series of questions that it then leaves open for the audience to consider. Who is to judge what is moral or immoral, ethical or not? Are not many acts of judgement, to an extent, acts of hypocrisy?

The clown, Pompey, points out to Escalus, from the perspective of Mistress Overdone's brothel where he works as a procurer (Act 2, Scene 2), the impossibility of curtailing sexual activity:

ESCALUS	How would you live, Pompey? By being a bawd? What do you think of the trade, Pompey? Is it a lawful trade?
POMPEY	If the law would allow it, sir.
ESCALUS	But the law will not allow it, Pompey; nor it shall not be allowed in Vienna.
POMPEY	Does your worship mean to geld and splay all the youth of the city?
ESCALUS	No, Pompey.
POMPEY	Truly, sir, in my opinion, they will to't then.

(2.1.220–30)

Pompey makes the point that laws are artificial restraints and in this case incompatible with nature. Just as in *Love's Labour's Lost* the vow of celibacy and the self-imposed exile from female company made by the aristocratic scholars is ridiculous, so laws enacted against natural instincts are impossible to enforce without removing the means of that instinct by general castration. It is farcical but it opens a debate that extends beyond lechery to authority. If in *Hamlet* the Prince can metamorphose Caesar into becoming a stopper for a beer barrel, so even the clown Pompey's name reduces a historic Roman general to being a bawd.

HYPOCRISY

The Duke is unable to cure the evils within Vienna, and he announces at the start of the play that he is to leave the city for a time, appointing Angelo as his deputy to rule in his place. But the Duke then disguises himself as a friar and returns to the city to witness how things are going. In doing so, he becomes involved in attempts to correct the errors which the hypocritical Angelo makes, as well as their impact on certain other inhabitants, especially Isabella who initially expresses the desire to become a nun.

Meddling friars – who the Wife of Bath saw as responsible for getting rid of the fairies – do not generally fare well in Shakespeare. Shakespeare's comedy, however, also ridicules Puritanism. In Act 2, Scene 2 the Duke's deputy, Angelo, who has introduced harsh sexual laws, himself falls into temptation. Although he has condemned Isabella's brother, Claudio, to death for getting his girlfriend, Juliet, pregnant, the hypocritical Angelo lusts after Isabella. She pleads for mercy for her brother. Angelo's puritanical mind tries to reconcile his feelings with the law by debating, at first, whether the fault for his temptation lies with her or him:

> What's this? What's this? Is this her fault, or mine?
>
> The tempter, or the tempted, who sins most, ha?
>
> Not she; nor doth she tempt; but it is I
>
> That, lying by the violet in the sun,
>
> Do as the carrion does, not as the flower,
>
> Corrupt with virtuous season.

(2.2.163–8)

But Isabella is also a problematic character, as I have shown elsewhere:

Isabella's wish for a stricter regime provides an association with the severity of the Puritanism found in the character of Angelo, which is at the heart of the play's issues. Even in Angelo's confession (5.1.363–71), his rationalization may appear corrupt – as possessing a self-delusory satisfaction with his own guilt. Angelo's reference to the Duke as 'divine-like', once his sexual hypocrisy and cruelty have been revealed, remains consistent with his character. He is saying that the Duke must be like a god in finding him, in seeing his inner being, therefore justifying his humility and his punishment. It is the construction of the hypocrisy that pervades his conduct. He has been found out by a 'god-like' figure and is forced to repent. He, nevertheless, continues to distance himself from the deed. Shakespeare in this play takes us into very deep territory in relation to truth, ethics and morality.

THE QUESTIONS RAISED BY THE PLAY

The kind of objections that have been raised about the play may simply confirm us in our prejudices, foreclosing the debate inherent in the drama rather than opening our minds to the ways in which the play manipulates our responses and reactions. So the questions we might ask are ones that the play is prompting us to make. Questions such as why is the Duke going to such great lengths in the first place? And what is his motive? Does he go away, as he says to the Friar, because he is unable to control the situation that he has himself created in Vienna? Does he temporarily abdicate in favour of a stricter man? If so, why doesn't he just disappear? Does he know what kind of man Angelo is? Surely he would have known if he had knowledge of him as his deputy? Is the Duke testing Angelo? If that is so, does it make his opening explanation one of irony that is deepened by his conduct in the rest of the play? Is Isabella right or wrong in refusing to sleep with Angelo in order to save her brother? Is Mariana merely being used and, if so, why? Is she a victim of Angelo's callousness or is she prepared to participate in a female form of rape? Does Isabella accept the Duke's proposal of marriage at the end of the play? If she does, how can she, after all the misery he has caused her while looking on in his disguise? These kinds of questions that the play throws up may be infuriating for some, but actually they are intrinsic to our appreciation of the work.

Key idea

The questions raised by the play don't just draw us into the play, or emanate from it: they are the play. We should be able to accept that Shakespeare may actually want us to ask these questions of his play since human conduct itself is complex, as indeed are the multiple motivations of the characters that Shakespeare portrays.

'Measure for Measure *is about the opposition between law and passion, but nothing in the play can really be understood unless the full significance of "law" is grasped. Law can be seen as an essential restraint on individual action, and thus a negative force: it is seen like this frequently in the play, both by those who dispense justice and by those who are its victims. But law has a positive aspect as well, one which makes criticism of those who break the law deeper and more subtle.'

Eagleton, T. (1970: 66), *Shakespeare and Society: Critical Studies in Shakespearean Drama*. London: Chatto & Windus

THE STRUCTURE OF THE PLAY

If we look at the structure of *Measure for Measure*, we can
see that it operates to an extent according to the formulae
that we have outlined earlier – problem, journey/disguise,
complexity, recognition – but then leaves us not necessarily with
reconciliation but with issues about ethics and authority that the
play has addressed, if not resolved. As Isabella says of Angelo:

> But man, proud man,
>
> Dress'd in a little brief authority,
>
> Most ignorant of what he's most assur'd –
>
> His glassy essence – like an angry ape
>
> Plays such fantastic tricks before high heaven
>
> As makes the angels weep, who, with our spleens,
>
> Would all themselves laugh mortal.
>
> (2.2.118–24)

We have a choice. We can listen to this passage and consider it
to be about the hypocrite, Angelo, which, of course it is.
He is the "proud man" in question. Or we can go beyond him
to include anyone's authority in any role, be it Duke or Deputy,
Friar or Bawd, Spectator or Reader, Teacher or Student. Does
Isabella accept the Duke's proposal of marriage at the end?
Will he enforce such a proposal if she does not? *Measure for
Measure* is a play with no answers but plenty of questions, and
its conclusion continues to surprise and perplex, prompting
audiences to ask them. That is the measure of the play.

26

Cymbeline (1609–10) and a note on the poems

Categorized as a tragedy, *Cymbeline* was the last of Shakespeare's plays to be printed in the First Folio of 1623. Written in 1609–10, it does not, however, easily conform to a particular genre and is now often termed a 'tragicomedy'. Here Shakespeare uses his dexterity to take risks with the structure that underpins many of his plays, in particular his comedies, and to startling effect. It took an artist who knew more than just the basics of his profession to be able to create a play such as this one.

Spotlight

Shakespeare's plays allow a freedom that many find difficult to accept but some, however, continue to impose strictures upon him. If they did not, how could John Drakakis, in 1985, edit a book entitled *Alternative Shakespeares*, a collection of radical critical essays that challenged the orthodoxy of the then current trends of Shakespearean scholarship? Yet Drakakis would be the first to note the danger of any form of literary criticism, including new historicism or cultural materialism, as being the 'key' to Shakespeare's meaning. New ideas and new interpretations will continue to appear in times and ages to come. That is part of the greatness of Shakespeare.

It is said that, when some aspiring poets asked T. S. Eliot to instruct them on how to write free verse, he told them to learn first how to write a sonnet. Similarly, the contemporary artist David Hockney has complained that aspiring artists are no longer, at some art schools, being taught how to draw. As we have noted earlier, radical artists usually owe their creativity to an understanding of the established rules of their craft. Beethoven's last symphony tantalizingly begins almost as if trying to find its way, as if the orchestra is warming up, and then builds up through the first three movements to the fourth in which, with artistic courage, the choral voice enters as a glorious instrument, taking the symphonic form to a new height. It is perhaps a metaphor for the way great artists, writers and composers constantly work from the first principles of their art, from the inheritance of others' endeavours, through the continuing experimentation with forms and ideas to produce their work.

As we have moved from play to play, genre to genre, we have seen in Shakespeare's works the way in which he structures his plays, how he makes them work as drama with an artistic integrity, an expression of linguistic beauty and an eye to the market. The plays needed to entertain. They needed to bring in the spectators to form the audience. We have seen how some commentators through the years have tried to appropriate Shakespeare for themselves, at one extreme deifying him, at the other denying that a man from the provinces with no aristocratic or university background could have written these texts. We have also seen how through the ages some have appropriated him for themselves and have rewritten, 'improved' or rejected acts, scenes, speeches and even entire plays. In this we have noted, however, that drama is a fluid art form, not entirely owned by the dramatist but in being dynamic, living in performance from age to age, agile enough to be reconstituted for new audiences and new generations.

The genre debate

Jacques Derrida was one of the writers who exerted an influence on the alternative Shakespeare movement:

> 'As soon as the word "genre" is sounded, as soon as it is heard, as soon as one attempts to conceive it, a limit is drawn. And when a limit is established, laws and interdictions are not far behind ...
>
> [quoting Gerard Genette] 'The history of genre theory is strewn with these fascinating outlines that inform and deform reality, a reality often heterogeneous to the literary field, and that claim to discover a "natural" system wherein they construct a factitious symmetry heavily reinforced by fake windows.'
>
> Derrida, J. (1980: 203, 207), 'La loi du genre/The Law of Genre', *Glyph Textual Studies*, vol. 7, quoted in Brown, R. D. and Johnson, D. (eds) (2000: 24), *Shakespeare 1609: Cymbeline and the Sonnets*. London: Macmillan

Because it does not conform to the generic rules implied by the term 'tragedy' which was how it was first categorized in 1623, *Cymbeline* has been a victim of critical uncertainty that has coloured its reception. Irrespective of theoretical warnings, some have argued that it might, therefore, be considered a 'comedy' but it does not abide by the rules of that genre either. The discussions will continue. Is it a pastoral? Is it a history? Is it a Roman play? Is it a tragicomedy, a term which has attracted some critical favour as evidenced, for example, by Ruth Nevo who in her analysis of the play makes a persuasive case based on structural generic understandings?

> 'In Shakespearean tragic structure we regularly find protagonists in Act IV facing a great void, an annihilation of the values which have sustained them. Deprived of their objects of love or faith or hope, they experience despair, so that possible remedy, tantalisingly just within reach, is occluded from their view, or, if perceived, is snatched away by the circumstances which have swept beyond control. In his comic structures, Act IV initiates the remedial phase of the narrative, exorcising precedent errors and follies by maximizing them to the point of exhaustion. In Cymbeline, the most intricately interlocked of the tragicomedies, both vectors coexist, and are synchronized in the play's most phantasmagoric event – the mock death of Fidele.'
>
> Nevo, R. (1987), 'Shakespeare's Other Language', reprinted in Thorne, A. (ed.) (2003: 107–8), *Shakespeare's Romances: Contemporary Critical Essays*. New Casebooks. Basingstoke: Macmillan

But to engage in the 'genre debate' over this play is nevertheless still a means to compartmentalize and formalize structures. The questions to be asked of this play are not necessarily about genre. Does *Cymbeline* work as drama to attract the audience for which it was originally intended, or audiences today? Sadly, perhaps, today the answer is no since it is not regularly performed, but nor are some of the other late plays such as *Pericles, Henry VIII* or *The Two Noble Kinsmen* – plays that were written in collaboration with other dramatists. *Cymbeline*, however, appears to have been solely written by Shakespeare.

Provenance

The play, apparently, was enjoyed by both James I and Charles I, which may give us a clue about its provenance. It was possibly written with an eye to King James, who was attempting to revise recent history by asserting a new relationship with Spain, even though the Catholics had tried to assassinate him through the Gunpowder Plot. He wished to be regarded as a new Caesar Augustus and maybe he would have fancied himself as the masque-like Jupiter of Act 5, descending to take control of the 'petty spirits of region low', and so to calm their conscience in a promise to 'uplift' the tribulations of Posthumus:

> His comforts thrive, his trials well are spent:
> Our Jovial star reign'd at his birth, and in
> Our temple was he married. Rise, and fade.
> He shall be lord of lady Imogen,
> And happier much by his affliction made.
>
> (5.4.104–8)

Similarly, the King may well have associated himself with Cymbeline who supports the mercy shown by Posthumus to Iachimo, and that would allow him, the King, similarly to show mercy and forgiveness in his kingdom:

> Nobly-doom'd!
> We'll learn our freeness of a son-in-law:
> Pardon's the word to all.
>
> (5.5.421–3)

Whether of course this was the kind of bountiful mercy King James showed in reality is a different matter altogether. What is interesting is that it seems to echo the perception that the King had of himself.

Some, of course, might criticize Shakespeare for appearing to write with such flattering intent. We have seen earlier how he was able to take associations between the contents in the plays and royal approval/disapproval to the very limit but, without the King, Shakespeare would have had no profession. A little sycophancy was no bad investment given the commercial nature of the theatre. When Marston, Jonson and Chapman openly satirized the King in their collaborative *Eastward Ho!* (1605), Jonson and Chapman were arrested and threatened with having their noses sliced and ears cut, while Marston, who some believe had fled to Norwich, decided on his return, having been involved in frank 'Palace' discussions, to terminate his career as a dramatist, marry the daughter of the King's chaplain and take Holy Orders himself! Playwriting could be a precarious profession and, having been patronized by James, the King's Men would have taken this protective association seriously.

Shakespeare in the age of King James

King James was building a new Britain. He had joined the crowns of England and Scotland the year before this play, in which Wales also has a prominent function in the action, was first staged. There is a political dimension culminating in a need for peace, a rejection and indeed condemnation by Cymbeline of 'our wicked queen,/Whom heavens in justice both on her, and hers,/Have laid most heavy hand' (5.5.464–6). The collocation 'wicked Queen' has often been acknowledged as a 'fairy story' circulated in an oral tradition. The phrase, however, might, in this case, interest us in a different way. It must be doubtful that Shakespeare would have concluded any play during the reign of Elizabeth I with such a phrase, however much related to fairy stories. Was it possible that his flattering of the King who was making his peace with Elizabeth's most ardent enemy, Spain, allowed him a freedom of expression not available to him under the previous monarch?

The failure to pay tribute to Rome in the play was the Queen's, and so the reconciliation with Augustus' Rome takes place allowing for 'A Roman, and a British ensign wave' since 'Never was a war did cease/(Ere bloody hands were wash'd) with such a peace' (5.5.481, 485–6).

Structural convention and innovation

All of this comes at the end of a long final act in which recognitions and expressions of forgiveness come quickly one after the other, in an almost bewildering and yet well-controlled manner. With the earlier comedies, as we have seen, characters escape from, or resolve, the problems posed at the start, through geographic relocation or physical disguise or both. Although discomforts, sadness, melancholy and difficulties are present in the relocations, dramatic characters are nevertheless able to reassess themselves and confirm their identities. But in this possibly more challenging play, Shakespeare innovates upon that structure, almost, but not quite, dismantling it.

Innogen (wrongly first printed in 1623 as Imogen but still spelled thus in the *Arden Shakespeare Complete Works*) is already married to Posthumus; he is banished by the King at the start, and has relocated to Rome where he has undertaken an improper wager with Iachimo concerning the fidelity of his wife. Iachimo hides in a trunk to gain access to her bedroom – you may recall that in *The Merry Wives of Windsor* Falstaff is forced to hide in a 'buck basket' to escape from his attempted adulterous escapades – and fails in his seduction but nevertheless slanders her to Posthumus.

'Iachimo's entry into Imogen's [sic] bedroom from the trunk is an event of fairy-tale surrealism superimposed upon a scene of the most exact realism. The dramatist names the time ... the length of Imogen's bedtime reading ... and the time of her morning call ... As she sleeps, the trunk lid opens and Iachimo steps into the silence of her room ... Some readers believe that Iachimo kisses Imogen ... "That I might touch!/But kiss, one kiss!/Rubies unparagon'd,/How dearly they do't" (2.2, 16–18). Surely the point is that he does not touch, no matter how close he comes, that even his expression of a wish to do so is a figurative comment upon Imogen's beauty, not upon his desire for it.'

Brownlow, F. W. (1977: 139), *Two Shakespearean Sequences.*
London and Basingstoke: Macmillan

The slanders can be achieved because he is able to give not only a description of her bedroom but produce the bracelet he has removed from her arm. It was a gift from her husband – you may remember a similar vaginal symbol of Portia's ring in *The Merchant of Venice*. Further, as she lay sleeping while Iachimo was in the room, he observed:

On her left breast

> A mole cinque-spotted: like the crimson drops
> I'th' bottom of a cowslip.

(2.2.37–9)

Shakespeare's mastery here lies in his drawing on and adapting the various dramatic conventions, especially recognition, which have helped him develop the structure of many of his plays. The use of the 'mole' as a proof of Imogen's infidelity draws, for example, on the convention of anagnorisis, or recognition, which usually resolves the complexities of the plot. Here, though, it will produce an incorrect recognition by Posthumus of Imogen's behaviour. A physical proof of one's identity, such as a mole, may normally be required for identity in a recognition scene to be assured, as it is in *Twelfth Night* when Viola and her brother Sebastian are reunited:

> VIOLA   My father had a mole upon his brow.
> SEBASTIAN   And so had mine.

(5.1.238–9)

More particularly in *Cymbeline*, it is a 'mole' that provides identity when the King probes for proof that Belarius' revelation of his lost sons are truly who they are:

> CYMBELINE   Guiderius had
> Upon his neck a mole, a sanguine star;
> It is a mark of wonder.
>
> BELARIUS   This is he,
> Who hath upon him still that natural stamp:
> It was wise Nature's end, in the donation
> To be his evidence now.

(5.5.364–9)

Of course, it was not 'Nature's end' of proof but the dramatist's to provide a satisfactory resolution. But in this drama Shakespeare uses the mole as recognition in two ways:

- to exacerbate and to verify Iachimo's evil story, diverting the plot into a further problematic course

- at the end, to prove the identity of the long-lost sons in order to help resolve the complex narrative.

Further, when Imogen, disguised as the boy Fidele, awakes to find her/himself lying next to the headless body of Cloten, there is no physical proof, such as a mole, to denote the victim's identity, only Posthumus' clothes that Cloten had borrowed. Imogen, however, in her anguish searches for physical proof and ironically believes she finds it:

> A headless man? The garments of Posthumus?
> I know the shape of's leg: this is his hand:
> His foot Mercurial: his Martial thigh:
> The brawns [muscles] of Hercules: but his Jovial face –
> Murder in heaven! How – ? 'Tis gone.

> (4.2.308–12)

Shakespeare here again distorts an important element of his comic formula to provide tragic effect in a horrific moment that is clearly not comic. It is neither tragic nor comic, nor is it tragicomic. It is simply the way the drama's narrative works, playing off different dramatic conventions. It is possible – and is certainly believed to be so by Terry Hands – that the same actor in Shakespeare's company played both Posthumus and Cloten. This would have added a further dimension to the action, leaving the audience unsure of the relationship between the two characters. Is one the distorted image of the other?

The dirge for Fidele

Earlier, Fidele – the disguised and now drugged Imogen who is assumed to be dead – is laid to rest by Guiderius and Arviragus, while a dirge is sung which has become one of the most famous of Shakespeare's lyrics. In the context of the movement of the play, however, this song serves the purpose of gradually varying the dramatic tone as the complicated plot moves towards the horror of what is to come: Imogen's mistaking of the dead Cloten for Posthumus. The dirge begins:

> Fear no more the heat o' th' sun,
> Nor the furious winter's rages,
> Thou thy worldly task has done,
> Home art gone, and ta'en thy wages.
> Golden lads and girls all must,
> As chimney-sweepers, come to dust.

> (4.2.258f.)

Key idea

Perhaps we should note, with Juliet Dusinbere (1975: 182), that *Othello* is not far away in composition or theme: 'Posthumus's decision to write against women in revenge for Imogen's faithlessness (2.4.183) becomes, in a more passionate man [Othello], the strangling of a wife.' Posthumus, of course, also instructs Philario to murder her. Further, the bedroom scene, with Iachimo's desire 'to kiss' Imogen, may remind us of Othello's 'Once more, and that's the last' (*Othello*, 5.2.19). There are interesting dramaturgical comparisons to be made between these two plays.

It is no wonder that scholars and critical observers become perplexed at this play's genre but it is a pity if such uncertainty on their part is one of the reasons why the work is not performed or indeed read as widely as some of the other great plays. Perhaps, as Ruth Nevo asserts, tragicomedy is a useful term for it in that its proliferation of motifs draws the audience into its narrative, after what is a difficult opening in which so much information has to be given. Once, however, into its stride, the play twists and turns, demonstrating Shakespeare's wealth of dramatic experience, drawing on other plays and culminating in the complicated, though well-executed, series of final recognitions in the last act.

Shakespeare's poems

Cymbeline was probably being written in 1609, the same year in which Shakespeare's *Sonnets* and *A Lover's Complaint* were published. The *Sonnets* show the strict discipline of a poetic form and suggest a narrative sequence that had been developed over a number of years from the 1590s onwards. *A Lover's Complaint*, whose authorship textual critics now question, is a young woman's story of her seduction told to a stranger. It was probably written by John Davies of Hereford (c.1565–1618) in imitation of Shakespeare's style.

There are 154 poems in the sonnet sequence, the first 126 addressed to a young man of high social status; the next ones, from 127 to 152, are addressed to a dark lady, an unfaithful mistress of the narrator, and involve a rival lover. The final two poems concern Cupid and Diana. Some regard the *Sonnets* as autobiographical, but there is no firm evidence to suggest that they are. Shakespeare created characters and narrators in his plays, so why not in his poems? In form, they differ from the Italianate Petrarchan sonnet in that the 14 lines are divided not as eight and six but as four quatrains and a concluding couplet. This form, as we saw in Chapter 5, has come to be known as the Shakespearean sonnet.

In the *Sonnets* and in the narrative poems, *Venus and Adonis* and *The Rape of Lucrece*, Shakespeare demonstrates his dexterity as a poet. *Venus and Adonis* (1593) was written while the theatres were closed because of plague. It became a very popular work, making his name prior to the fame to come with the plays. It is a dramatic poem in which Venus detains Adonis from the hunt, proposing that they should make love:

> 'Fondling,' she saith, 'since I have hemm'd thee here
> Within the circuit of this ivory pale,
> I'll be a park, and thou shalt be my deer:
> Feed where thou wilt, on mountain or in dale;
> Graze on my lips, and if those hills be dry,
> Stray lower, where the pleasant fountains lie.'

> (lines 229–34)

With such 'steamy' lines of sexual innuendo the poem probably secured its success. The animal and landscape imagery predominates, as bantering between the two characters takes place. Adonis repels love:

'I know not love,' quoth he, 'nor will not know it,
Unless it be a boar, and then I chase it ...'

(lines 409–10)

The poem presages many elements of the later plays, from
Much Ado About Nothing to *Antony and Cleopatra* and *All's
Well That Ends Well* and also the *Sonnets* as, for example, in
Venus's reference of mortality being defeated by posterity:

What is thy body but a swallowing grave,
Seeming to bury that posterity,
Which by the rights of time thou needs must have,
If thou destroy them not in dark obscurity?
If so, the world will hold thee in disdain,
Sith in thy pride so fair a hope is slain.

(lines 757–62)

But Adonis leaves her for the hunt and is killed by a boar.

The Rape of Lucrece (1594) has a dark theme as the title
implies, in Tarquin's assault on Lucrece, for which, as The
Argument preceding the poem records, 'with one consent and a
general acclamation the Tarquins were all exiled, and the state
government changed from kings to consuls'. As with *Venus and
Adonis*, we find presaged within it much to be found in later
dramas. Read the following lines, for example, and think about
issues we've discussed during our journey through the plays:

Why should the worm intrude the maiden bud,
Or hateful cuckoos hatch in sparrows' nests?
Or toads infect fair founts with venom mud,
Or tyrant folly lurk in gentle breasts?
Or kings be breakers of their own behests?
But no perfection is so absolute
That some impurity doth not pollute.

(lines 848–54)

The Rape of Lucrece is written in what is known as rhyme
royale, with a seven-line stanza ababbcc in contrast to the
six–line stanza ababcc of *Venus and Adonis*.

These are both dramatic poems written by a young enthusiastic poet, displaying a tight control of his medium. The sonnet sequence, not published until 1609 but composed over time while he was writing many of his plays, is similarly disciplined. It may be tempting to consider these poems as ones that Shakespeare had been writing on and off and forming into a sequence for his own intellectual amusement and enjoyment, away from the pressure of getting his plays on to the stage. Such a view, however, maybe regarded as reductive, in a similar way that some of the biographical identification theories can be regarded as distracting. Jonathan Bate has his own speculations over the identities of the various characters possibly related to the lovers' 'tryst', but referencing the final couplet of Sonnet 152 he is prompted to ask, 'Does love come from the "I" or the "eye", is it a "truth" or is it a "lie"?' (Bate, J. [1998: 53]).

'We will never know whether ... the sonnets are knowing imaginings of possible intrigue ... their reticence on this matter is essential to their purpose: we must be denied knowledge of the original bed deeds, because the sonnets are interested not so much in who lies with whom as in the paradoxes of eyeing and lying.'

Bate, J. (1998: 58), *The Genius of Shakespeare.*
London: Picador

Although scholarship now generally considers the publication of the *Sonnets* to have been authorized, the poet W. H. Auden wrote in the 1960s, 'Of one thing I am certain: Shakespeare must have been horrified when they were published' (Auden, W. H. [1964: xxxvi]). It is an interesting quote, whatever the circumstances of their publication. That first publication did not attract at the time the same level of success that was seen with the earlier publications of the narrative poems.

There is a lovely little poem 'To the Queen' which was found only at the end of the last century and is not included in the Arden edition but is readily available in other editions. Written as an epilogue to a Court performance in 1599, it plays on the 'dial of time', a familiar theme that we have encountered. *The Passionate Pilgrim* is an unauthorized anthology of 19 poems published by William Jaggard in 1599. It claims to be 'By W. Shakespeare' and thereby was trading on his name and success presumably to make the publisher some money. It opens with two of Shakespeare's sonnets, 138 and 144, which must have been in private circulation at the time, and contains two further sonnets and a poem from *Love's Labour's Lost*. These last three had been published in quarto in 1598: Poem 5, Sir Nathaniel's 'If love make me foresworn, how shall I swear to love?' (4.2.106–20), and Poem 3, Longaville's 'Did not the heavenly rhetoric of thine eye' (4.3.59–72), together with Poem 16, which in the comedy is Dumaine's 'ode that I have writ', 'On a day – alack the day! –' (4.3.98f.). Although they were attributed to Shakespeare when first published (1598/9), his involvement with any of the other poems is uncertain. What is known is that Shakespeare was unhappy about their publication.

Shakespeare's poem *The Phoenix and Turtle* (1601) has perplexed critics because of its obscurity. Some see it in relation to a poem by Robert Chester, *Love's Martyr*, pertaining to Elizabeth I and the death of a courtier, although relatively recent scholarship has suggested that it concerns a real-life event referring to the execution of a Catholic widow, Anne Line, who had received a Catholic priest into her home. The historian Michael Wood believes it to be a poem that 'may take us nearer to Shakespeare's feelings about a real event of his time than anything else he wrote' (Wood, M. [2003, 2005 p/b: 259]).

Key idea

The *Sonnets* were published in 1609, the same year that *Cymbeline* was first performed. If some people categorize this as an inferior play, they are, I believe, misguided. Shakespeare knew how to write a sonnet. He knew how freely to experiment with his dramatic structure. He knew his business. He knew how to write a play. *Cymbeline* may be something of an enigma because it resists clear definition. That resistance is possibly its strength.

The Tempest (1611) and the collaborative plays: *Henry VIII* (1613); *The Two Noble Kinsmen* (1613–14); *Pericles* (1608); and *The Shakespeare Apocrypha*

The Tempest is often regarded as Shakespeare's last play, which leads some to read into it what they like to think were Shakespeare's final thoughts about his profession. It may not, however, have been his final play: *Henry VIII*, *The Two Noble Kinsmen* and the lost play *Cardenio* may have followed. Although in some ways a problematic play, *The Tempest* shows Shakespeare returning to a neoclassical model, but one which includes a masque. With the earlier collaborative play *Pericles*, he uses a sprawling narrative structure to good effect. In *Henry VIII* he and his co-writer, John Fletcher, adeptly use the form of the masque, which had become a new fashion in the aristocratic class of Stuart London. Shakespeare and Fletcher's *The Two Noble Kinsmen* is based on a story from Chaucer's *The Canterbury Tales*. There are also a number of other plays over which there is speculation that Shakespeare had a hand in their composition.

On 29 June 1613 the thatched roof of the Globe Theatre caught fire during a performance of Shakespeare and Fletcher's play *Henry VIII*. The wooden building was burned to the ground. There were no fatalities but one man's breeches were reported to have caught fire, only to be quenched by a bottle of beer. The fire is often taken to mark the symbolic end of Shakespeare's theatrical career. However, within a year a new theatre had been erected, with a tiled roof, but less than three years later Shakespeare was dead. He was buried in Holy Trinity Church, Stratford-upon-Avon on 25 April 1616, where, if you visit, you can see the place where he lies and read the doggerel versed inscription, which tradition has it was written by him:

Good friend for Jesus sake forbeare,

To digg the dust encloased heare:

Bleste be the man that spares thes stones,

And curst be he that moves my bones.

Scientific investigation has recently revealed that there may be some truth to the old story that Shakespeare's skull was once stolen from his grave. It is still, nevertheless, his last resting place. On the wall to the left is a bust, which is the most contemporary likeness we have of him, although it is somewhat crude and stiff.

Henry VIII

It is perhaps ironic that the Globe fire broke out during a play about Henry VIII. Henry was the tyrannical, self-obsessed, ruthless, psychotic monarch who had been responsible for much of the religious and social turmoil in sixteenth-century England. It may be that some unpleasant personality traits were exacerbated following a severe blow to his head after a fall from his horse. The end, however, of what he began, it could be argued, came, ironically enough, with the execution in 1649 of the monarch himself, Charles I, but certainly Henry left a legacy of intolerance and bitterness that has continued for centuries. But, despite all that, Henry VIII, whom Erasmus referred to in the early years of his reign as 'a universal genius', promoted education and began the forging of a national identity which to a limited extent continues to the present day. Often, however, lionized by future generations, in Shakespeare's play Henry is less vividly characterized than some of those about him: the Duke of Buckingham, Cardinal Wolsey and Queen Katherine. The structure of the play works, as Ralph Berry (1985: 128–41) has pointed out, like a masque and does not provide an opportunity for the wider historical perspective found in the other history plays by Shakespeare.

Spotlight

Holbein's famous painting of Henry – standing erect with legs astride and large codpiece symbolizing the King's masculine power and virility – helps establish the iconic image of this self-centred king. Shakespeare, however, chooses to provide a different focus. In the play he presents a series of vignettes or 'staged pieces' that concentrate on the characters surrounding the King rather than on the monarch himself. This is no more so than with Katherine of Aragon (spelled with a K in the text), who in Act 2, Scene 4 comes for judgement before the tribunal presided over by the two cardinals Wolsey and Campeius; they are charged with determining the legality of her marriage to the King.

The stage directions are more detailed generally throughout this play than is usual in Shakespeare's Folio text, as, for example, in Act 2, Scene 4 with the entry of the King, the Cardinal, nobles and officials, which give an indication of the play's great theatricality, which productions have continued to exploit over the centuries. Particularly in the nineteenth century, they allowed for great pageants and ornate stage designs to be created. Despite this theatrical emphasis, the play is a historical drama whose subtitle is *All is True*.

In Act 2, Scene 4 Queen Katherine is called formally into the Court, although she is already seated in the room. The Folio stage direction reads: 'The Queen makes no answer, rises out of her chair, goes about the court, comes to the King, and kneels at his feet: then speaks' (stage direction, 2.4.10). What she says is calm, measured and dignified – reminiscent, perhaps, of Hermione's defence in *The Winter's Tale*, as she seeks to counter the unjust cruelty of her husband's attitude and action. This scene has, however, a historical accuracy that gives it even greater poignancy. Historian Michael Wood, for example, conjectures that if *Henry VIII* was performed in the indoor Blackfriars theatre – it was not unusual that the same play might be performed at both the Globe and the Blackfriars after Shakespeare's company had succeeded in acquiring the latter for their own use in 1609 – the audience may have recalled that they were in the very hall where Queen Katherine's tribunal took place. Her speech, one of the great set pieces in Shakespeare, begins, 'Sir, I desire you do me right and justice' (2.4.11 f.).

'Is there a sense here [2.4.11f.] that history has moved on – the clock cannot be turned back? As in The Winter's Tale, Pericles *and* The Tempest, *the theme is recognition and forgiveness; here, however, it is not in fiction but in English history. The way is prepared after her trial by the boy singing a beautiful (Robert) Johnson song on Orpheus, and then fully expressed in the mystical scene of Katherine's dying vision, when to "sad and solemn music" she falls asleep to see, in one of Shakespeare's longest stage directions, six angels descend "clad in white robes, wearing on their heads garlands of bays, and ... branches of bays of palm in their hands ..." (4.2.82).'*

Wood, M. (2003: 367–8), *In Search of Shakespeare.* London: BBC Books

Robert Johnson (*c.*1583–1633) was a royal lutenist and composer who worked with Shakespeare from *c.*1610 on songs for *Cymbeline, The Winter's Tale* and *The Tempest*, and on the collaborative plays with Fletcher, *Henry VIII, The Two Noble Kinsmen* and perhaps the lost play *Cardenio*. His music reflects the masque tradition and the ambience created in the indoor Blackfriars theatre, which is indicative of the change of compositional style in Shakespeare's last plays. (There is a recent CD release of a 1993 Parlophone recording, *Shakespeare's Lutenist*, which brings together many of Johnson's songs.)

The masque-like play, *Henry VIII*, maintains a sharp focus on Queen Katherine but concludes with the birth of Elizabeth and the prophecy of the greatness that will come with her accession to the throne. But the play also indicates a new direction in writing as Shakespeare moves towards retirement.

The Two Noble Kinsmen

The Two Noble Kinsmen, like *Henry VIII*, is by John Fletcher and William Shakespeare and draws on Chaucer's *The Knight's Tale* telling the story of friends Arcite and Palamon and their love for Emilia, the sister of Hippolyta, who loves them both as much as each other. It harks back to earlier Shakespearean plays, for example the friendship of Valentine and Proteus in *The Two Gentlemen of Verona*, the contest between Theseus and Hippolyta in *A Midsummer Night's Dream*, and in *Antony and Cleopatra* to the choice between Cleopatra's Venus, the goddess of love, to whom, in this play, Palamon holds allegiance, and Antony's Mars, the god of war, to whom, here, Arcite is dedicated. It also has a girl, the Jailer's daughter, who, reminiscent perhaps of Ophelia, loses her sanity in this play because of her impossible love for Palamon.

Theseus rules that Arcite and Palamon should meet in a chivalric tournament and that the winner will gain Emilia, while the loser will forfeit his life. Palamon prays to Venus, Arcite to Mars and Emilia to Diana, goddess of chastity, that the one who loves her the most might be victorious or that they should both die, allowing her to remain a virgin. As in Chaucer's tale, the gods' answer is that Arcite wins but he is then accidentally killed in his victory parade, leaving Palamon to marry Emilia. As Theseus says:

> Never Fortune
> Did play a subtler game. The conquered triumphs;
> The victor has the loss; yet in the passage
> The gods have been most equal.

> (5.4.112–15)

It is an engaging story, raising issues of heterosexual and same-sex love, and reminiscent not only of the plays mentioned but also of the *Sonnets*. W. H. Auden noted, for example, in reference particularly to Palamon's prayer to Venus (5.1.77–136), an expression of 'the intensity of the disgust expressed at masculine sexual vanity', and asked, in relating the passage to the *Sonnets*, 'Did Shakespeare later feel that the anguish at the end was not too great a price to pay for the glory of the initial vision?' (Auden, W. H. [1964: xxxvii]).

Cardenio/Double Falsehood (?)

Collaboration on the writing of plays was common practice during this period. You may recall that Thomas Nashe (1567–1601), and possibly others, probably worked with Shakespeare on *1 Henry VI* and that Thomas Middleton (1580–1627) may have contributed to *Timon of Athens* and to a minor extent even to *Macbeth*. Then, towards the end of his career, there are the plays we are discussing here, where it appears he worked with John Fletcher (1579–1625) in particular, who was to succeed him as the Company's dramatist: *Henry VIII*, *The Two Noble Kinsmen* and possibly the lost play *Cardenio* (1612–13), based on the story of Cardenio's madness in love found in Cervantes's *Don Quixote*, which may or may not be a play called *Double Falsehood*, discovered and subsequently published in 1727/8 by Lewis Theobald. The editors of the Arden Shakespeare believe that a possible relationship with the lost play is sufficiently interesting to include it in their edition of *The Complete Works*, but the scholastic jury is still out. But both it and *The Two Noble Kinsmen*, another play not found in the First Folio, have had revivals particularly by the Royal Shakespeare Company over recent years, with another one of *The Two Noble Kinsmen* occurring in 2016–17.

We have seen earlier (in Chapter 21) how texts were pirated in one way or another. It is possible, also, that popular authors' names or initials might have been assigned to texts in print, whether or not their contribution had been significant or slight, or perhaps even non-existent. Similarly, some collaborations or editing may have gone unrecorded. So the issue of collaboration with Shakespeare, or Shakespeare's collaboration with others, including the musician Robert Johnson, is an area of interest and academic research. The fact that the masque, popular with King James, altered the nature and form of the last plays is something which theatre productions and audiences in modern times find challenging. Often the masque elements of the play sit uneasily with the acting styles that some modern companies promote. In the twenty-first century attempts have been made to realize the influence of music and masque on the style of an entire play as, for example, with Jonathan Holmes's Jericho House production of *The Tempest* at St Giles, Cripplegate, Barbican BITE Festival in 2011, with music by Jessica Dannheiser.

The Shakespeare Apocrypha

In 1908 C. F. Tucker Brooke published a collection of 14 plays under the title *The Shakespeare Apocrypha* as part of a then ongoing debate 'to provide an accurate and complete text … of all those plays which can, without entire absurdity, be included in the "doubtfully Shakespearian" class' (Tucker Brooke, C. F. [1908: Preface], *The Shakespeare Apocrypha*. Oxford: Oxford University Press). These plays and some additional ones have continued to interest scholars. One of them, *The Two Noble Kinsmen*, is now included in most Complete Works published in the latter part of the twentieth century and since then.

More than a century after Tucker Brooke, Jonathan Bate and Eric Rasmussen, with others, published *William Shakespeare and Others: Collaborative Plays* which, newly edited, comprises eight of the 14 plays included in *The Shakespeare Apocrypha* (1908), together with Lewis Theobald's *Double Falsehood* or *The Distressed Lovers* (1728), the source story for *Cardenio* and also Thomas Kyd's *The Spanish Tragedy* (with additions). Modern research using computer technology, we are told, detects the hand of Shakespeare in additions to *The Spanish Tragedy* and in *Arden of Faversham*, although some serious doubts still exist. The history play *Edward III* includes 'a superb seduction scene by Shakespeare' (publisher's blurb). *Sir Thomas*

More is included as the only play we have containing a scene in Shakespeare's handwriting. Of the other plays included, *The London Prodigal* and *A Yorkshire Tragedy* were ascribed to Shakespeare – probably to make money from his name – during his lifetime, while *Locrine* and *Thomas Lord Cromwell* contained, on the title page of their first publication, the initials 'W.S.' which Bate proposes 'were intended to give the impression that [Shakespeare] was the author' which 'alone make the plays worth reading: even if they were not by Shakespeare, they are plays that were plausibly passed off as his' [Introduction: 10–11]. Initials are a minefield for speculation and research, as the debates through the centuries over the identity of Mr W.H., 'the only begetter' of Shakespeare's *Sonnets*, testifies.

The other play included in Bate and Rasmussen is *Mucedorus* (with additions), a comedy that Tucker Brooke also included, about which – linking it with *Fair Em: The Miller's Daughter* (not in Bate) – he commented, 'they bear the mark of vagabondage on every feature' (1908: vi). It was possibly Tom Stoppard's knowledge of this latter play, *Fair Em*, that inspired 'Ethel, the Pirate's Daughter', a clever bit of comedy in the film *Shakespeare in Love* (1999). Over the last century or so some plays have retained at least a claim of a possible association with Shakespeare, while others in Tucker Brooke, like *Fair Em*, have fallen by the wayside or been assigned elsewhere: *Sir John Oldcastle, The Puritan, The Merry Devil of Edmonton* and *The Birth of Merlin*. Nevertheless, every now and again someone will announce that one or other of these is a 'lost play' by Shakespeare or written in collaboration with Shakespeare. For the moment, Bate and Rasmussen et al., with their reservations and qualifications, are where the matter resides – as well as the challenges to them, of course.

Pericles, Prince of Tyre

Pericles is a significant play excluded from the First Folio, not appearing in a collected edition until the second printing of the Third Folio in 1664. It was published in a poor-quality quarto, bearing only Shakespeare's name as author in 1609. It is now generally accepted by scholarship and theatre practitioners that this play was written in some form of collaboration with George Wilkins, a hack writer but more particularly a 'brothel keeper'.

The structure of *Pericles* is one that must have led neoclassical scholars to near distraction. It darts across the seas from one country to another and lurches from one catastrophe to another with remarkable rapidity: Antioch, Tyre, Tarsus, Pentapolis, Ephesus, Mytilene. It is not often performed but I have seen a number of productions and none of them has ever left me disappointed. In one by the RSC in the Newcastle upon Tyne Studio Theatre, I was in the first row of the gallery looking down on to the stage. At the point in the play where a coffin/trunk containing the 'corpse' of Thaisa, Pericles' wife who has 'died' in childbirth at sea, is washed ashore and opened by the doctor, Lord Cerimon, I found myself looking down immediately into it. As Cerimon worked on the body to restore it to life, the person next to me – whom I didn't know – suddenly grabbed me and squealed 'She's alive!' It was a moment of great theatre and great tension for audience and the play. (The woman concerned was much embarrassed!) In his experimentation with the play's structure, Shakespeare uses the choric figure of John Gower, the medieval writer from whom he borrowed much of the story, as a frequent narrator, moving along with the shifts of location and thereby giving the narrative a discipline, and the audience a confidence, to be taken from one phase of the action to another.

'... the narratorial interventions of Gower achieve the abbreviated convergence of desire and reality by enlisting the audience's collaboration at every stage ... The deliberately naive, archaic doggerel that distinguishes the choric couplets of "ancient Gower" ... distances the brazenly concocted universe of *Pericles* ... [sharpening] ... the audience's sense of the contrasting modernity, and hence the historicity, of the world in which they themselves, "born in these latter times", ... watch the play.'

Ryan, K. (2002, 3rd edn: 110), *Shakespeare.* Basingstoke and New York: Palgrave

It is the first of 'the last plays' in which Shakespeare upholds the dignity of women wronged by husbands or guardians.

> 'In the romances (last plays), the feminine principle is reasserted, but ... is being hounded by the masculine. The situation is one of outright war. The conclusion the playwright aims for, however, is that bitterly discussed and bitterly won in All's Well: the supremacy of the feminine, rather than the masculine principle. Each play provides a different form, but all of them are experiments in achieving a vision in which "feminine" values are triumphant within the world of earthly power.'
>
> French, M. (1983: 286), *Shakespeare's Division of Experience*, London: Abacus, Sphere Books

During the play, Marina, Pericles and Thaisa's daughter, is sold by pirates to a brothel keeper (thus the interest of George Wilkins?) but, much to his, his wife's and their pimp's displeasure, Marina is able to persuade each customer not to violate her. This includes the governor of Mytilene, Lysimachus, who at the end of the play is betrothed to her. Some critics believe this to be an inappropriate conclusion to the complex romance, but possibly they protest too much. In production it appears to work well enough. Even if he had met her first in the brothel, it was there that she managed to reform his erstwhile profligate behaviour.

The play moves at a good pace, with a galaxy of different one-dimensional characters knitted together by Gower's chorus function and by Pericles himself on his quest, that allows for different episodes or tales to be told. It is a much-underrated enjoyable narrative drama. The budget version for the BBC Complete Shakespeare, directed by David Jones, with a thoughtful articulate performance of Pericles by Mike Gwilym, is a good evening's entertainment to be recommended. Not all productions need lavish expenditure, which in itself says a great deal about Shakespeare.

The Tempest

The Tempest (1611), although the first play printed in the 1623 First Folio, is often regarded as Shakespeare's farewell to the stage. As we have seen above, it is not his last play but in regarding it as his last solely authored work some have regarded it as his retirement goodbye, linking Shakespeare the writer with Prospero the usurped duke and magician. Prospero's breaking of his magic staff at the end of the play is given an autobiographical force as a personal gesture by Shakespeare, marking the public ending of his dramatic career. In such readings he then returns to Stratford to his family and his large house, just as Prospero is to return to Milan as Duke.

Prospero tells us:

> ... – I have bedimmed
> The noontide sun, called forth the mutinous winds,
> And 'twixt the green sea and the azured vault
> Set roaring war

(5.1.41–4)

Has not, metaphorically some might ask, Shakespeare done the same for his audiences throughout his career? Moreover:

> ... graves at my command
> Have waked their sleepers, ope'd and let 'em forth
> By my so potent art.

(5.1.48–50)

Shakespeare places the bookish Prospero on an island because of his misdeeds when in power as much as because of the machinations of others. There he uses his magic, but even so Prospero can only 'prosper' by opportunism. Although he can raise a tempest, he only does so when:

> By accident most strange, bountiful fortune
> ...
>   hath mine enemies
> Brought to this shore; and by my prescience

I find my zenith doth depend upon
A most auspicious star, whose influence
If now I court not, but omit, my fortunes
Will ever after droop.

(1.2.178–84)

These lines seem to express and affirm a positive vision of the future as an extension of Renaissance values. Those values, however, the play itself proceeds to challenge. Certainly, Shakespeare's 'art' has been potent and regarded as such through the centuries. But here his last great character relinquishes his power. He will break his staff and bury his art deeper than a grave, so that it cannot be restored:

... But this rough magic
I here abjure;
...
... I'll break my staff,
Bury it certain fathoms in the earth,
And deeper than did ever plummet sound
I'll drown my book.

(5.1.50–51, 54–7)

In the Epilogue, Prospero speaks with what some have thought to be autobiographical references:

Now my charms are all o'erthrown
And what strength I have's my own,

Prospero then appeals to the audience to release him from his 'bands/With the help of your good hands.' He continues:

... Now I want
Spirits to enforce, art to enchant;
And my ending is despair,
Unless I be relieved by prayer,
...
As you from crimes would pardoned be,

Let your indulgence set me free.

(Epilogue, 13–16, 19–20)

His last appeal is to the audience to release him from the (stage) island, to allow him to be free; otherwise, he says, 'my project fails,/Which was to please' (Epilogue, 12–13).

Recent literary criticism, however, goes beyond the association of the character with the author, and of a farewell to the theatre. Rather than the play embodying a romantic, sentimental farewell, Stephen Greenblatt regards this sentiment in the 'Last Plays' as an apotheosis of Shakespeare's artistic direction and the ethical climate of his time.

'The conclusion towards which these stories tend is not the cynical abandonment of all hope for decency in public life, but rather a deep scepticism about any attempt to formulate and obey an abstract moral law, independent of actual social, political, and psychological circumstances. This scepticism set Shakespeare at odds with the dominant currents of ethical reflection in his period. It is not that he set out, like Marlowe, to swim against these currents or to stage violent protests against them; he seems simply to have found them incompatible with his art.'

Greenblatt, S. (2010: 82), *Shakespeare's Freedom.* Chicago and London: The University of Chicago Press

Greenblatt perhaps does not give enough credit here to the ethical dimension of Michel de Montaigne's influence, particularly his essay 'Of the Cannibals' (1580, trans. Florio 1603). Shakespeare may well have been familiar with Montaigne's writings through the translations of John Florio, tutor to the young Earl of Southampton who some think is the subject of the first 17 of Shakespeare's sonnets. Many late twentieth-century interpretations of the play sought to emphasize the play's colonial context. Laurie Maguire and Emma Smith, for example, point to a particular production that changed theatrical interpretations:

'After Jonathan Miller's 1970 staging of the play it has been difficult to recover a sympathetic Prospero unmarked by colonial guilt. As reviewers described that landmark production, Prospero was "a solemn and touchy neurotic, the victim of a power complex" who 'has arrogated to himself the god-like power of the instinctive colonist ... by the end the cycle of colonialism is complete: Ariel, the sophisticated African, picks up Prospero's discarded wand, clearly prepared himself to take on the role of bullying overlord. Recent Prosperos have tended to be so unpleasant that any association with Shakespeare would reflect very badly on the playwright himself.'

Maguire, L. and Smith, E. (2013: 135), *30 Great Myths about Shakespeare*. Malden, Oxford and Chichester: Wiley-Blackwell, quoting reviews by Eric Shorter and Michael Billington, recorded in excerpts in O'Connor, J. and Goodland, K. (2007: 1357–8), *A Directory of Shakespeare in Performance, 1970–2005*. Vol. 1: *Great Britain, 1970–2005*. Basingstoke: Palgrave Macmillan

This, however, is now as much a theatrical commonplace as associating Shakespeare with Prospero, and new interpretations are likely to emerge as new 'spirits' are conjured by Shakespeare's revels in modern critical evaluations and theatrical production. What remains relatively steady, however, is the play's firm structure and narrative.

Spotlight

Shakespeare displays in Prospero iconographic characteristics in his manipulation of a world portrayed through the metaphor of a dream. Shakespeare seems to have gone back to the dream plays of his early comedies, and to the iconic frame of plays such as *Richard II* and *Henry V*. What we find in *The Tempest* is a gallery of characters who all have a particular relationship with the icon Prospero, who in turn reflects images of an audience watching the play. Shakespeare does this in a virtuoso display while he actually returns to the neoclassical rules of the three Unities – place, time and action – which he had more or less abandoned

DANCE OF DEATH?

In conventional readings of the play, Prospero appears to control everything, as does an author writing a play or other work, but do they? In a crude sense the symbol of his total command is found in Caliban as the representative of the earth:

> ... – What ho, slave! Caliban,
> Thou earth, thou: speak!

(1.2.14–15)

Within the creation of the two contrasting characters, Caliban and Ariel, Shakespeare could be staging twin resistances to the magician's authority, but equally he might also be expressing the dual constitutive elements of the icon's identity, which at the end of the play are allowed to go their separate ways: Caliban, the body, remains firmly of the earth; the other, Ariel, takes to the air.

> ... Then to the elements
> Be free, and fare thou well!

(5.1.319–20)

Thus an argument can be made that *The Tempest* works as a dance of death with the breaking of the staff at the end of the concluding dance of the play, representing the moment of death itself. The iconic Prospero takes centre stage in a dreamlike dance that will result in release.

THE TIME LIMIT

The narrative of the story, however, limits the credibility of such an interpretation since the plot doesn't demand that Prospero die but return to Milan, where he will resume his dukedom. He does so within a play that not only observes the Unities but does so, as Jan Kott (1967: 238–9) proposes, by using a time limit which actually coincides with how long it will take for the play to be performed. Within this tight time limit, the action is also limited. There is the shipwreck, the dispersal of the passengers, the meeting of Ferdinand and Miranda, the plot against Alonso, the plot against Prospero and the recognition of all when at the magician's cell.

THE DREAM MOTIF

That tight structure allows yet again for the Shakespearean dream motif – a state of mind that distorts reality and its otherwise mundane temporal order. It is through this dream that Shakespeare reveals the artistic power of Prospero. He is the controller of everyone's sleep. He instructs his daughter:

> … Here cease more questions.
>
> Thou art inclined to sleep; 'tis a good dullness,
>
> And give it way. I know thou canst not choose.

$$(1.2.184–6)$$

Similarly, Ferdinand, hearing strange music and seeing veiled sights, says:

> My spirits, as in a dream, are all bound up.
>
> My father's loss, the weakness which I feel,
>
> The wreck of all my friends, nor this man's threats
>
> (To whom I am subdued) are but light to me, (1.2.487f.)

Gonzalo, Adrian and Francisco are charmed into sleep in Act 2, soon followed by Alonso and, as in *A Midsummer Night's Dream*, the implication is clear that the play itself is as a dream:

> … Be cheerful, sir.
>
> Our revels now are ended. These our actors,
>
> As I foretold you, were all spirits and
>
> Are melted into air, into thin air;
>
> …

We are such stuff

As dreams are made on, and our little life

Is rounded with a sleep.

(4.1.147–50, 156–8)

The relationship between the play, the dream and life merge, so that the question of reality itself is raised – the 'parted eye' of *A Midsummer Night's Dream* is reflected also by Miranda when talking of her early childhood as being:

... rather like a dream than an assurance

That my remembrance warrants.

(1.2.45–6)

Shakespeare here reworks his tried and trusted formula, utilizing the dream in different ways, as we have seen through many of his plays. The controller of the dream finally includes himself in his fantasy: 'We are such stuff / As dreams are made on'. He is the dreaming artist.

The structure of the dream defies logic – in dreams the movement of images challenge the seeming coherence of the narrative. Thus it is with Prospero, who, still as controller is enrapt in the revels, distractedly enjoying them to the point that he '... had forgot that foul conspiracy / Of the beast Caliban and his confederates / Against my life' (4.1.139–41).

Francis Barker and Peter Hulme argue that '... conventional criticism has no difficulty in recognizing the importance of the themes of legitimacy and usurpation for *The Tempest* ... However, these rebellions, treacheries, mutinies and conspiracies, referred to here collectively as usurpation, are not *simply* present in the text as extractable "Themes of the Play". Rather, they are differentially embedded there, figural traces of the text's anxiety concerning the very matters of domination and resistance.' (p. 198). Earlier in their essay they contend that criticism points not only to the presence in the text of alternative viewpoints to the dominant one of Prospero but through 'Discourse', which is 'the *field* in and through which texts are produced':

Shakespeare has Prospero elucidate the meaning of the 'revels' within the framework of dream and play, but Prospero isn't actually the only authority in the play, nor is his discourse isolated. The danger is that we fall into the trap of the play and believe him to be the sole arbiter of meaning.

TAUNTING, COMFORTING, IDEALISTIC, CRUEL

A creative experience is found within the conduct of this remarkable play, which reflects a mutability within the discipline of Aristotelian or neoclassical structure, allowing the dream to be ambiguous: simultaneously taunting, comforting, idealistic and cruel:

> ARIEL [*SINGS*]   Full fathom five thy father lies,
>   Of his bones are coral made;
>   Those are pearls that were his eyes,
>   Nothing of him that doth fade
>   But doth suffer a sea-change
>   Into something rich and strange.
>   Sea nymphs hourly ring his knell.
>
> SPIRITS   Ding dong.
>
> ARIEL   Hark, now I hear them.
>
> SPIRITS   Ding dong bell.

(1.2.397–405)

It is the play which is the song, which suffers the sea-change, that through the tightness of its structure retains a valid trans-historical continuity. Even though the performance ends and Prospero's books are to be discarded at the culmination of his sojourn, the play will continue to be re-enacted. It will emerge from the waters of time through interpretation, debate and discourse as rarified as the corals and the pearls that we now see and discuss. *The Tempest*, through its form and function, is a prophetic play.

28

The Winter's Tale
(1610–11)

As we come to the end of our journey through the plays, we discuss the play of winter, in which life decays and is ultimately regenerated from the seemingly dead earth. The play is centrally concerned with a process of atonement for a woman deeply wronged, but although a 'sad' tale is thought best for winter, the action points forward to new growth in spring and to a rapprochement between the generations that, as we have seen, is characteristic of Shakespeare's comedies.

An 'improbable fiction'

Have we lost our sense of the wonder of Shakespeare's plays? This is a question that has nagged at me through the writing of this complete introduction. No more is this so than in *The Winter's Tale*. So many critics appear to want to 'condemn it as an improbable fiction' (*Twelfth Night*, 3.4.128), rather than accept it as such and admire and enjoy its wonder, 'Like an old tale still,' (*The Winter's Tale*, 5.2.62).

The first time I encountered the play was in Trevor Nunn's 1968 RSC production, with Judi Dench playing both the role of Hermione and of Perdita, and the two great actors Charles Wood as Leontes and Richard Pasco as Polixenes. I did not know the story and was advised not to read it or a synopsis of it before I went. It was good advice. Even as I write, I can see Judi Dench's Hermione slowly crumple to the floor as Leontes' jealousy showed no regard for the oracle. Nunn used an ultraviolet light to depict the jealousy that led his wife to her 'death'. She was, for all I knew, dead until that final scene when not only did she move but she spoke in a soft voice that almost cracked as the words were delivered. Here was the wonder of breaking through the 'pity of it' (*Othello*), the 'rough magic' (*The Tempest*) of Shakespeare in performance.

In 2015, having seen many good (and some not so good) performances in the meantime, I had the privilege of seeing Judi Dench in the play once more on this occasion, again playing two roles, Paulina and the Chorus, Time. The person who crumpled in this production at Hermione's 'death' was Kenneth Branagh's Leontes. It was a beautifully staged, romanticized production that made no apologies or excuses for the play's improbabilities but rather allowed the narrative to work its wonder. Sadly, as the exhilarated audience left the West End theatre that Friday night, 13 November 2015, news started to filter through about the so-called Islamic State atrocities and murders in Paris. We had all experienced such beauty, presented by some of the greatest actors of our generation, while others in our allied European city had experienced a tragedy and horror for which no theatrical performance could ever compensate.

So much in Shakespeare is about 'remembrance' and my lasting memory of that night will be a fracturing between art, as we had seen it so professionally enacted, and the barbarity of which human beings are capable.

The impact of history on the play

Throughout this book we have been considering how the plays work and how they allow for a variety of meanings and interpretations that can emerge through performance, criticism, discussion and reflection. We have looked at history and histories, at tragedy and romantic comedy and at what Northrop Fry refers to as a 'diptych' in which comedy is followed by tragedy or tragedy is resolved by comedy. We have also seen epic narrative translated into drama; we have challenged some long-held perceptions about the nature of drama and genre, and we have looked at comparisons with other plays and fictions and at history in many of its manifestations.

It is with the last of these that I would encourage you to begin your consideration of *The Winter's Tale*, a late play that concentrates on the jealousy of a king. As implied in earlier chapters, it is hard, if not impossible, for us to imagine fully the horrific impact of the reign of Henry VIII on Tudor England: his decision to have his marriage to Catherine of Aragon annulled and then, further, his accusations, made through Cromwell, of Anne Boleyn's adultery and incest, that led to her execution. As with the brutal execution of his chancellor, Thomas More, Anne Boleyn's demise was an act of unwavering royal pragmatism that exemplified the masculine power game in which Henry was engaged. Jealousy, the consuming desire for a male heir, and the abuse of power all manifested themselves in the accusations of adultery which condemned Anne to death at a trial, which like that of Sir Thomas More was 'fixed' in accordance with the King's authority. As you no doubt will have realized, I am offended by any popular sentimentality that some might have extended towards Henry VIII.

Spotlight

Catherine of Aragon's defence and Anne Boleyn's last words find their echo in Shakespeare's drama, as we have seen in our discussion of the collaborative play written with Fletcher, *Henry VIII*. In *The Winter's Tale* we have a similar defence, offered by Hermione:

> Since what I am to say, must be but that
> Which contradicts my accusation, and
> The testimony on my part, no other
> But what comes from myself, it shall scarce boot me
> To say 'not guilty': mine integrity,
> Being counted falsehood, shall, as I express it,
> Be so receiv'd. (3.2.21f.)

It is the plea of a queen against accusations that she knows it will be to no avail to counter, just as in history such appeals were to no avail before Henry. Voltaire was later to note that it is difficult for the innocent to be right when those in power are wrong. *The Winter's Tale* comments on Tudor history but also, perhaps, on the Stuart king, James I.

> *'Leontes' mad claim that "There is a plot against my life, my crown;" (2.1.47) echoes James's paranoid fear that he was surrounded by assassins, just as his method of disposing of those he distrusted may well be reflected in Leontes' plan to have Camillo poison Polixenes's drink.'*
>
> Lucas, J., 'Freedom and Hospitality in The Winter's Tale', *Loughborough University Conference Paper*. See Overton, B. (1989: 63), *The Critics Debate*

In similar vein, Bill Overton argues that Shakespeare cleverly exposes the King's proclivities without James realizing it, through the very theatricality and the progress of the narrative, which is very different from what happens in, say, *Hamlet*'s 'mousetrap'. He references Simon Shepherd's (1981) point that in Polixenes' condemnation of Florizel in 4.4.420f., there is an historical parallel with an event in 1610–11 when the King's refusal to allow his cousin Arabella Stuart to marry William Seymour was disobeyed, leading to their imprisonment.

The power of kings in essence was such that they could enforce their will, as the husband Petruchio did over his wife Katherina in *The Taming of the Shrew*, to make the sun the moon and the moon the sun. This may have been a problem for some of King James's courtiers, as it proves to be for Camillo in the play.

'Possessed by jealousy, Leontes has in effect the power to define reality according to his fantasy ... Through a show trial he seeks to impose belief on his subjects, who can resist only at personal hazard. Camillo ... cannot believe Leontes' charge against Hermione, and his outspoken denial (1.2.282–3) ... is a dangerous risk. When Leontes insists even more violently, only one reply will keep Camillo safe: "I must believe you, sir" (333). Here "must" can mean compulsion as well as conviction.'

Overton, B. (1989: 60), *The Winter's Tale: The Critics Debate*. Basingstoke: Macmillan

Shakespeare, as we have seen so many times, was in *The Winter's Tale* once again treading on dangerous political ground, and yet he always managed to survive.

Jealousy

Leontes' jealousy is the 'green-eyed monster' that needs no goading from an Iago. It is self-inflicted but on the basis of flimsy evidence of the kind that Iago fabricates. There is no handkerchief, just looks, hands joined and the fact that at Hermione's entreaty, not the King's, Polixenes agrees to stay longer at the court – an insult perhaps also to Leontes' authority. The question we have to ask here is why does all this happen so quickly? The answer lies in the conversation between Hermione and Polixenes about the two men's childhood experiences. She characterizes maturity as 'falling' into the world of adult sexuality, but says that this 'fall' can be excused so long as the spouse remains faithful to one partner. This becomes the cue for Leontes to misinterpret Hermione's and Polixenes' gestures, and to speculate that he is not the father of Hermione's unborn child. This, perhaps, can all happen more quickly in the later play because it has already happened in a more protracted form in the earlier *Othello*.

The result of Leontes' error is the death of his heir and condemnation to a winter life, when there can be no celebrations until the oracle's prophecy is acknowledged. As in C. S. Lewis's *Narnia*, it is a state of existence where it is always winter and never Christmas.

Time

As you would expect, neoclassical critics dislike the time gap between the two halves of the play and even some modern critics have seen the introduction of the character Time as a contrived convenience. Shakespeare designed it to be so, as a necessary element of the story he was telling:

> I that please some, try all: both joy and terror
> Of good and bad, that makes and unfolds error,
> Now take upon me, in the name of Time,
> To use my wings. Impute it not a crime
> To me, or my swift passage, that I slide
> O'er sixteen years ...

> (4.1.1–6)

As we have seen in play after play, he encourages the audience to think that they have been asleep, although in this play, it is the entire 'tale' that is the 'dream':

> ... Your patience this allowing,
> I turn my glass, and give my scene such growing
> As you had slept between:

> (4.1 15–17)

Yet the dream, like a play and like life itself (*The Tempest*, 4.1.146–58), is subject to Time, paradoxically to an awakening and an ending. So, in many of Shakespeare's works, Time plays a prominent part. It is, as we have seen, a formative motif in the *Sonnets* and an agent of mutability reflected in the comedies, as in *Twelfth Night*:

> Then come kiss me, sweet and twenty:
> Youth's a stuff will not endure.

> (2.3.51–2)

In that play it is also the one to 'untangle' error's 'knots' (*Twelfth Night*, 2.2.40–41). In *As You Like It*, when Rosalind asks 'I pray you, what is't o'clock?' Orlando replies, 'You should ask me what time o'day; There's no clock in the forest', only to receive the humorous correction, 'Then there is no true lover in the forest, else sighing every minute and groaning every hour would detect the lazy foot of Time, as well as a clock' (3.2.295–300). People can affect the experience of Time, as Rosalind proceeds to explain (3.2.303–27), but Time is still Time, 'that old common arbitrator', as Hector calls him in *Troilus and Cressida*, which 'Will one day end it' (4.5.225–6). These are just a few examples of references to Time that permeate the poems and the plays, whether comedies, histories or tragedies.

With *The Winter's Tale* towards the end of Shakespeare's writing career, we may feel, therefore, that it is fitting that Time makes an actual appearance as a Chorus between the two narrative movements of the play. There is an old tradition that Shakespeare even played the role, but in that supposition there is a danger of creating self-fulfilling interpretations in a way that, as we've noted, has sometimes occurred with *The Tempest*. So let us concentrate on Time's role in the play.

Time and remembrance

Time, as Chorus, goads the neoclassicists, calling on our remembrance:

> ... imagine me,
> Gentle spectators, that I now may be
> In fair Bohemia, and remember well
> I mentioned a son o'th' king's, which Florizel
> I now name to you;
>
> (4.1.19–23)

and teasing his audience in expectation by talking of Perdita:

> ... What of her ensues
> I list not prophesy; but let Time's news
> Be known when 'tis brought forth.
>
> (4.1.25–7)

So time in this play bridges the stages of action found in the development of the narrative, through a traditional structure, but it cannot do it for everyone. The threat of death at the start of the play becomes a reality. Mamillius dies and Leontes, and the theatre audience, think that Hermione has died too. 'A sad tale's best for winter:' innocently says Mamillius, 'I have one / Of sprites and goblins.' He begins, 'There was a man – ... Dwelt by a churchyard: I will tell it softly, / Yond crickets shall not hear it' (2.1.25–6, 29–31). But we hear no more. He is the victim of time, of 'the man' and 'the churchyard' as surely as Antigonus is, in the form of his assailant, the Bear.

Spring

The boy dies because of the violation of the oracle's truth and the treatment of the mother by the 'man' Leontes. Hermione's heart 'dies', turning her to stone – the statue that will be erected in her memory. But can art imitate the seasons? Can spring release the fertility of the earth after the frosts of winter? To survive through the winter is one of the basic challenges of life. Antigonus is eaten by a hungry bear and his companions perish at sea but, elsewhere, spring gradually dawns – but not as some paradise. The daffodils begin to appear, Autolycus, the roguish pedlar sings, 'With heigh! the doxy over the dale, / Why then comes in the sweet o'th year, / For the red blood reigns in the winter's pale' (4.3.2–4). The daffodils will bloom, as will the prostitutes (doxy), in the spring sunshine, escaping the cruel winter's hold but still within its domain (the pale).

This provides the opportunity, as it does for Marina in *Pericles*, for the unblemished life to flourish, in spite of the brothel. In the case of Perdita, the 'lost one', goodness also flourishes. This is not to imply some form of rural quaintness or a panacea or some sentimentalizing loss of a world that was. It is rather a movement towards what is to occur at the end of the play. The country dancing, the festivity and the comedy are part of the entertainment. The queen of the festivity is the woman, the lost Perdita, about to be found as the prophecy – an agency of time – has foretold.

> 'The author of The Winter's Tale *was not a folk artist, and he made it clear in many ways that he was not. A sheep-shearing festival performed on the stage of the Globe as part of a sophisticated tragicomedy was not in fact a sheep-shearing festival; it was an urban fantasy of rural life, informed by knowing touches of realism but also carefully distanced from its homely roots.'*
>
> Greenblatt, S. (2004: 40), *Will in the World: How Shakespeare Became Shakespeare.* London: Jonathan Cape

The art of grafting

The Winter's Tale is a story with sadness, humour, song and dance: it is a story of life and death, of tribulation and new birth. It is controlled not by a fictionally created Chorus such as Gower but by the dramatist controlling his creation within the agencies of Time itself. The experiences of time sometimes reflect one another. Polixenes becomes, in his rage with Florizel, a parallel figure to Leontes in the first half of the play. His patience in seeing the frivolity of his son's courtship of Perdita turns into the scene of a marriage bargain as something that as a parent he must control: 'Is it not too far gone? 'Tis time to part them' (4.4.346); but after some gentle pleading over the issue of allowing a son to be able to choose a wife (a cultural flashpoint, as we saw in the case of Bertram in *All's Well*), he loses patience and exercises his regal authority:

> Mark your divorce, young sir,
> Whom son I dare not call; thou art too base
> To be acknowledg'd:

(4.4.419–21)

We might imagine King James sympathizing with this response, but it reflects in its particular tyranny a control over nature.

Spotlight

Earlier, Polixenes had tried to persuade Perdita that the art of control was better than untempered nature:

> Yet nature is made better by no mean
> But nature makes that mean: so, over that art,
> Which you say adds to nature, is an art
> That nature makes.

(4.4.89–92)

For Perdita and Florizel, however, the art of the court or the adherence to patriarchal values is in distinct contradiction to the Polixenes argument. The debate about 'grafting' concerns the attachment of a branch to a root in order to strengthen the plant. At this point it is thought that Perdita is a country maiden, but of course she is a princess. In the conclusion, 'nature' will harmonize with the social order and provide a means of social regeneration. But here, in the play, Florizel's flouting of Polixenes' authority has significant social repercussions.

Recognition

Shakespeare has returned to issues that interested him at the beginning of his career, with old Egeus' demands over whom Hermia should or should not marry, Demetrius or Lysander, but Egeus is not even a king. Florizel and Perdita's relationship is one of genuine love that is not to be controlled by patriarchal authority, nor is it to be commodified, but cherished as the newborn flowers, as the daffodils, which had opened in Autolycus' song. Even if nature is to be tampered with ('grafting'), it can be improved, and Perdita sees her relationship at this point in the play with Florizel as just such an improvement.

The disguised King certainly cannot agree and so is forced out of his disguise to prohibit the marriage. As we have seen earlier from *The Comedy of Errors* onwards, so much of the dramatic action in the comedies revolves around disguise and unknown identity, eventually reconciling errors through anagnorisis, or recognition. In *The Winter's Tale*, Shakespeare provides us with multiple recognitions but certainly not in the first of them –

Polixenes throwing off his disguise – in order to reconcile. Instead, the King discards his disguise in order to prohibit, but in doing so he sets in motion a series of events that will lead to a further two recognitions. The first of these is the discovery of Perdita's true identity, which is reported by the three Gentlemen (Act 5, Scene 2) rather than enacted, since the second, even greater revelation, is to prove the final moment of revelation and reconciliation.

Autolycus

While Autolycus opens Act 5, Scene 2, in which the Gentlemen report the finding of Perdita, he has, as many critics have noted, little function in the context of pushing forward the narrative. He complains that the revelation of Perdita as Leontes' daughter was delayed because of seasickness. In the context of the entertainment value of the play, however, he serves a major function, entering into the feast with first expectation and then as a flourish, as the Vice character would have done in the old morality plays.

> CLOWN   Prithee bring him in; and let him approach singing.
>
> PERDITA   Forewarn him, that he uses no scurrilous words in's tunes.
>
>   (4.4. 213–16)

His function in entertaining the country festivities is to modulate the rural idyll by introducing an element of deception and trickery and to highlight the culture of the community, including its trials and tribulations. Perdita's stricture draws Shakespeare's urban audience into the play. True, Autolycus steals from those he encounters, but this is a 'realistic' part of life that can infiltrate even the most rural of scenes. The Clown never recognizes him and, though he says he 'was cozened by the way and lost all my money?' (4.4.252–3), he shows no vehemence, no hatred.

But, for the expectation of Polixenes, this spring is a cruel beginning of something. In Sicilia, Paulina has refused

Leontes, the King of Winter, the warmth of consolation, while secretly maintaining Hermione, feeding her a 'little life' until regeneration, an acknowledgement of loss and ultimately forgiveness can take place through the re-awakening of Leontes' 'faith'. So the Chorus has indeed prophesied to 'make stale / The glistering of this present' (4.1.13–14). Aligned with the role of the author, the Chorus, Time – whether originally played by Shakespeare or not – will move on 'To th' freshest things now reigning' (13), and will promise the audience to 'let Time's news / Be known when 'tis brought forth' (26–7).

Key idea

Time provides a dramatic function of expectation. That expectation comes, therefore, not with the reported recognition of Perdita, but with the coming to life of the statue of Hermione.

The theatrical wonder

Thus we come to the theatrical wonder itself. Shakespeare perhaps imitated the sexual titillation of Marston's *The Metamorphosis of Pygmalion's Image* (1598), taken from Ovid, to bring the statue to life in a scene of mystery. It has been suggested that necromancy is being hinted at in this episode but Paulina defends what she is doing by highlighting the theatricality of the scene and the legitimacy of the 'magic' that she will now perform:

> ... Then all stand still:
> Or – those that think it is unlawful business
> I am about, let them depart.
>
> (5.3.95–7)

In a progression built up carefully through the scene, Hermione comes alive only when she moves, and she moves only when Leontes renews his faith in her. The Second Gentleman notes that Paulina 'hath privately twice or thrice a day, ever since the death of Hermione, visited that removed house' (5.2.106–8), where, it is revealed, Julio Romano has been carving Hermione's statue. (Shakespeare is being particularly astute in naming the artist, since works by Guilio Romano (*c*.1499–1546) were particularly liked by the Stuart family. Romano's engravings of his mentor Raphael's work had been used, for example, as the basis for the costumes of Ben Jonson and Inigo Jones's *Masque of Queens* performed at Whitehall Palace in 1609.) The climax is that Hermione turns out to be alive. The statue miraculously has 'aged' and breathes and moves. As Leontes suggests, 'art' and 'life' come together and this is something for which there should be legislation:

> ... O she's warm!
>
> If this be magic, let it be an art
>
> Lawful as eating.

(5.3.109–11)

She embraces him and, prompted by Paulina, she turns and speaks to the lost daughter who has been found:

> ... You gods, look down,
>
> And from your sacred vials pour your graces
>
> Upon my daughter's head!

(5.3.121–3)

Shakespeare has moved the polarity once again, from the male who appears as the protagonist to the female, whose 'spring' regeneration is the hope of the play. Today we might recall the first lines of T. S. Eliot's poem *The Wasteland* (1922):

> April is the cruellest month, breeding
>
> Lilacs out of the dead land, mixing
>
> Memory and desire, stirring
>
> Dull roots with spring rain.

as the spring of *The Winter's Tale* is confirmed by Hermione's voice:

> ... For thou shalt hear that I,

Knowing by Paulina that the Oracle
Gave hope thou wast in being, have preserv'd
Myself to see the issue.

(5.3.125–8)

Is Leontes forgiven? Another production of the play in 2015 –
but one which was rather dull – at the Royal Shakespeare
Theatre in Stratford played against any forgiveness on
Hermione's part. In the conclusion, Leontes, it was made clear
through the body language, was still rejected. The production
played against, thereby, the clear stage directions in the lines
from Polixenes, 'She embraces him.' Surely, Hermione's
embrace of Leontes and Camillo's words 'She hangs about
his neck!' (5.3.111–12) indicate her forgiveness. Had the
conferment of meaning by the director in this case been in
blatant contradiction of authorial stage direction and intent?
Branagh's interpretation, in contrast, as most do, expressed
Hermione's forgiveness for Leontes, and his wonder and joy.

Branagh's production, sadly, in the remembrance of 'my time'
will, nevertheless, always be tarnished with the actual atrocities
of that November night, 2015, in Paris. In a sombre way, my
experience, however, illustrates some of the issues we have been
discussing throughout our journey. Shakespeare's plays are works
of art, representations of reality, but not actual life and death.
We enjoy Shakespeare. We are entertained and intellectually and
emotionally challenged by him but we project our experiences,
ideologies and meanings upon him. We appreciate the way in
which his plays work, drawing us into them, pushing us this way
and that, as he varies his structural templates for the narratives he
imparts. We begin to understand his plays, considering them as
complex mechanisms. We locate them in their historical moment,
and appreciate them in our own time.

Conclusion

The line of enquiry in this book has followed Shakespeare's plays more or less chronologically but also by genre, with six 'critical perception' chapters and one on language breaking the journey. Various alternative structures could have been followed. I could, for example, have grouped the plays according to the different theatres where they were first performed, or related them to known facts about Shakespeare's life or according to their order in the First Folio, or I could have taken an even stricter chronological approach, irrespective of genre. There were many options but whatever the approach taken it would have had an effect on my critical judgements which, implicitly or explicitly, I have been making along the way. To discuss the plays chronologically and/or according to genre is to impose upon the *oeuvre* a certain rigidity of interpretation, but so would any other critical arrangement. There is no key that will fully unlock Shakespeare's drama; there are just gates to open, paths to follow. Quite deliberately, I did not conclude with *The Tempest*, which many chronological interpretations do, because there is no firm authority for regarding it as Shakespeare's final play.

Yet not to do so may obscure something that might have been the case. It could have been his last play and it might have reflected his own feelings about his art and the theatre. I chose a different path simply to make the point that other paths are there. Similarly, when I've deliberately discussed plays out of their usually accepted chronological order – as with *Pericles*, for example, or possibly in discussing *All's Well That Ends Well* (the date of which is uncertain) before *Measure for Measure* or *Timon of Athens* before *Troilus and Cressida*, or discussing *Julius Caesar* within the chapter on Greeks and Romans rather than as a play chronologically written almost in tandem with *Henry V* – I have inevitably downplayed some possibilities in favour of my overall interpretative approach. Shakespeare, as we have seen, was mercurial and interpretation should follow suit in registering that fact.

What is important in criticism, as in performance, is the discussion, the debate that is found in and through the plays, and that the plays and their interpretations prompt according to our predilections and ideologies. If this is so, then, within certain parameters, there is no right or wrong. Important, too, is the quality of the argument and the judgement through interpretation and contemporary performance, and through subsequent performances. Samuel Johnson's views in the eighteenth century, Coleridge's views in the age of the Romantics, Bradley's views influenced by realism – all laid claim to truth in their time, as, for example, is the case with C. L. Barber in the mid-twentieth century and Stephen Greenblatt in the late twentieth century.

Key idea

In an important sense, the views of the past have helped evolve a continuity of criticism that informs, in one way or another, our current thinking. Early twenty-first-century views will no doubt join with them in likewise informing the development of further different interpretations in the future.

The same is the case with performance. Although there are acting traditions and histories about how great actors have played particular parts, the modern actor of his or her time, while usually, but not always, consulting information relating to past performances, is influenced by the culture and ideologies of his or her particular time. However daunting the concept of the acting tradition might be, every individual interpretation is that of a particular actor, with a life of his/her own, within the time, age, decade, even the year of the performance, and also of the place, time (morning, afternoon, evening), theatre (large, small, open air, indoor), company (professional, amateur, establishment, fringe, experimental), and the audience of each performance. The critic considers and evaluates the plays with his or her own time and ideology but the actors interpret and perform before an audience that reacts within the process of the play as it unfolds before them. Once the performance is over it has gone, and when the actors take to the stage again the performance is necessarily new and the audience different. Shakespeare's plays, however, endure through all of this because they remain open to interpretation and receptive to the changes of time.

Shakespeare the man

But what of Shakespeare the man? As previous chapters have shown, we know more about him now than we formerly did because of some meticulous academic research. My own feeling –

and it is no more – is that he may have been a very private man, as some actors tend to be in contrast to their public personas on stage, and yet a 'company man'. He knew his talents and steered a difficult course through the politics of his day. Unlike Marlowe or Kyd, he survived and, unlike Jonson, he was not threatened, as far as we know, with having his nose split or, like Marston, given no option but to abandon the theatre.

Outside of being a 'company' man with his fellow actors, musicians and influential patrons, he probably spent many hours on his own, creating and writing out his plays. In London, he may have led something of a solitary life, away from his family in Stratford-upon-Avon, but he appears to have felt love and loyalty towards his parents and siblings and to his wife and children. I, personally, don't read into the matters of his will or his legal issues anything more than pragmatism to avoid disputes and concern to get matters right. He was right to think that enclosure of his Stratford lands would not occur in his lifetime. Who knows the real significance of leaving his 'second best bed' to his wife? Was that thoughtful – it may have been her bed – or not? It may have been the bed kept for visitors, indicating that the legacy might have been a compliment to her. Or was it done in a rush as he neared his end to protect her legally, especially since his daughter Judith had just married a rakish character, Thomas Quiney, who had apparently humiliated her and the family by his previous sexual misdemeanours. These statements are speculative, but let me risk another. The law in relation to inheritance was patriarchal. Perhaps a situation which previously he had taken for granted, that his wife would be looked after by his sons-in-law, had suddenly taken a different turn and Anne's name had to be formally entered late into the will to make a general point for his sons-in-law to understand. They would be judged by history if they did not look after her properly. The 'second best bed', whether 'her bed' or a 'visitor's bed', was perhaps a message to them about her home.

Great figures are lauded and praised but are invariably subject to attempts to knock them off their pedestals. As you may have perceived from Chapter 3, I don't have much time for those who contest the authorship issues, and neither do most serious academics. The authorship question is reminiscent of a mindset that likes to indulge in conspiracy theories. Many who have promulgated these are content to subscribe to a cultural or class-oriented elitism. Some of the argument, as we have seen, is based on fraudulent documentation. There were people who continued to believe that the world was square even after it had been circumnavigated!

The 1580s are sometimes termed 'the lost years' because no definitive document has been unearthed to show where Shakespeare was or what he was doing. It is, as a result, a decade of his life prone to theory. Was he in Lancashire working as a teacher in a Catholic household? Did he stay for a while, at least, not far from St Asaph in north-east Wales? Or was he in London working as an actor with the Queen's Men (established in 1583)? A number of scholars currently think the last of these is the most likely scenario but, as noted in Chapter 24, Critical perspectives 6, there is no firm evidence to support this claim.

Whether he was a Catholic, a Protestant or an agnostic is something that can be argued about, but what is clear is that he was well versed in the religious disputes of his time. His parents appear to have been loyal to the old faith, and the region of the Midland counties, in which Stratford is situated, was known to have Catholic sympathizers. But the Borromeo letter, found some time in the eighteenth century in the eaves of the house at Stratford, and used to support the claim that Shakespeare's father harboured Catholic sympathies, is thought to be of doubtful provenance. Whereas Ben Jonson was known to be a Catholic, there is no clear indication concerning Shakespeare one way or the other.

An enigmatic, company man, undertaking, most likely, much solitary work writing for the public stage, he certainly wanted recognition for his family and his father, at least through obtaining a coat of arms, and for himself through acquiring significant properties in Stratford-upon-Avon and London. Shakespeare appears also to have been intimate with friends and family but possibly a 'little distant' with others, as often many great artists tend to be. His public voice was his art. Throughout this book I have tried to come to an understanding of Shakespeare in both a historical and a contemporary context, by considering how the plays work as drama, which is one means of interpretation. I trust, however, that it has provided you with a complete enough introduction to Shakespeare to serve your purpose, and, like me, you will continue your journey in the exploration, appreciation, enjoyment and excitement of his work.

Appendices

1 Dates of Shakespeare's works

1589–92?	*The Taming of the Shrew*
1591	*2 Henry VI*
1591	*3 Henry VI*
1591–2	*The Two Gentlemen of Verona*
1591–2	*Titus Andronicus*
1592	*1 Henry VI* (with Thomas Nashe and others?)
1592–4	*Richard III*
1593	Narrative poem: *Venus and Adonis*
1593–4	Narrative poem: *The Rape of Lucrece*
1593–1608	*Sonnets*
1594	*The Comedy of Errors*
1595	*Love's Labour's Lost*
1595–6	*A Midsummer Night's Dream*
1595–6	*King Richard II*
1595–6	*Romeo and Juliet*
1595–7	*King John*
1596–8	*The Merchant of Venice*
1596–7	*1 Henry IV*
1597–8	*2 Henry IV*
1597–1601	*The Merry Wives of Windsor*
1598–9	*Much Ado About Nothing*
1599	*Henry V*
1599	*Julius Caesar*
1599	Poem *To the Queen*
1599–1600	*As You Like It*
1600–1601	*Hamlet*
1601	Poem *Let the Bird of Loudest Lay* (*The Phoenix and Turtle*)
1601	*Twelfth Night; or, What You Will*
1601–2	*Troilus and Cressida*
1604	*Othello*
1604	*Measure for Measure*

1605	*All's Well that Ends Well*
1605	*Timon of Athens* (with Thomas Middleton?)
1605–6	*King Lear*
1606	*Macbeth*
1606–7	*Antony and Cleopatra*
1608	*Coriolanus*
1608	*Pericles* (with George Wilkins)
1609–10	*Cymbeline*
1610–11	*The Winter's Tale*
1611	*The Tempest*
1613	*Henry VIII* or *All is True* (with John Fletcher)
1613–14	*The Two Noble Kinsmen* (with John Fletcher)

Lost plays: *Love's Labour's Won* 1595–7; *Cardenio* (with John Fletcher) 1612–13

2 Some key dates, 1485–1633

1485	Battle of Bosworth, death of Richard III, accession of Henry VII
1509	Accession of Henry VIII
1532	Divorce of Catherine of Aragon
1533	Marriage of Anne Boleyn and birth of Elizabeth
1534	Formal breach with the Church of Rome
1535	Execution of Thomas More, Chancellor of England
1536	Execution of Anne Boleyn
1547	Death of Henry VIII, accession of Edward VI
1553	Death of Edward VI, accession of Mary I
1554	Marriage of Mary and Philip of Spain
1556	Burning of Thomas Cranmer
1558	Death of Mary I, accession of Elizabeth I
1559	Elizabethan Church Settlement Acts of Uniformity and Supremacy
1563	John Foxe's *Acts and Monuments* ('Book of Martyrs') published

1564	Death of Michelangelo, birth of Galileo, birth of Christopher Marlowe. Birth of William Shakespeare, 23 April (?); christened at Holy Trinity Church, Stratford-upon-Avon, 26 April
1568	Mary Queen of Scots escapes to England
1570	Excommunication of Elizabeth I by Pope Pius V
1576	James Burbage opens The Theatre in Shoreditch, North London
1577–80	Francis Drake circumnavigates the globe
1582	William Shakespeare marries Anne Hathaway
1583	Shakespeare's daughter Susanna born
1584	John Lyly: *Sappho and Phao*
1583	Formation of the Queen's Men
1585	Shakespeare's twins, Hamnet and Judith, born
1587	Mary Queen of Scots executed
1587	Christopher Marlowe: *Tamburlaine the Great*
1588	Defeat of Spanish Armada
1588–92	Christopher Marlowe: *Doctor Faustus; Edward II; The Jew of Malta*
1589–92	Thomas Kyd: *The Spanish Tragedy*
1592	Plague in London: playhouses close for two years
1593	Christopher Marlowe killed in Deptford, 30 May
1594	Thomas Nashe: *The Unfortunate Traveller* – precursor of the novel form
1595	Shakespeare by now established as actor and writer; named as one of the players performing before Elizabeth I
1596	Shakespeare's son Hamnet dies
1597	Shakespeare buys New Place, Stratford-upon-Avon
1599	Essex's expedition to quell Ireland ends with truce made with Earl of Tyrone
1599	John Marston: *Antonio and Mellida*
1600–1601	John Marston: *Antonio's Revenge*; Shakespeare: *Hamlet*
1601	Shakespeare's father John Shakespeare dies. Earl of Essex rebellion and execution

1603	Death of Elizabeth. Accession of James I, son of Mary Queen of Scots
1603–4	John Marston: *The Malcontent*; *The Dutch Courtesan*
1605	Ben Jonson, George Chapman, John Marston: *Eastward Ho!*
1605	The Gunpowder Plot
1605–6	Ben Jonson: *Volpone*; Shakespeare: *King Lear*
1606	Shakespeare: *Macbeth*
1608	Shakespeare's granddaughter Elizabeth Hall born; his mother Mary Arden dies
1609	Ben Jonson and Inigo Jones: *Masque of Queens*
1610	Ben Jonson: *The Alchemist*
1611	Authorized version of the Bible
1611	Thomas Middleton: *A Chaste Maid in Cheapside*
1611	Shakespeare's *The Winter's Tale* and *The Tempest* performed at Court
1612	Death of James I's eldest son, Prince Henry
1612	John Webster: *The White Devil*
1613	Globe Theatre burns down; Shakespeare retires from theatre?
1613	John Webster: *The Duchess of Malfi*
1614	New Globe theatre opens
1616	Shakespeare dies (23 April?); Ben Jonson publishes his own *Works* in folio
1620	The *Mayflower* sails to New England, where the Pilgrim Fathers establish a colony
1621	The poet John Donne becomes Dean of St Paul's
1622	Thomas Middleton and William Rowley: *The Changeling*
1623	First Folio of Shakespeare's *Complete Works* published by John Heminges and Henry Condell
1625	James I dies; accession of Charles I (executed 1649)
1629–33	John Ford: *'Tis Pity She's a Whore*; *Love's Sacrifice*

3 The English monarchs, 1154–1649

THE HOUSE OF PLANTAGENET

Henry II	(1133–89)	reigned 1154–89
Richard, Coeur de Lion	(1157–99)	reigned 1189–99
John	(1166–1216)	reigned 1199–1216
Henry III	(1207–72)	reigned 1216–72
Edward I	(1239–1307)	reigned 1272–1307
Edward II	(1284–1327)	reigned 1307–27
Edward III	(1312–77)	reigned 1327–77
Richard II	(1367–1400)	reigned 1377–99

The sons of Edward III were:

1 Edward, Prince of Wales, The Black Prince (1330–76)

2 Lionel, Duke of Clarence (1338–68)

3 John of Gaunt, Duke of Lancaster (1340–99)

4 Edmund of Langley, Duke of York (1341–1402)

5 Thomas of Woodstock, Duke of Gloucester (1354–97).

Richard II was the son of Edward the Black Prince, eldest son of Edward III, who predeceased his father, the throne thereby going to Richard. He was deposed by Bolingbroke, son of John of Gaunt, Duke of Lancaster, who became Henry IV.

THE HOUSE OF LANCASTER (EMBLEM THE RED ROSE)

Henry IV	(1366–1413)	reigned 1399–1413
Henry V	(1386–1422)	reigned 1413–22
Henry VI	(1421–71)	reigned 1422–61; 1470–71

THE HOUSE OF YORK (EMBLEM THE WHITE ROSE)

Edward IV	(1422–83)	reigned 1461–70; 1471–83
Edward V	(1470–?83)	reigned 1483
Richard III	(1452–85)	reigned 1483–85

1 King Edward IV, the son of Richard, Duke of York (1411–60), was killed by Queen Margaret (1429–82, wife of Henry VI) and the Lancastrians at the Battle of Wakefield. Edward IV's brothers were Clarence and Richard of Gloucester. Edward IV's claim to the throne came from the fourth son of Edward III, Edmund of Langley, first Duke of York.

2 Edward V, son of Edward IV, was one of the two princes, the other being his brother, Richard, reputedly murdered in the Tower of London by Richard III.

3 Richard III, Richard, Duke of Gloucester, was brother of Edward IV and George, Duke of Clarence. He was killed at the Battle of Bosworth, 1485, by Henry Tudor, son of Margaret Beaufort (1441–1509), who was descended from John of Gaunt, third son of Edward III. She had married Edmund Tudor, Earl of Richmond, son of Katherine of France by Katherine's second husband, Owen Tudor. Katherine's first husband was Henry V. For some, the Tudor's claim to the throne was thereby somewhat doubtful.

THE HOUSE OF TUDOR (EMBLEM THE TUDOR ROSE, COMBINING WHITE AND RED)

Henry VII	(1457–1509)	reigned 1485–1509
Henry VIII	(1491–1547)	reigned 1509–47
Edward VI	(1537–53)	reigned 1547–53
Mary I	(1516–58)	reigned 1553–8
Elizabeth I	(1533–1603)	reigned 1558–1603

1 Henry VII attempted to strengthen his newly created dynasty, combining the red rose of Lancaster with the white rose of York, by marrying on 18 January 1486 Elizabeth of York (1466–1503). She was the eldest child of Edward IV, niece of Richard III and sister of Edward V and Richard, the princes 'murdered' in the Tower.

2   Henry VIII had six wives, the first being Catherine of Aragon (1485–1536), whom he married in 1509, following the death in 1502 of Catherine's first husband, Henry's elder brother Arthur Tudor, Prince of Wales (1486–1502).

3   Edward VI's mother was Jane Seymour (1508?–37), Henry's third wife, who died 12 days after the birth of Edward in 1537.

4   On the death of Edward VI in 1553, Lady Jane Grey (1536/7?–54), the great grand-daughter of Henry VII through his younger daughter Mary, was proclaimed queen in accordance with the Protestant Edward VI's instructions. She 'reigned' for only nine days (10–19 July) before being deposed. She was subsequently executed in February 1554.

5   The Catholic Queen Mary I's mother was Catherine of Aragon, Henry VIII's first wife.

6   Queen Mary I in 1554 married Philip of Spain (1527–98), who became co-regent with Mary (1554–8).

7   Queen Elizabeth I's mother was Anne Boleyn (c.1501/7–36). She was executed for adultery, incest and high treason on 19 May 1536.

THE HOUSE OF STUART

| James | (1566–1625) | reigned as James VI, King of Scotland 1567–1625 and as James I, King of England 1603–25 |
| Charles I | (1600–1649) | reigned 1625–49 |

1   King James I was the son of Mary, Queen of Scots (1542–87), who was descended from Margaret Tudor (1489–1541), elder daughter of Henry VII and Elizabeth of York. Mary, Queen of Scots, having fled to England in 1568, was executed by Elizabeth I in 1587. The two queens never met.

2   Charles I was executed in 1649 at the end of the English Civil War, after which Oliver Cromwell (1599–1658) ruled the country as the Commonwealth. The monarchy was restored in 1660 with the son of Charles I becoming Charles II (1630–85), who reigned 1660–85.

4 Selected bibliography and further reading

Alexander, N., *Poison, Play and Duel: A Study in Hamlet* (London: Routledge and Kegan Paul, 1971)

Auden, W. H., Introduction to *The Sonnets and Narrative Poems* (New York: Knopf, 1992)

Barber, C. L., *Shakespeare's Festive Comedy* (Princeton, NJ: Princeton University Press, 1959)

Bate, J., *The Genius of Shakespeare* (London: Picador, 2008)

Bate, J., *Soul of the Age: The Life, Mind and World of William Shakespeare* (London: Penguin, 2009)

Belsey, C., *Shakespeare and the Loss of Eden: The Construction of Family Values in Early Modern Culture* (Basingstoke: Macmillan, 1985)

Bennett, S., *Performing Nostalgia: Shifting Shakespeare and the Contemporary Past* (London and New York: Routledge, 1996)

Berry, R., *Shakespeare and the Awareness of the Audience* (Basingstoke: Macmillan, 1985)

Berry, R., *The Shakespeare Metaphor: Studies in Language and Form* (London and Basingstoke: Macmillan, 1978)

Bethell, S. L., *Shakespeare and the Popular Dramatic Tradition* (London: P. S. King and Staples, 1944)

Bulman, J. C., (ed.), *Shakespeare, Theory and Performance* (London and New York: Routledge, 1996)

Briggs, J., *This Stage-Play World: Texts and Contexts, 1580–1625* (Oxford: Oxford University Press, 1997)

Brown, J. R., *Shakespeare and his Comedies* (London: Methuen, 1968)

Brown, J. R., *Shakespeare in Performance* (Harmondsworth: Penguin Shakespeare Library, 1969)

Brown, R. D. and Johnson, D. (eds.), *A Shakespeare Reader: Sources and Criticism* (Basingstoke: Macmillan in association with the Open University, 2000)

Bryson, B., *Shakespeare* (London: Harper Press, 2007)

Cartmell, D., *Interpreting Shakespeare on Screen* (Basingstoke: Macmillan, 2000)

Cartmell, D. and Scott, M. (eds.), *Talking Shakespeare: Shakespeare into the Millennium* (Basingstoke: Palgrave, 2001)

Crawforth, H., Dustager, S., and Young, J., *Shakespeare in London* (London: Bloomsbury, 2015)

Crystal, D., *'Think on My Words': Exploring Shakespeare's Language* (Cambridge: Cambridge University Press, 2008)

Dollimore, J. and Sinfield, A. (eds.), *Political Shakespeare: New Essays in Cultural Materialism* (Manchester: Manchester University Press, 1985)

Dollimore, J., *Radical Tragedy: Religion, Ideology and Power in the Drama of Shakespeare and his Contemporaries* (London: Palgrave Macmillan, 3rd edition, 2010)

Drakakis, J. (ed.), *Alternative Shakespeares* (London: Methuen, 1985)

Drakakis, J. (ed.), *Shakespearean Tragedy* (London: Longman, 1992)

Duffy, E., *The Stripping of the Altars: Traditional Religion in England 1400–1580* (New Haven and London: Yale University Press, 2005)

Duncan-Jones, K., *Shakespeare: An Ungentle Life* (London: Arden Shakespeare, Methuen Drama, 2010)

Dusinberre, J., *Shakespeare and the Nature of Women* (London: Macmillan, 1975)

Evans, B., *Shakespeare's Comedies* (Oxford: Oxford University Press, 1960)

Evans, M., *Signifying Nothing: Truth's True Contents in Shakespeare's Text* (Brighton: Harvester Press, 1986)

French, M., *Shakespeare's Division of Experience* (London: Jonathan Cape, 1982)

Frye, H. Northrop, *A Natural Perspective: The Development of Shakespearean Comedy and Romance* (New York: Columbia University Press, 1965)

Greenblatt, S., *Will in the World: How Shakespeare Became Shakespeare* (London: Jonathan Cape, 2004)

Greenblatt, S., *Renaissance Self-Fashioning: From More to Shakespeare* (Chicago: The University of Chicago Press, 1980)

Greenblatt, S., *Shakespeare's Freedom* (Chicago: The University of Chicago Press, 2010)

Greenblatt, S., *Shakespearean Negotiations: The Circulation of Social Energy in Renaissance England* (Oxford: Clarendon Press, 1992)

Gurr, A., *Playgoing in Shakespeare's London* (Cambridge: Cambridge University Press, 3rd edition, 2004)

Hawkes, T., *Meaning by Shakespeare* (London and New York: Routledge, 1992)

Hawthorn, J., *A Concise Glossary of Contemporary Literary Theory* (London: Edward Arnold, 1992)

Holden, A., *William Shakespeare: His Life and Work* (London: Little, Brown, 1999)

Holderness, G., *Shakespeare: The Histories* (London: Palgrave Macmillan, 2000)

Holderness, G., *Visual Shakespeare: Essays in Film and Television* (Hatfield: University of Hertfordshire Press, 2002)

Honigmann, E. A. J., *Shakespeare: Seven Tragedies: The Dramatist's Manipulation of Response* (Basingstoke: Macmillan, 1976)

Jardine, L., *Reading Shakespeare Historically* (London and New York: Routledge, 1996)

Jardine, L., *Still Harping on Daughters: Women and Drama in the Age of Shakespeare* (New York and London: Harvester Wheatsheaf, 1983)

Jones, E., *Scenic Form in Shakespeare* (Oxford: Clarendon Press, 1971)

Kantorowicz, E. H., *The King's Two Bodies: A Study in Mediaeval Political Theology* (Princeton, NJ: Princeton University Press, 1998)

Karim-Cooper, F. and Stern, T. (eds.), *Shakespeare's Theatres and the Effects of Performance* (London and New York: Bloomsbury Arden Shakespeare, 2014)

Kastan, D. S., *A Will to Believe: Shakespeare and Religion* (Oxford: Oxford University Press, 2014)

Klein, H. and Wymer, R. (eds.), *Shakespeare and History – Shakespeare Yearbook,* Vol. 6 (Lewiston: Edwin Mellen Press, 1996)

Knight, G. Wilson, *The Wheel of Fire* (Oxford: Oxford University Press, 1930; London and New York: Routledge, 2001)

Kott, J. (trans. Taborski, B.), *Shakespeare Our Contemporary* (London: Methuen, revised edition, 1967)

Leggatt, A., *Shakespeare's Comedy of Love* (London: Methuen, 1974)

Leggatt, A., *Shakespeare's Political Drama: The History Plays and the Roman Plays* (London: Routledge, 1989)

MacGregor, N., *Shakespeare's Restless World* (London: Penguin, 2012)

Maguire, L. and Smith, E., *30 Great Myths about Shakespeare* (Chichester: Wiley-Blackwell, 2013)

McAlindon, T., *Shakespeare and Decorum* (London and Basingstoke: Macmillan, 1973)

Milling, J. and Ley, G., *Modern Theories of Performance* (Basingstoke: Palgrave, 2001)

Nevo, R., *Comic Transformations in Shakespeare* (London: Routledge, reprint edition, 2004)

Nicholl, C., *The Lodger: Shakespeare on Silver Street* (London: Allen Lane, 2007)

Peck, M. and Coyle, J., *Literary Terms and Criticism* (Basingstoke: Macmillan, 1993)

Ryan, K., *Shakespeare* (Basingstoke: Palgrave, 3rd edition, 2002)

Ryan, K. (ed.), *Shakespeare: Texts and Contexts* (Basingstoke: Macmillan in association with The Open University, 2000)

Salinger, L. *Shakespeare and the Traditions of Comedy* (Cambridge: Cambridge University Press, 1974)

Scott, M., *Renaissance Drama and a Modern Audience* (London: Macmillan, 1982)

Scott, M., *Shakespeare and the Modern Dramatist* (Basingstoke: Macmillan, 1989)

Scott, M. (gen. ed.), *The Critics Debate* (Basingstoke: Macmillan):

Daniell, D., *The Tempest* (1989); Davison, P., *Othello* (1988); Hattaway, M., *Hamlet* (1987); King, B., *Coriolanus* (1989); Knowles, R., *Henry IV Parts I & II* (1992); Overton, B., *The Winter's Tale* (1989); Thompson, A., *King Lear* (1988); Wharton, T. F., *Measure for Measure* (1989)

Scott, M. (gen. ed.), *Text and Performance* (Basingstoke: Macmillan):

Davison, P., *Hamlet* (1983); Draper, R. P., *The Winter's Tale* (1985); Hirst, D. L., *The Tempest* (1984); Holding, P., *Romeo and Juliet* (1992); Mason, P., *Much Ado About Nothing* (1992); Nicholls, G., *Measure for Measure* (1986); Overton, B., *The Merchant of Venice* (1987); Page, M., *Richard II* (1987); Potter, L., *Twelfth Night* (1985); Salḡado, G., *King Lear* (1984); Scott, M., *Antony and Cleopatra* (1983); Warren, R., *A Midsummer Night's Dream* (1983); Wharton, T. F., *Henry the Fourth Parts 1 & 2* (1983); Williams, G., *Macbeth* (1985); Wine, M., *Othello* (1984)

Scott, M., *Shakespeare's Comedies* (London: Hodder & Stoughton, 2014)

Scott, M., *Shakespeare's Tragedies* (London: Hodder & Stoughton, 2015)

Selden R., *A Reader's Guide to Contemporary Literary Theory* (Brighton: The Harvester Press, 1985)

Shell, A., *Shakespeare and Religion* (London: Bloomsbury, 2010)

Shapiro, J., *Contested Will: Who Wrote Shakespeare?* (London: Faber and Faber, 2010)

Shapiro, J., *1599: A Year in the Life of William Shakespeare* (London: Faber and Faber, 2005)

Shapiro, J., *1606: William Shakespeare and the Year of Lear* (London: Faber and Faber, 2016)

Tennenhouse, L., *Power on Display: The Politics of Shakespeare's Genres* (London and New York: Methuen, 1986)

Traversi, D. A., *An Approach to Shakespeare*, Vol. 1 (New York: Doubleday, 1969)

Vickers, B., *Appropriating Shakespeare. Contemporary Critical Quarrels* (New Haven and London: Yale University Press, 1993)

Wells, S., *Shakespeare, Sex & Love* (Oxford: Oxford University Press, 2010)

Wells, S., *Shakespeare For All Time* (London: Macmillan, 2002)

Wilson, R. N., *Julius Caesar* (Basingstoke: Palgrave Macmillan, 2001)

Wood, M., *In Search of Shakespeare* (London: BBC Books, 2005)

Index